This book is to be returned on
or before the date stamped below

UNIVERSITY OF PLYMOUTH

PLYMOUTH LIBRARY

Tel: (0752) 232323
This book is subject to recall if required by another reader
Books may be renewed by phone
CHARGES WILL BE MADE FOR OVERDUE BOOKS

POLITICAL EDUCATION IN FLUX

SAGE Annual Reviews of Social and Educational Change

POLITICAL EDUCATION IN FLUX

edited by DEREK HEATER
and JUDITH A. GILLESPIE

SAGE Annual Reviews of Social and
Educational Change   Volume 3

SAGE Publications · London and Beverly Hills

For information address
SAGE Publications Ltd
28 Banner Street, London EC1Y 8QE

SAGE Publications Inc
275 South Beverly Drive
Beverly Hills, California 90212

British Library Cataloguing in Publication Data

Political education in flux. —
   (Sage annual review of social and educational change,
   ISSN 0140-2196; v.3)
   1. Political socialization
   I. Heater, Derek   II. Gillespie, Judith A.
   306'.2   JA76   80-42090

   ISBN 0-8039-9822-8

Contents

III   NEGLECTED AREAS

Preface

Throughout the 1970s interest in the need for more and better political education flowered in many countries. It is therefore fitting that the 1981 SARSEC yearbook should be devoted to this topic. The movement in favour of political education in schools has been hesitant: hesitation among the teachers concerning the most effective ways of satisfying the general need; hesitation among the authorities concerning the advisability of fostering the activity at all. As a consequence, in many countries, the matter is in a state of flux.

Much has been written about these problems since the revival of interest in the question in the late 1960s. But most commentary has been confined to the experiences of single countries and to addressing immediate problems. What this volume tries to do is to draw upon the experiences of the North Atlantic world — of North America and Western Europe — and to use them to take stock of where we have reached. There is a certain coherence of tradition and experience in this segment of the globe, though we would by no means wish to deny the crucial importance of Communist and Third World experiences in this field. There is not room, however, for everything within the compass of a single volume.

Our contributors indicate what has been achieved and what is still left to be done. Yet the whole volume implicitly raises the question of cross-national exchange of research findings, doubts, achievements and experiences. An *International Journal of Political Education* exists and the International Political Science Association has established a Research Committee on Political Education. These initiatives need to be strengthened and added to. If this volume encourages connections and interchanges, it will have served its purpose.

Derek Heater
Brighton, 1981

Introduction

Judith A. Gillespie

People often find road maps very useful. They show historic places, businesses and how to get from one town to another. They are easy to understand, and they are useful because they get you to where you want to go. Whatever their shap , size or variety, most people own one or more road maps, and mot use them frequently.

A road map is a simple geographic map. Mapping an education or social science field is not as easy as plotting places and roads. Some fields naturally congeal around some major concepts. In economics, the concepts of supply and demand are important. In sociology, the concept of role is paramount. Yet, there is a great deal of diversity in most social science fields; and particular theories and concepts help to arrange only part of the mapping. Actually, different road maps of political science would look quite different because the terrain of theories and concepts that would be utilized would be divergent. It would be as if a person owned three maps of the state of Indiana, each of which told him or her vastly different information about how to get from Bloomington to Indianapolis.

Mapping the political education field is an especially difficult task. Its major concepts have different meanings to different people. Its practices vary widely. It is not only difficult to draw the map, but it is difficult for people to make equally efficient use of any map that is drawn. All of this is compounded when one considers the international or transnational aspects of political educa-

3

tion. There is no common epistemology for discourse, nor is there a set of common practices on which to draw.[1]

This volume attempts to map the political education field in space and time. It does so from a transnational perspective. While we know that the map will be incomplete, and, in many cases, different terrain will be covered, the purposes of the volume can be listed. First, our purpose is to share information about what is happening in political education, and to begin to dialogue across nations. Second, our purpose is to highlight key questions in political education, and to afford comparisons of responses to those questions. We shall also highlight promising ideas and practices currently being utilized across the globe. Finally, we shall consider the future of political education and the possibilities for transnational cooperation.

MAPPING POLITICAL EDUCATION

Here we attempt to draw a map of political education utilizing major approaches and definitions. We show various ways of developing that map, and recognize that any map will change dramatically over time. What we will end up with is a series of ideas and approaches and ways of thinking and acting in political education.

One of the key definitions necessary to begin our task is the definition of political education. Here we will define political education as the development of competencies in thinking about and acting in political arenas.[2] The 'education' part of the definition is the development of competencies. This is the essence of education and is internationally understood. Which competencies need to be developed and how they are developed is a persistent question for debate and discussion.

The second part of the definition involves thinking and acting. In this case we are referring both to inquiry and values. We refer to rote thinking as well as divergent thinking. We include values which support the system as well as those which engender criticism in considering social and political issues. In this case, thinking is viewed in the generic sense of developing competencies to inquire into problems, and to propose alternate solutions while thinking of the consequences.

Another key part of the definition involves acting. Here, both individuals and groups are a focus. Individual actions affect political life; yet most individuals make an impact on the political system in group activity. Whether this be formal or informal, developing competencies in acting in and through groups is an important part of the definition of political education.[3]

Political arenas are also important. They are as diverse as any landscape. Here when we speak of political arenas, we are thinking of standard governmental arenas as well as non-governmental economic and social arenas. Schools, families, the workplace, as well as political parties and government agencies, are all considered to be political arenas. What we are concerned about is developing competencies of thinking and acting in these arenas. What makes them political is that values, or valuable things, are distributed as a result of action in these arenas as a result of group activity.[4]

Once a common definition is set, approaches to political education continue to vary widely. Not only do they vary across approaches; but within any given approach, there is a great deal of diversity in core ideas and practices. Here we will be concerned both with the diversities within approaches and between approaches.

Valuing Approaches

Four approaches will be discussed here. The first is what might be called a valuing approach. This approach is concerned with values, commitments and loyalties to groups, to nations or to the global political system as part and parcel of a discussion of political education. The approach often involves indoctrination, ceremony and social criticism in a complex web of ideas and practices.[5]

Within the valuing approach, there are a wide variety of perspectives. In developing nations, people are often concerned about nation-building and about loyalty to the state.[6] Sometimes this takes the form of nationalistic tradition and ceremonies that are performed in schools. At other times, it takes the form of teaching students self-respect and initiative, and values crucial to the society are a major concern. Across the globe in nations, states and local communities core values are viewed as an important part of political education. In fact, this particular concern with core values is part of every other approach that will be listed in the pages following.

Another kind of view that falls under the values approach is a concern for justice and moral education.[7] Here students are taught to think through value situations and to determine their consequences. In effect, schools wish to teach skills in valuing as well as a set of values which confirm loyalty to the polity. Still another focus within this approach involves global education with its concern for transnational values and common human concerns.[8] Here the value focus becomes more diverse and transnationalized, although the approach is still one which shows central concern for human values and international understanding.

Information Approaches

The second approach to mapping political education involves a focus on information. Here people are concerned about the knowledge base that students acquire. They are concerned about students' knowledge of the structures and functions of government and how the political process works at the local, state, national and international levels.[9]

Although information is a key approach to political education, what information will be included and what purpose it will serve varies across local school systems. Approaches to government can have a local base or a national base. They can focus on people, institutions or issues. They can also attempt to inject new social science knowledge or practical knowledge for future citizens. Another distinct part of the imformation approach includes the movement in legal education. Here, both local and national laws become the basis for teaching political education.[10] The legal tradition is a strong one and the new law-focused educational efforts involving more 'street law' ideas have attracted a great deal of attention.

These perspectives permeate the information approach to political education. It is distinctly different from the valuing approach; yet its variants are as wide as those in valuing. The fact-value continuum is in evidence here. Often people teach information about governments expecting loyalty as a result. When they teach values, they often do so from a solid information base. Many political education programs combine valuing and information approaches.

Inquiry

A third approach which involves a very wide variety of perspectives is that of inquiry. Many people believe that political education is basically an inquiry process, regardless of its content. There is a strong movement for students to inquire and be responsible citizens by seeking evidence for their arguments and considering the consequences of their actions.

Inquiry approaches vary considerably. There are those that are interested in inquiry as an analytical technique for viewing different perspectives and initiating a consideration of alternatives. There are others who view it as a means for student self-expression and the clarification of ideas and values. Still others attempt to use inquiry approaches in practical ways to train citizens to participate effectively in individual or group action through decision-making processes.[11]

Still another perspective within the approach involves that of critical theory. Here, a world view and an instructional view combine to teach students methods and means of constructive change through both analysis and action. Critical theory approaches are most popular in Europe where dialectical methods allow students to explore issues in a variety of ways and to see change as a constructive part of political life.[12]

Participation

A fourth general approach to political education involves participation. Here, students are taught basic roles and activities in individual and group action which promote citizenship skills and opportunities for participating in community, state and national policies.[13] Some participation approaches involve internships and social action in the community. Here, students learn from experience the general characteristics of the political process as well as the unique characteristics of particular agencies with particular purposes. The community in effect forms a laboratory for students to acquire important citizenship skills.

Still another perspective under this approach involves students simulating roles and taking part in classroom and school activities in order to learn important ways to work in groups, initiate tasks and implement them. In this case, the school becomes a laboratory for citizenship instruction; and the goals are not so much to solve the problems in the school or community, but to provide appropriate transfer experiences for the skills students are learning. The approach is more oriented toward the development of competencies than the solution of particular problems. Programs in political literacy in England are examples of this type of approach, and often extend beyond the boundaries defined here.

Still other perspectives on participation approaches involve students in events in the school or community. Model United Nations efforts are constructed so that students can learn to participate as if they were part of that organization. Election campaigns are simulated so that students can participate in voting processes. These types of created situations within and outside the school are typical of participation approaches, but are distinctly different from either the attempt for students to systematically learn skills or to develop realistic roles through internships and other activities in communities.

With all of the approaches combined, it is a diverse and vast array of possible approaches to mapping political education. At first, it does not seem to have any common core, nor is it clear what using different approaches means for individual citizenship skills. A further problem involves aggregation. When individuals aggregate in groups or as a whole polity, we do not know what will result from a variety of types of political education strategies which train citizens. In effect, further research and development work needs to be done that will determine what the consequences of different approaches are for students and what they mean for the polity in general.

Core Aims of Political Education

It seems that what needs to be constructed, at least at first, is a kind of political education consensus where, regardless of what one calls them — competencies, skills, or different concepts — those who are active in the field of political education can understand both the language of political education and the variety of approaches which are used. We will make an effort to define some core aims here, regardless of the particular use of particular words by people from different schools or different nations.

It seems to us that there are some core aims in the political education map, regardless of the approach that one uses. Every approach is concerned with *values*. Values are considered from different perspectives and take a different place in political education depending upon the approach, but everyone is concerned about the values that students hold regarding politics and political participation. People are also concerned about *information*. Here, whether the information is about politics or self or law or appropriate behavior for citizens, information is a key; and it becomes a core domain of objectives in political education. In a very real sense, information links those whose aims are chiefly cognitive with those who teach utilizing more affective objectives. Information becomes a rich and complex umbrella linking a variety of approaches.

Inquiry is also a key aim, whether this means analysis or critical theory approaches or more practical ones. Inquiry involves the manipulation of evidence and ideas, and without that there would be no translation into active citizenship. Finally, all of the approaches in some way involve *participation*. They can be geared toward teaching appropriate values, or information that will help citizens to participate, or they can be geared to improve skills in participation, whether one is thinking or acting politically.

Values, information, inquiry and participation are then important core aims for mapping the field of political education. However, there is a need to flesh out the list of core ideas with some aims that are not common across approaches and not even treated by some approaches. We claim here that *change, complexity* and *respect for human dignity* are equally important ideas.

The change concept is very important. Too often students think of political processes as static ones. They do not see how individuals grow and change politically. Nor do they see how political systems develop and change over time. The change process is probably as important a part of the understanding of citizens as knowledge or thinking skills. Students who comprehend both the variety of processes of change and the context and limitations on change processes will be much better able to cope with citizenship in any particular society.

In the current era where transnational events and processes affect individuals as much as local ones, there is still another need. Students do need to understand both the complexity of modern society and the abstractions of many of its institutions.[14] A transnational economic organization, for example, is a concrete institution in and of itself, but many of the monetary processes which are now carried out involve very abstract ideas. For example, whereas once money was the basis for exchange, credit is now that basis. A credit card is a concrete object, but the money exchange itself needs to be understood in abstract terms. The same is true of arms negotiation or other processes that are conducted politically. The adeptness which students exhibit in handling the complexity of issues and their abstractness is a key quality of effective citizenship, both in the national and in the global community.

Finally, a key concept of respect for human dignity is fundamental to the mapping of concepts in political education.[15] Too often approaches neglect this basic concept, which involves individuals' rights and responsibilities to themselves and to others. Without some basic focus on this type of concept, the knowledge and skills that are learned will not be put to use in ways that make an important contribution to either the local or the global communities.

Here we have seen how we might weave a fabric of political education by mapping its central concerns and approaches. We have also seen where some of the holes are and where concepts are needed in order for approaches to reflect the necessary concerns of the global community in the 1980s. Throughout this volume, we will be drawing different pieces of this map of political education. Hopefully, we can learn from each other and work together to form a more complete picture of both the variety of types of approaches and the types of maps that can be drawn.

POLITICS AND POLITICAL EDUCATION

People often think of political education as it has been described in the previous section. They think of a course of study or an approach to teaching about politics or government. Even in such a narrow definition, political education has natural applications to politics at the local, national and international level. Teachers who teach politics are constantly making applications from the local and national news, as well as describing international events.

Yet, the definition always has been, and increasingly is, more extensive than this. People are becoming aware of the political education opportunities that exist in the workplace, the home, the community, churches and other such organizations.[16] In effect these institutions are, in themselves, political. They are laboratories for political education. They help to expand and confirm the natural linkage between political education and political activity in nearby as well as more distant settings. Therefore, political education, in and of itself, has natural linkages into more partisan political arenas at various levels.

Our task will be to describe some of these linkages. There are linkages between instruction and practice. There are also linkages between people, between arenas and between events in those arenas, which make the mesh of politics and political education both tight and intricate, both delicate and conflictual.

Within the School Curriculum

Within the school curriculum, the initial link between politics and political education is set by the very approaches to study that are taken. Whether approaches are prepared at the national, local or individual level, they reflect political assumptions and content. Not only the facts which are selected for teaching, but the goals and objectives reflect more or less clear political strategies. Sometimes these strategies are quite plainly prescribed. A curriculum is designed to promote nation-building, for example. Sometimes they are more covert, especially in complex technological societies, content is often couched in a scientific focus. Yet, it is important to note that even science is molded and presented in a way which carries political assumptions and produces different types of political socialization influences and implementation strategies.

Perhaps the most important political vehicles within the school curriculum are the students themselves. Students are not apolitical beings who appear in courses to be filled with political content. Even as they enter primary school they have assumptions about and perceptions of the political system which give context and application to the facts which they assimilate and the approaches which they take. As students get progressively older, these political beliefs become more well-defined. They are always largely molded by influences outside of the school curriculum either within the school environment itself, in the family or in the local community. Therefore, students are political animals, and they contribute to the politicization of the curriculum within the school in significant ways.

Teachers are also an important political variable. They carry more or less well-formed partisan political beliefs and values. Regardless of the particular approach teachers make, it is impossible to keep these values and assumptions out of the curriculum. Either they are clarified and well-articulated, or they are reserved as hidden assumptions which structure what is taught, which enter into political discussions, and which formulate the rules and regulations that surround the political action in the classroom. No matter how professional a teacher may be, his or her political attitudes are revealed in the very act of teaching. As teaching involves changing behavior, it involves influence, and is basically a political act in and of itself. It is most often an act of political communication. The role models that teachers set for political action are also very apparent, if only subliminally to the students who are being taught.

The course of study or books that are being used also reflect political biases. A book cannot be written on the subject of politics which does not reflect certain ideas more than others, as well as value biases. The choice is not a text which either does or does not reflect political biases, but rather one which clearly articulates its point of view or reveals alternatives. Value neutrality is an impossibility. Clarifying assumptions and basic biases within a text is necessary if conscious political education is to be achieved. It has been common in the United States, for example, for teachers to attempt to select textbooks that reflect various points of view. The problem is that the assumptions behind the textbook are often never revealed. In selecting a 'value neutral' book, the teacher is actually selecting one which does not specifically define its political viewpoint.

For all of these reasons, the school curriculum itself is a political instrument. It is intimately involved in outright politics, let alone political education, as it reflects political viewpoints and demonstrates effective political strategies and role modeling on the part of teachers.

Within the School Environment

The constituency of the school environment is a distinctly political one. If students and teachers are politicized within the classroom, their activity outside the classroom reflects political ideology, political strategies, political goals and outcomes. Students and teachers are politicized; so are administrators. As they make rules and decisions, they operate in a political arena within the school environment that is sometimes highly charged and volatile. Activities in the environment are usually more routine, but they involve basic issues of representation, budgeting and human interaction which are at the heart of political activity.

The political structure of the school is most often reflected in the rules and regulations which surround it. Rules and regulations regarding attendance and punishment, regarding dress and behavior, are only one set of political decisions which distribute values and valuable things within a school. Scheduling, course selection and monetary distributions also reflect essentially political decisions. Although not everyone would view these rules and activities as strictly 'political', there is increasing information being gathered on their distinctly political impact on school participants.[17]

The processes of decision-making within the schools are highly political. They involve choices between alternatives which advantage some groups and disadvantage others. They involve questions of representation and participation on the part of students, teachers and administrators that are as highly political as those of congressional districting or representation in a national legislature.

In all of these ways, the school environment is a political arena. It is one in which political habits are acquired on the part of youth. It is one in which political actors make significant decisions on a regular basis. It is also one which national and local events enter with enough regularity to be judged as significant in the lives of school participants.

Within the Community

In some nations, community control characterizes the school system. This gives the community a great deal of political leverage. In the United States, community participation has been increasing over the years. More and more community norms and values are permeating both the curriculum and the extracurricular activities of school participants. Parents who once were largely involved only in school boards are now becoming more involved in such activities as textbook selection, course planning, teacher assignments and student participation.

The decision-making process in local communities is a significantly political one. Communities contribute in large measure to the socialization process of all participants in the school community. These unconscious decisions of norms and values and role modeling are equally as significant as the ones that are made determining financial support and direction for the goals and purposes of most schools. Even when the curriculum is more nationally directed, parental support for youths involved in schooling is critical to not only performance, but to the types of experiences and opportunities which students are given in political arenas.

The State and the Nation

Both the state and the nation contribute to the socialization of youth and adults in significant ways. This indirect political process has demonstrable effects on the attitudes and behaviors of those involved within the school community. Partisan politics becomes part of the teaching laboratory of the school as elections are simulated, and voting is actually done within the school settings. More indirectly, the values and ideologies set forth in national and state documents are taught to students in direct ways in the classrooms.

States and nations contribute major guidelines and financial sustenance for local schools that provide obvious reminders of the appropriate political stance that schools must take. Whether it is state or federal legislation, often directions in education are charted which are built from partisan political considerations.

Nor can one ignore events at the state or national level that permeate the walls of school buildings. These events can be an oil crisis or the assassination of a president. Regardless of their nature or scope, they become subjects for discussion, objects of action and certainly influence political processes within the everyday life of most school buildings.

In these and other ways, the mood of the nation or its specific activities is transmitted not only into the classroom, but into the extra-classroom environment in most schools across the globe. The twinning of political pressures and education needs is apparent walking into any classroom, whether it be in the United States, Japan, India, or the Federal Republic of Germany.

International Influences

For far too long, schools have ignored the international influences upon them. Not all of these are political. There are as many economic and social influences as there are political ones. The most obvious influences are probably events. International events, such as the SALT negotiations or political revolutions, are all discussed in schools on an everyday basis. They can serve to stimulate, or horrify, an entire school population.

Yet, the more regularized politics of the school are also influenced by more direct international influences. Student exchanges are common. The study of foreign languages and foreign newspapers is routine in most schools. Direct evidence of international contact is plentiful across the globe.

Yet, it is also true that with increasing complexity of international events and processes, global influences are less easy to trace and their consequences are far more difficult to analyze and address. The transnational 'processes' are harder to pin down, yet, they exist on an everyday basis. The influence of teaching methodology, of travel, of educational communication is increasing. Just as the economic sphere has been transnationalized, the educational sphere is beginning to show signs of global communication linkages. These linkages are fundamental. The linkages between politics and political education are based on the people that are involved, the political arenas that are touched, the goals that are shared and the dependency of schools on global decision-making.

The problem, then, is to clarify those linkages and to explicate them as well as to recognize their consequences. Part of the problem is to successfully mesh the need for political decision-making and the need for improved political education. There is usually a tension between the two. It is manufactured out of a difference in scope between official political actors and those interested in promoting the education of youth. The teaching of conflict management strategies is important if solid linkages between politics and political education are to be managed successfully.

Yet, there is another problem that increases as we move into a transnational age, and that is the problem of transnational problem-solving. Here we face problems of awareness. Students in local communities are often isolated from knowledge of international events and activities and international role models which could be effective for them. Their knowledge base of international affairs is dismally low. One significant part of that knowledge base needs to involve the study of transnational activities and processes.

It is also true that the kinds of skills that are needed for transnational cooperation are bound to be different from those that are required in small-group decision-making. What skills are needed and how they need to be emphasized has not yet been fully articulated by either educators or practitioners in the field.

All of this need for awareness, knowledge and skills leads to the basic need for transnational educational problem-solving. Without such problem-solving, which is institutionalized and routinized in terms of its participation and communication patterns, education will remain behind other fields that have successfully mobilized their efforts on a transnational basis.

What is needed for transnational cooperation and education to be effective is an established communication process that allows for knowledge and information to be transmitted relatively quickly and in non-subjective form to not only major leaders in education but to those involved in everyday political education in schools, communities, workplaces and families. Communication, however, is not enough. Participation is also an important variable. Without participation, problem-solving could not exist. Therefore, the organization of both formal and informal groups that can tackle major problems of awareness, knowledge and skills is necessary in order for education to proceed on a transnational basis.

Finally, some successes are needed in order to set models for transnational cooperation. If people can successfully solve even the smallest problems, the success will serve as a stimulus for further cooperation. It is one of the attempts of this volume to provide a success story in communication that will provide one vehicle for improving awareness and knowledge in the political education field by linking politics and political education on a transnational basis.

VOLUME RATIONALE AND OUTLINE

Purposes

The purposes of the volume are several. They are each equally important. If one of these purposes is accomplished for any given reader, it will have fulfilled its function.

The first and primary purpose is to share information. Here we are interested in increasing awareness about activities and ideas in political education across the globe, and in contributing to new research and development work through the cross-fertilization of efforts. If people read this volume, information will be distributed. If as a result of the volume they contact other authors and share mutual interests, the full purpose of awareness and information will be satisfied.

A second purpose of the volume involves highlighting important questions in political education and providing responses from a variety of perspectives. The central purpose of the volume is reflective. It is to analyze rather than to describe, to pinpoint key ideas and needs rather than to provide detailed outlines about research or practice. In this way the reader should be asked to question, to think, to reflect, rather than to seek out detailed information in the volume.

The volume also will promote comparisons across Europe and the United States. It will promote the juxtaposition of a variety of ideas so that readers can determine not only what is going on where, but how activities, ideas and purposes are compared across countries. The volume will also promote the exchange of new ideas and practices. Each section of the volume will highlight key ideas

and will outline significant practices stemming out of a particular
topic which is under discussion. The volume will highlight needs in
research and development in political education for the future. The
entire third section of the volume focuses on gaps in our knowledge
and understanding of political education. Each article within each
section will focus on needs that are seen by the author for future
progress in the exchange of ideas and practices across nations.

Finally, but not less importantly, a sixth goal of the volume
focuses on needs for transnational cooperation. An information
base is a key need for the promotion of transnational cooperation
and problem-solving. Hopefully, this dialogue will be the beginning
of an ongoing effort in a variety of areas between authors and
readers over educational problems and their solutions.

Outline

The volume is divided into three sections. The first section surveys
recent developments in the field. In this section, authors from different nations talk about what is going on in their own and other
countries, the current promising ideas and practices, as well as what
needs to be done in the field.

Section I focuses on approaches to political education. The introductory essay sketches a wide variety of approaches which are
taken to the topic. Subsequent essays focus on developments in two
specific countries. The tone is reflective and contemplative. Ideas
are more important than descriptions. Hopefully, this section sets
the information base for the volume.

Section II focuses on politics in political education and the types
of linkages we have been talking about in this introduction. The introductory essay focuses on the variety of ways in which politics
and political education interrelate. The subsequent essays in this
section take up different topics which demonstrate ways in which a
variety of agencies and ideas reciprocally influence each other in
order for political education to be advanced.

Section III focuses on two neglected areas: adult education
and international education. In these cases, many new ideas and
practices are introduced as springboards for future cooperative
research across authors and readers.

Finally, the conclusion stresses comparisons and transnational cooperation. It highlights ideas from each of the articles and draws comparisons. It draws interpretations and conclusions based on the findings from the previous chapters and lays out a plan for transnational cooperation.

As a result, the volume should provide both a general view and a special view of political education across the globe. It gives some basis for transnational cooperation. Hopefully, readers of this volume will contact authors and initiate an ongoing dialogue that will result in new models of cooperation in problem-solving in political education across the globe.

NOTES

1. One example of this idea occurs with the use of the term 'political education'. The concept has a different meaning in the United States, where it becomes generally equated with citizenship education in schools. In Britain or Germany, the term has a much more partisan focus with much broader applications to the community and workplace.

2. This is a standard definition used in many places. One well-known source is Fred Newmann, *Education for Citizen Action*, Berkeley, California: McCutchan, 1975.

3. This definition is detailed in Judith A. Gillespie and John J. Patrick, *Comparing Political Experiences*, Washington DC: American Political Science Association, 1974, monograph.

4. The definition stems from Harold D. Lasswell's seminal work, *Power and Society*, New Haven: Yale University Press, 1950; and its dimensions are clarified by several authors in David Easton (ed.), *Varieties of Political Theory*, Englewood Cliffs, NJ: Prentice-Hall, 1966.

5. For a detailed explanation of these and other approaches see Robert Barr, James Barth and S. Samuel Shermis, *The Nature of the Social Studies*, Palm Springs, California: ETC Publications, 1978.

6. See especially Rajni Kothari, *Footsteps Into the Future*, New York: The Free Press, 1974.

7. Various approaches are outlined in Douglas Superka's, *Values Education Source Book*, Boulder: Social Science Education Consortium, 1976.

8. See James Becker (ed.), *Schooling for a Global Age*, New York: McGraw-Hill, 1979.

9. Barr, Barth, Shermis, op. cit.

10. American Bar Association, *A.B.A. Directory on Law Related Education Project*, Chicago: ABA Special Committee on Youth Education for Citizenship, 1978.

11. See Bruce Joyce and Marsha Weil, *Models of Teaching*, Englewood Cliffs, NJ: Prentice-Hall, 1972.

12. Jurgen Habermas, 'Towards a Theory of Communicative Competence', *Inquiry* 13, 1970, pp. 360-375. Jurgen Habermas, 'The Analytical Theory of Science and Dialectics', pp. 131-162, in Theodor Adorno (ed.), *The Positivist Dispute in German Sociology*, New York: Harper Torchbooks, 1976.

13. For a typology and various applications see Fred Newmann, *Skills in Citizen Action*, Madison, Wisconsin: University of Wisconsin Press, 1977. One program which features action of the type described here is Judith A. Gillespie and Stuart Lazarus, *American Government: Comparing Political Experiences*, Englewood Cliffs, NJ: Prentice-Hall, 1979.

14. See Lee F. Anderson, *Schooling and Citizenship in a Global Age: An Exploration of the Meaning and Significance of Global Education*, Bloomington, Indiana: Social Studies Development Center, 1979.

15. One example is Gerald and Patricia Mische, *Toward a Human World Order*, New York: Paulist Press, 1977.

16. See Elizabeth Farquhar and Karen Dawsen, *Citizen Education Today: Developing Civic Competencies*, Washington DC: US Office of Education.

17. See especially Judith A. Gillespie, et al., *School Environments and Their Impact*, Bloomington, Indiana: Program in Educational Policy and Change, Indiana University, 1979.

I

RECENT DEVELOPMENTS:
AN OVERVIEW

1

Political Education: Pros and Cons

Willem Langeveld

In educational sociology little attention has been paid to the social and political forces demanding the introduction of 'civics', 'the constitution' or 'political education' in schools. In the course of this century educationalists and pedagogues have supplied a whole range of arguments for including this kind of subject in the curriculum; many of them wished it to be an integral part of every subject taught in schools. However, this is only one side of the picture and probably not the most important one. A more fundamental analysis of factors influencing the start of political education (under perhaps a more neutral name) seems necessary in order to help us understand its (hidden) goals, its limits and its possibilities. Of course, there are all sorts of differences between countries, or rather between political cultures, as regards the circumstances under which political education has been initiated and I would need much more space than I have to work out one or two examples. Instead I shall try to give a kind of theoretical construct with which decision-making processes in this particular field may be analyzed.

In the first part of this chapter a general view of some political functions of education in western industrialized countries is presented. Next the implications for political socialization will be discussed, after which the above-mentioned construct will be developed. In the course of my essay I shall bring in as many examples from various countries as I see fit.

THE SCHOOL AS AN AGENT
OF POLITICAL SOCIALIZATION

In general, schools have three main functions in western societies:
— an allocative one, providing students with qualifications for jobs and in connection with that, status;
— a socializing function, inculcating norms and values prevalent in society;
— the conservation of the cultural heritage, as well as the provision of modest support for social change.

The first function is not without political significance, as through various processes of selection it helps to maintain the social stratification notwithstanding tangible examples of external democratization in many western countries.[1]

The second function is more directly relevant to my theme, as schools have been socializing in a political way ever since this institution was founded in ancient times. Schools in our day are more important than ever before in this respect, since traditions, churches and elites no longer do this job.[2] General social norms and values are now transferred to the new generation by educational institutions. A portrayal of this process is at the same time an explanation of the functions of these norms and values in society. This is difficult because we cannot distance ourselves enough from our own way of life. The picture I give is therefore necessarily incomplete and impressionistic.

Educational systems are in their external and internal organization, as well in the ways they have to function, products of political decisions. Whether there are Protestant and Catholic schools or not, whether comprehensive schools can be founded and whether eleven-plus choices have to be made are all results of political discussions. However, in schools hardly any attention is paid to this kind of decision which is out of bounds for all students — 'let sleeping dogs lie . . .' So students do not learn about their own political situation.

Parliamentary democracies are ruled by delegation. This principle of delegation lies at the root of our socio-political system and it implies that a citizen feels little inclination to be politically active.[3] Voting once every so-many years is all the responsibility he or she is supposed to take and only very few politicians hope he or she will take more than that. In schools all main decisions are taken by the board or the principal. In many classrooms the teacher is still the authority whose opinions and knowledge may not be doubted. He must be respected and obeyed, even if the reasons for his actions are completely unclear to his pupils. Many controversial problems are said to be too difficult for students and this is an excuse not to touch upon them at all. They should be left to people who are older and know better.[4]

In many ways schools operate to create alienation. The students are often completely in the dark about the importance of the things they have to learn; learning takes place by extrinsic motivation, with sheer verbalism as a result, as everybody knows from his or her own experience. This alienation is a very useful non-quality in many types of work and social situations.

Political convictions belong to the private domain. This holy acquisition which was won by the bourgeoisie in a long struggle in the eighteenth and nineteenth centuries and which served as a protection of individual citizens, has stimulated individualism and weakened solidarity amongst like-minded people. The consideration of political opinions as private affairs has been an important obstacle to the treatment of highly controversial political problems in schools. Instead the present social and political situation is portrayed as optimal and as the end of a long tiring road.

Individualism is a major characteristic of western educational systems. Not only does a complicated selective pattern of notes, examinations and tests give rise to a competitive mentality, but it is also the source of feelings of personal guilt in cases of failure. Bad results are attributed to lack of motivation and attention, laziness and unsuitability. Blame the victim! No wonder students, when they are adults, have the same attitude towards the poor, minorities and other groups in unfortunate situations. Poverty is not seen in its socio-economic context, but rather as a contingency that can be changed by personal initiative.

The economic organization under capitalism is highly individualistic and it is not by chance that education instills these values in its pupils. In fact, cooperation and mutual aid are punished and a premium is set on conforming to individualistic standards.[5] Well-known is the dislike teachers have for students who do not accept their position of power, which always gives them the last word. Students who comply are rewarded, and so students learn that inequality in power is efficient. No wonder so many

people are politically inefficacious and leave decisions to experts or
to people they deem powerful.

   More important than what is taught is the way in which it is
taught. Whatever innovations are introduced in many schools, a
large part of the hours students spend in schools are still reserved
for teacher-centred lessons in which they cannot move and must
listen to the teacher and believe what he says in order to memorize
and reproduce it. Creativity is not a quality much appreciated in
students: it is often misinterpreted by their teachers as insubordina-
tion or pedantry. Students have no say in what they study and after
some years of this 'training' they do not want it any more. In fact,
they are totally dependent on their teachers in every aspect of the
learning process. It is tremendously difficult for them to work independently or in small groups when on occasion they are asked to
do so. Students are not confronted with the principle that different
solutions may be had to problems and that different viewpoints
lead to different conclusions. It seems to them that there is one and
only one right answer to almost any question and that doubt has
nothing to do with critical thinking, let alone wisdom. They do not
learn to listen to arguments for and against a solution, weighing
costs and benefits, even ending up with a more or less arbitrary
solution and hoping for the best, as is the case in many political
situations. Such practices are threatening to them, as they have not
learned to live with uncertainties. Political leaders who offer simple
clear solutions to very complicated problems may count on wide
support and many of them have learned this lesson — also in
school.

   The content of the curricula in most schools generally is remote
from the facts of life. The approach to many topics is necessarily a
theoretical one and many students (older adolescents) are often
helpless when they have to solve simple practical problems; talking
together, discussing, organizing, helping each other and many
other social skills are not taught.[6] What is more, in schools for the
elite there is usually a more advanced curriculum than in schools
for the lower strata of society. Children from families with higher
socio-economic status get a better preparation for political activity,
although in fact they need it less, as their milieu already helps them
along.

   This lack of confrontation with the world outside the school —
even TV programmes that students watch are normally not discuss-

ed in classrooms — has an infantilizing effect on youngsters, who have to spend more years at school than ever. The extension of adolescence stands in sharp contrast to the lowering of the age of legal maturity to 18 years, as is now the case in many countries. Youngsters are kept passive and dependent on the one hand, while they have rights (youth did not fight for them, they were rather easily given) they hardly know what to do with. The voting right is a good example: a high percentage of voters between 18 and 21 do not make use of it at elections.

Schools still maintain the differences in roles of men and women. Books and teaching aids have a sexist character, as research in various countries has demonstrated.[7] Discrimination of women in society is reflected in education, especially in vocational schools, boys having far more options than girls, though theoretically they have equal chances. On one point, however, they receive equal treatment, and that is as regards stratification. From the first day they enter school children are grouped according to age, sex, test scores, behaviour, achievement, school types, school classes, intelligence, etc. A person who is once classified in a group has very little chance of escaping, and of the perhaps ten percent who do escape, half go down rather than up.[8] Moreover, 'bad' groups get an education of lower quality than 'good' groups. This is revealed at first glance by the budgets for different school types. Schools for children from the lower classes — with the highest percentage of pupils — get relatively far less money than schools for the children of the elite. Children accept their positions and blame themselves for not being intelligent enough to enter 'better' schools.[9] Students who rank higher in the school's pecking order imitate the behaviour of their teachers with the less able pupils.

Schools inculcate a work ethos that is in strange contrast to an automated world where youth unemployment can only be remedied by an extension of compulsory education. Work is a private affair, with as its goal the reaping of personal rewards. Knowledge is private property, hopefully to be sold on the labour market.

Perhaps the most important way in which schools exercise political influence is through the total lack of alternatives to the existing situations. In general alternatives are depicted as bad, as deviations from the norm. Freedom in society is idealized and is hardly given any specific content in various social settings. By disparaging alternatives an attitude of resignation is formed, which makes students accept what seems to be the best of all possible worlds, like Dr Pangloss.

In conclusion I assert that schools do socialize politically in many ways, not usually openly but through the 'hidden curriculum'. Education reflects the social system rather closely. Its main function is to legitimize the existing power relations and configurations. At the same time, by its particular methods, it creates alienation — in fact education reproduces the alienation that prevails in society and particularly in work — that in turn gives rise to political apathy. Individualism, achievement, competition, obedience, order, trust in authorities in objective science are some important values that education transfers.

I understand that this picture will appear too black to many readers. I agree that many students, though they form a minority, do not become politically apathetic. In my opinion this is in spite of what education tries to do to them. They are the salt of the earth. Unless they are offspring of the elite, who get a better political socialization anyway, they set up a kind of counter-school culture with its own norms and values. Disobedience, truancy, cribbing, sabotaging school rules, impoliteness and disorderly behaviour are some salient marks of this youth subculture. Many students are conscious of the fact that school learning has little or nothing to do with the outside world, with real life. Early on in life, working class youth is aware of differences between rich and poor and accepts these as inevitable.[10] On the other hand, they refuse to internalize middle class values as conveyed by schools like industriousness, postponement of consumption and sex, dependence on adults, learning as something good in itself, and the solution of problems by reasoning instead of by force and aggression. They understand that as a class they will never have a chance of emancipation, certainly not by educational means alone. This is a political fact that no school can deny, let alone change.

This is not a conspiracy model of education invented by some shrewd politicians, capitalists and educational mafia. Education is organized and paid for by the state, it is founded on bureaucratic schemes, it preserves the cultural heritage and it has its own built-in rules and norms, which teachers do not like to reflect on too much. The internal functioning of such a system makes it a priori impossible for it to work in any other direction than the one that I indicated. Teachers express and transmit the prevalent norms and values of society more by how they act than by what they teach. In this way they are agents of political socialization without being aware of it. Many objections arise to teaching politics openly and particularly to doing this in such a way that students are able to criticize — God help us — oppose the system.

IS A SPECIAL SUBJECT NECESSARY?

Educational systems in western countries are not monolithic; the highly centralized French system cannot really be compared with the very decentralized British one. All systems have their own narrower or wider margins for autonomous actions by schools or individual teachers. Some are real kings in their classrooms; in other countries they have to fear school leaders or inspectors, or parents' organizations. But in all countries education is a subject of public discussion. Many groups with different interests — sometimes rather antagonistic ones — try to get it in their grip, and no group can really have 100 percent success. This situation provides opportunities for some teachers and some schools to deviate somewhat from the general rules and standards. Sometimes this kind of small-scale autonomy gets innovations started. The structure of the system itself, however, functions as a barrier against innovations generating 'from the base'. This is why many experiments done in individual schools with positive results hardly have any effect on the rest of education, and remain isolated incidents. Sometimes they have a legitimizing function for the immobility of the system as a whole.

Indeed, some teachers, making use of the 'holes' in the system, teach politics — without mentioning this dismal word — in a realistic and controversial way. What they do is not illegal, but from the viewpoint of the system it could be called subversive. It is not this kind of political education that I intend to look at now, as there are hardly any facts available that are based on research. This is not to say that it is not important. Our schools could perhaps have real impact by using what is said and done in their margins, where teachers go beyond the bounds of what they are supposed to say and do on formal grounds. It might also be that, for this reason, vested authorities and interests want to make those margins as small as possible. This could have led to the introduction of a new subject ('civics'), but this is only one of many hypothetical motives I shall discuss in the next paragraphs.

For the sake of clarity I differentiate between the manifest and the latent socialization processes. The aims of the manifest process are revealed in official curricula, tests, examination programmes, school regulations, official educational policy, schoolbooks and aids and in many publications which take the system for granted. The latent process can only be discovered by exposing the curriculum and showing the hidden forces at work.

As I demonstrated above, schools are supposed to be politically neutral, at least manifestly. On the other hand they are latently socializing their students politically, but whether they are successful is another question. The opinion one has about this depends on one's point of view. If one has a vested interest in the status quo, it might be that this interest is best served by widespread political alienation and apathy, or second best by passive acceptance and consent. If one regards democracy as a system that has to be improved politically and that has to be applied to all sectors of society (industry, government bureaucracies, tertiary sector), for which the support and participation of as many people as possible is required, then one cannot be satisfied with the manifest and latent functions of schools as agents of political socialization. To put it another way — and I am aware that I am simplifying things — politically conservative people like schools that put people in their place by whatever methods that serve this end; politically progressive people want politically emancipated students and schools to turn the latent process into a manifest one directed at further democratization.

In reality schools are subject to the same contradictory forces that are at work in capitalist societies.[11] The privileged classes want to keep their positions and need the passive support of the deprived masses, or at least non-resistance brought about by lack of interest or apathy. At the same time they need more and better-qualified workers with a broader kind of general education, which makes them more flexible on the job. For this reason they want schools to help implant an ideology that defines the existing situation as the best imaginable one: political apathy and alienation have a bad influence on the mentality of the workers; lack of trust in the system spreads to the job in office or factory, and people who feel this way are susceptible to anti-system forces in times of crisis.

Progressives also have mixed feelings about a more effective political education because of their doubt about the direction the effect would take. If the main goal of political education is the legitimization of the status quo with (in their eyes) all its injustice, inequalities in power, knowledge and financial position — and as we saw, it is hardly possible for it to work in any other direction — it is understandable that progressives reject it. The less monolithic the system is, the more positive their attitude will be. For different reasons neither group is very happy with the political socialization function of schools; both groups (again from different angles) work towards the improvement of that function, e.g. by adding a special subject to the curriculum.[12]

Until now I have only viewed the situation from the standpoints of two important groups in society. The state and the educational system itself, however, have a say in it as well. The political education function of schools is very controversial in all western democracies and every country has its examples of conflicts that have been discussed in Parliament.

The main function of the state in modern capitalistic societies is to maintain the balance between the powerful classes with capital, high incomes and specialized knowledge and the classes that do not have these things.[13] The state (including all kinds of administrative organizations, welfare institutions, education etc.) is the biggest employer in many countries. For this reason alone the interests of the state are strongly intertwined with capitalist society as a whole; the state is heavily dependent for its income (taxes) on private industry (multinationals!). The state supports industry financially with orders, and in times of recession or depression with subsidies. Individual states cannot really attack the powerful positions of big business — in the improbable case that they should intend to do so — as the interests of of multinationals and banking capital are internationally interwoven in such a way that the one to suffer would be the country, not business. In capitalist countries the state maintains law and order. The state legitimizes not only existing differences in power positions but also its own function in maintaining them. As the influence of the state on society is continually growing — caused by such factors as the greater difficulties the state encounters in keeping society in balance and by the fact that non-profitable activities are delegated to the state — its oppressive aspects become more and more visible. Simultaneously an ideology which conceals these functions is produced: society is complex because it is open; different groups and interests play a game of countervailing powers; the state protects everybody but particularly the socially weak.[14] These are only a few of the myths or half-truths that are brought into circulation — but through what media?

Laws on education are products of capitalism. The main function of education in the nineteenth century was to discipline the lower classes and to educate the higher classes in order that the new generation could take over the leadership in society. Although social and political drilling was a general principle of the whole system, some subjects, such as history, physical training, singing and religion had a particular importance. With universal suffrage the need for a subject like 'civics' became pressing, especially for children from middle and high class families.[15]

The voting age in many countries was about 23 or 25. In general students in secondary education were considered too young to really understand politics. The state in its role of keeping society in balance has an interest in politically neutral education, at least manifestly. A special subject like 'civics' that explains the organization of the state and the constitution and that shuns any kind of critical reflection is needed, though even such a subject has its risks. But it also has a legitimizing function within education, which is meant to deflate the arguments of those groups that wish to improve the role of schools in political socialization.

This brings us to education as an autonomous factor in capitalist societies. This autonomy varies in degree from country to country and in one country at least it is even differentiated according to regions, types of schools and the rigidity of classifications and codes. However, an educational system as a whole, notwithstanding its internal contradictions and conflicts, may be seen as a socio-political factor of considerable power. It has developed its own traditions, norms, organizational principles and gates and filters through which it looks at demands from the outside. Education has developed a subculture of its own and it assimilates new demands which are then transformed into educational practice according to its own standards. However, these often do not resemble the original plan. In many cases a demand is kept outside the system by quite a range of procedures and methods, varying from installing a commission which drags on the discussion of the problem for years, or starting an experiment with insufficient means, the failure of which can easily be foreseen.[16] It is interesting to see how the system deals with innovations that come from within, sometimes started by individual teachers or a special school. Every system has its own internal filters and gatekeepers to deal with these 'withinputs'. Sometimes the internal social and formal control is not effective and it comes to public and political debate.

As to political education, until the sixties there has never been a strong pressure group recruited from the ranks of teachers in most western countries that supported the introduction of a special subject. As a group, teachers differ in profession, intellect and status from the rest of the population. The consequences of their political views and ideas may differ from country to country. In France a relatively high percentage of teachers are members of the Communist party,[17] but this is rather exceptional in comparison to other countries, where teachers generally affiliate with social-democratic or conservative parties. In the light of the system-maintaining function of education, their position is politically vulnerable. This vulnerability makes itself felt in those subjects that have a more manifest relationship to political questions, like history, geography, 'civics', social studies and possibly the native language. Research from various countries shows that teachers are well aware of their vulnerability and draw their consequences: in their lessons they avoid discussing current political conflicts, especially the national ones. International conflicts are safer topics, because they can be dealt with without making links to national politics.[18]

It is this vulnerability that keeps them from calling for political education even when they are convinced that it is necessary for emancipation. Demanding political education is asking for trouble and makes them suspicious in the eyes of their colleagues and educational authorities. Teachers tend to avoid the word 'politics' altogether: they can agree on content and methods, but they do not like to call a spade a spade.

Of course, teachers use all the arguments that can be heard elsewhere against political education as well. Schools could become the arena of party politics; political indoctrination will lie in wait at the threshold of every classroom; children are too young to understand politics anyway, especially the darker side of it; politics should be left to the parents; there is no time to do it well and in this field half-knowledge is worse than no knowledge, so schools had better stay away from it. Apart from the enormous amount of

energy that would have to be invested in a change in the curriculum
— a change that would also have consequences for the teaching
hours spent on other subjects — teachers who support political
education have to reckon with strong resistance from the system
and from forces outside it, like parents, press and political parties.
Many progressive teachers do not give very strong support to proposals for the introduction of political education because of a very
understandable fear that such a subject will in practice only serve to
reaffirm the system.

In the wake of the social upheavals of the sixties in various West
European countries, the term 'political education' could be used
openly and the demand for its introduction in education was made
by students and teachers, but without much effect. Some progress
has been made, however; the concept is legal currency in the educational shop.

To summarize, education as a political socializing factor comes
to the fore when the traditional forces can no longer be relied on to
do the job effectively, quieting groups that could become noxious
to the system. A special subject like political education is in fact introduced when the latent socializing forces in education are in their
turn no longer reliable and need some extra support. This need is
felt at different times in the history of various countries, depending
on their particular cultural and socio-political development. There
is a difference between the immediate and the more fundamental
causes for the introduction of this subject, as there is a difference
between the obvious reasons given by educational authorities and
the more basic ones that come from the economic and cultural
situation.

National history was brought into the curriculum in the nineteenth century to foster patriotism, love for one's country and
understanding of the mission it had to fulfill in the world. The
more fundamental reason was to make children believe a
mythology about the situation in their country and its relations
with the rest of the world. The American credo, 'to make the world
safe for democracy', is an example.[19] In Great Britain it was
'Britannia rule the waves', in France the superiority of French
culture, in Germany militarism was enhanced by the way history
was studied in schools.[20] It was no accident that this mythology was
accentuated in a period when the working class was protesting
against its miserable living conditions and was organizing itself

politically. In Germany history got this function of reinforcing official political myths in the period when laws against socialists were
in force. Old fashioned 'civics' in the USA was supposed to help
waves of immigrant children to understand better the blessings of
their new homeland. In fact they were supposed to internalize
values like freedom and equality and the concomitant enormous
possibilities of this open capitalist society for those who wanted to
work hard. This aim was to create resignation instead of protest in
cases of personal failure.

THE CASE FOR A SPECIAL SUBJECT

I shall now try to summarize the reasons for the introduction of a
special subject 'political education', or one that fulfils the same
function under another label. Those reasons may of course differ
from country to country and from period to period. What is an obvious reason in one country may be a hidden one in another. Only a
refined analysis of every particular situation can bring this to light.

Some reasons are strongly related to the political system in a narrower sense, others have a socio-economic or cultural character. To
the first category belong the following arguments:

a) Teaching people to accept the way governmental administration functions as the best possible way under the given circumstances. This need is felt by political actors when they have the
impression that support for the system is lacking, for example after
a change brought about by war, revolution or social turmoil such as
in 1968. The main aim of the educational activities is to foster con-
formity to state rules and laws, or to put it more bluntly, to maintain law and order. This kind of need is typical for times of crisis,
when the mythology which buttresses the system is unmasked and
new myths have to be created and spread. Political cynicism can
turn into political activity and endanger the system fundamentally,
at least in the eyes of those in power. In this situation it is possible
that the population hardly has a need for political education. Those
in power, however, do.

b) The wish to have it as a special subject can also be expressed
by other groups, for example trade unions or political parties. This
may happen in the struggle for universal suffrage, or after this right
is acquired. It is peculiar that in most countries I know of, so little

energy has been invested in efforts to help youngsters understand
more of politics after getting the right to vote. On the other hand,
as I pointed out earlier, education in schools was distrusted by progressives and conservatives, both parties being afraid of the other's
influence on innocent souls. Moreover, the question becomes more
urgent now that the voting age has been lowered to 18 and that
school careers are longer. Perhaps in the near future this may lead
to stronger pressure to have this subject in schools.

c) Nationalism might be an important factor.[21] In younger nations it still is, but also in countries with strong minorities or strong
socio-economic tensions, nationalism can be the remedy to dissolu-
tion. If there are outside forces at work which weaken the independence of the country in question, or when government needs
a myth of this kind for other reasons, political education can be
helpful. The wish to have it can either come from within or from
without the system, or both. These reasons should be clearly differentiated from political education for the integration of
minorities in society, or for the mitigation of class differences,
typical for the second category.

When we turn to this type of reasons, we find that they are supplied by persons or groups who stand outside the political system.
They are brought in by pressure groups of different kinds, including those working in education.

A plea is sometimes made — in this context rather unexpectedly
— by representatives of business, who avoid using the reprehensi-
ble concept 'political' in their formulation of what they feel to be
lacking in our schools. The attitude of business as regards education deserves a much deeper analysis than can be given here, but it
must be clear that the ideas about what the main tasks of education
should be were never uniform, as they reflect secondary contradictions in production under capitalist conditions, and that they are
changing with the historical process itself. So it can happen that in
a certain period employers wish education to stay away from
politics (e.g. a period when the educational system fulfils its
disciplinary functions in an optimal way). In other periods
employers are highly interested in more manifest approaches to
these problems, for instance in times of rapid social and political
change. There is also a relationship between the level of technology
and industry's expectations as to the achievements of education.
For instance, in early capitalism the main task of education was the

disciplining and drilling of working class children; in high capitalism this function was veiled by subjects which also had some significance for what was called the development of the personality, like drawing, painting, singing etc.; in late capitalism multi-purpose employees with flexible personalities are demanded and education has to turn to subjects like discussion techniques, consumer behaviour, teamwork training, computer knowledge, etc. Civics, that is knowledge and understanding of the functioning of state organs and the establishment of a strong conviction that the existing political system is the best that one can hope for, is deemed admissible in business circles.[22]

In every country there are all kinds of groups which are active outside the political arena where parties have their quarrels and strife, but which have their worries about democracy. These groups have varying ideologies and (hidden) intentions, but what they have in common is the pressure they put on the educational system to work for democracy as they understand it.

Some of these groups recruit their members from educational staff, teachers, parents, youth movements, consumer organizations and trade unions. When they ask for a special subject, they can differ strongly in opinion about its content and methods. Sometimes such groups are highly idealistic and have only a slight knowledge of the real possibilities of reaching their goals. They are a nuisance to many teachers who work hard for the same ideals and have to cope daily with all the troubles children can give who are not very interested in politics.[23] Some groups are interested in integrating minorities into society. They want to give children an understanding of the political system under which they live, of their duties (and sometimes their rights) in society and of the way the system works. Most often the picture given is a very harmonious one, completely contradictory to the experiences of the students.

Groups who work for this kind of education generally have other goals as well and they have different ideological points of departure. As the amount of power they can gain is usually small, their influence on education is generally marginal. It can become stronger when the minorities themselves join these groups. This is exceptional, however, as minorities have their own opinions about politics and, as a consequence, of what political education should be.[24]

Next to these kinds of explicit reasons many more can be inferred from the way in which the subject is formally introduced and from what happens after that. In the next section I shall try to make an inventory of the main issues that can arise when the subject is formally part of the curriculum.

PROBLEMS OF THE SUBJECT

As always in conflicts, much can be learned from those people who oppose an idea that is going to be realised. This is certainly the case wherever political education is a topic of discussion. Opposing persons and groups usually tell a lot about the real intentions of privileged groups. In various countries they continue to resist even after it has been decided that the subject should be incorporated. Authorities also take this opposition into account beforehand — especially when it comes from education itself — and define the subject in such a way and give it such a poor chance of being realised, that it cannot do much harm.

A very interesting indicator of how important new developments in society are to the political authorities is the time lag between the first call to include political education in the school curriculum and the factual accomplishment. What is needed is a measure of this time lag based on an average of various 'innovation periods'. New technological developments like calculating with computers have a very short period, whilst sexual education has a very long one.[25]

Another indication of acceptance by society would be the time lapse between the introduction of a new subject or method in the university and the point of time at which it percolates into primary education. Once multiplication and division were seen as difficult activities, to be taught at universities. It does not seem very probable that anything like a standard period of time exists, as the process of educational innovation is part of social change in society as a whole, which varies in rapidity in different historical periods.

It is typical for western democracies that prevailing opinion holds political education — even in an adapted form — unfit for children under the age of about fourteen. In totalitarian states political education — called indoctrination by western observers — starts very early in life, as early as kindergarten. In this way the system recruits its supporters, although the method is not as successful as one is inclined to expect. The political socialization process is extremely complicated and a perfectly organized educational system is no guarantee that it will produce docile citizens.[26]

From a viewpoint of psychological development totalitarian systems have an easier time of it than truly democratic systems. Totalitarianism is allergic to doubt and criticism and educates according to a rigid pattern of norms and values, convictions and prejudices. As young children (as far as we know) lack the ability to think in relative terms and have a need for certainties, it is clear that these systems have an advantage compared to teachers in democracies who really intend to help their pupils learn some fundamental principles of that system, like: 'Do not block the possibility of change with respect to social goals',[27] 'do not trust authority for itself but look for yourself in what or whose service it is exercised'; 'it is everybody's duty to make use of his or her democratic rights and this is the best defence of those rights'. In order to understand these and many other principles the child must be in the stage of 'formal operations' (Piaget) and there is no way to simplify the ideas to lower levels of abstraction.[28]

This long marginal note helps us to understand why political education has no access to primary education, although the more conventional reason is that children should be protected against the dirty aspects of politics, in other words against the stupid and 'childish' things that adults do to each other. In the TV era such a viewpoint sounds a little naive, but it is still valid, as it is used by opposing groups of different standpoints. This brings us to the age at which educational authorities judge children to be best suited for 'civic training'. In almost all countries I know of, this is after the age of fifteen. At that age they are able to think more rationally, but whether there is a possibility of modifying their attitudes is something else. But this is precisely what the opposition wants: political education — if it is unavoidable — must have as little influence as possible.[29]

Other well-known arguments against the subject are repeated again and again during the years after its introduction. One of the most persistent is that schools should not become a political arena in which the presumed pedagogical harmony changes into strife. Those who make this assertion generally mix up politics with party politics and are usually not informed about developments in political science and the discussions about political education.

Resistance to the subject also expresses itself in complaints about the time it takes and the lack of time there is for the 'really important subjects', like mathematics, science, language. This is related to the narrow outlook that political education is not based on an academic discipline, or that those social sciences are still in their infancy and that it is too early to bring them into schools. The subject is supposed to be too easy for the more intelligent students. In this context one may also hear the remark that the subject does not have a clearly defined field, goals and content. This leads to problems of qualifications, so important in educational systems with rigid classifications and codes.[30] Fortunately, teachers in many countries have some autonomy in what they do when the door of the classroom closes and they are at work with their students. This is not the case at all as far as teaching aids and studybooks are concerned — parents and authorities almost everywhere watch them with Argus eyes. The schoolbook largely determines the teaching process, and it is no coincidence that the opposition is very alert on this point, although as usual the influence of school learning on the pupils' attitudes and ideas is highly overestimated. Almost every country has its rows about 'indecent', indoctrinating books and materials.[31]

In order to understand more of the intertwining of education and politics, we must look not only at the opposition but also at the way it manifests itself. There are different methods of keeping teachers in line and the methods used depend on the country's political culture. In some countries non-complying teachers are silently disposed of, by giving them an impossible combination of teaching hours for example, or by asking them to do all kinds of extra work. In other countries a lot of screening is done before a teacher is accepted, laws are even made to ban so-called extremists from education. It is clear that the teacher of political education is in a very vulnerable position, and in many cases this knowledge induces the teacher to stay away from all really controversial topics, specially in domestic politics.[32]

Another question we have to ask is: in what form and by what means are conflicts made visible and solved? Some remain at the micro-level and are resolved in the school without much attention from outside. I think that there are many of these conflicts in every country, and making an inventory of them could throw a glaring light on the total situation.

Some draw the attention of colleagues in school and are fought on what I would call the meso-level. Sometimes parents and superintendents get involved, but as everybody tries to keep it out of the press, there is hardly any publicity and the problem does not get much attention.

Conflicts on the macro-level are those that are hotly debated in the media and that even get the attention of parliamentarians and government officials. They form the tip of the iceberg and compel the authorities to take decisions which affect the whole system. What appear to outsiders to be minor questions, incidents, storms in teacups, are in fact major conflicts between groups who defend the existing order and those who see democracy as an ongoing process of further democratization.

Those who fight for political education can only hope for some success if they conceive a strategy on the basis of a scrutiny of the political and educational system and their functions. Possibilities for political education are probably marginal everywhere. Being aware of this helps to prevent frustration.

EXAMPLES

To conclude I shall give some examples of conflicts about political education from various countries. Of course, what we need is a much closer analysis in every country and in each case, undertaken by teachers and political scientists in cooperation.

With the exception of the FRG, 'political education' is in no country that I know of regularly, let alone officially, used as a name. Almost everywhere a 'euphemism' for a subject with this kind of goal is given; for example, in the USA 'Social Studies', 'Civics'; in Britain 'British Constitution', 'General Studies', 'Modern Studies'; in the Netherlands 'Maatschappijleer'; in Belgium 'Maatschappelijke Vorming'; also in the FRG 'Gesellschaftslehre', 'Sozialkunde'; in Scandinavia 'Staatsbürgerkunde'. This already proves that politics is more or less contraband for schools, at least if openly advertised. In some countries like France and Italy the matter is hardly discussed at all. In Austria political education is a subject that can be chosen voluntarily by students in secondary education, a choice that 5-10 percent of them in fact make.[33]

A country that is a good example of the processes I tried to describe is Belgium.[34] There the subject 'Maatschappelijke Vorming' (Social Education) was introduced by a social-democratic minister of education in 1970 against resistance from outside and in the schools, where teachers of history attacked the new subject severely, not least because they had lost working hours. A fervent discussion started around the content of the subject, which gained a special character from the typically Belgian background, where some years before an agreement about 'neutrality of the schools' was signed by the political parties. Right-wing forces were afraid of the politicization of education. The new subject was introduced without sufficient preparation and it never really worked. A change of government brought a quick end to the newly born. The liberal minister of education who was in office in 1975 warned against the indoctrinating function of 'Maatschappelijke Vorming' and abolished the subject in the same and the next year almost totally. However, he introduced a new subject 'aesthetic education', a change that is self-evident.

Another interesting example originates from the 'Land' Hessen in the FRG. There a new curriculum plan for history, geography and 'Sozialkunde' was produced by a special committee in 1972.[35] This plan came under severe criticism from the Christian Democratic party and affiliated newspapers, like *Bild*. The accusations were that the plan was not based on the constitution of the FRG; that self-determination and participation in democratic procedures were the main goals; that conflicts were emphasized one-sidedly; that the class struggle was stimulated and particular interests fostered; and that by these goals the plan prevents the identification of students with the state.[36]

The whole affair ended with the retraction of the plan and the retirement from politics of the minister of education of Hessen, Ludwig von Friedeburg. Conflicts like this, although not with so serious consequences, happened also in other 'Länder' of the FRG.[37] In the Netherlands the subject 'Maatschappijleer' is still under the same threat as was 'Maatschappelijke Vorming' in Belgium. The subject was introduced by a general reform of secondary education in 1968, although nothing was done either before or after the introduction to give it sufficient support. Qualifications of teachers were not officially and efficiently settled and there was no in-service training for teachers. In fact almost all teachers were officially allowed to do the job. The subject is an obligatory one in all types of secondary schools, but without examinations. Up till now an official curriculum based on appropriate theory has not been produced. There have been several cases of teachers being accused of indoctrination, sometimes leading to debates in Parliament. There is strong resistance against changing the subject into political education and giving it that name.

Another good example could be found in Portugal after the revolution of 25 April 1974.[38] At that time there was a strong interest in political education, that has almost disappeared in more recent years, at least in governmental circles. In Britain, according to Entwistle,[39] there was interest in political education before and immediately after the Second World War, but this eruption had to do with the reinforcement of nationalism in that time of crisis. After that the interest flagged, but Derek Heater has noted a revival of interest at the beginning of the seventies.[40] One gets the impression that very different topics are brought under the label political education in Britain, although the subject may not bear that name, but has often been called 'British Constitution'.

In 1973 a very interesting conflict arose, as spokesmen of the Labour party were accusing Conservatives of making use of sixth-form conferences to indoctrinate school pupils. Here again is a specimen of the damage politics can do to the serene atmosphere of schools. In a typically British way, I might say, it was Bernard Crick, acting as president of the Politics Association — an organization once accused of being a 'socialist conspiracy' — who drafted ground rules by which the political parties agreed to go on with their informative work in schools.[41] Yet, political education in Britain still has many problems to cope with, especially in view of the very differentiated school system.

With these examples in mind, to which additions could be made from many other countries, from Finland to South Africa, from the USA to Australia, one may conclude that the standing of political education is a useful indicator for the democratic development of a society.

NOTES

1. See Samuel Bowles and Herbert Gintis, *Schooling in Capitalist America, Educational Reform and the Contradictions of Economic Life*, London and Henley: Routledge & Kegan Paul, 1976; Roger Dale, Geoff Esland, and Madeleine Mac-Donald (eds.) *Schooling and Capitalism, a Sociological Reader*, London and Henley; Routledge & Kegan Paul, 1976; Pierre Bourdieu and Jean-Claude Passeron, *Reproduction in Education, Society and Culture*, London and Beverly Hills: Sage, 1977.

2. Schools devote much of their time to the 'training' of good citizens. 'Estimates of time spent in such instruction range upward to over fifty percent of the entire elementary and secondary school educational experience. This fifty percent figure is reached when one considers that much of the work in English, music, health, and even in the neutral sciences has a strong nationalistic or citizenship component.' Russell F. Farnen, Jr., *Formulating a Comprehensive Index of Political Education in Contemporary America* (first draft), Mimeo., New York, 1977.

3. Compare Robert J. Pranger, *The Eclipse of Citizenship, Power and Participation in Contemporary Politics*, New York: Holt, Rinehart and Winston, 1968.

4. See for the ideological implications of this kind of 'training': Theo Jansen, *Ideologische aanpassing in het basisonderwijs*, Nijmegen: Socialistische Uitgeverij Nijmegen, 1975 (a report of research done in four elementary schools); Talcott Parsons, 'The School Class as a Social System', *Harvard Educational Review* 29 (4), Fall 1959, pp. 297-318; and Mieke van Haegendoren, 'Welke maatschappelijke vorming geeft de school?' *Persoon en Gemeenschap* 31 (5), January 1979, pp. 238-247.

5. See F. Wellendorf, *Schulische Sozialisation und Identität*, Basel: Weinheim 1974; Robert Dreeben, 'The Contribution of Schooling to the Learning of Norms', *Harvard Educational Review* 37 (2), Spring 1967, pp. 211-237.

6. Compare Paul Goodman, *Growing up Absurd*, London: Sphere Books, 1960.

7. See Angelika C. Wagner et. al., *Mann — Frau, Rollenklischees im Unterricht*, Munich: Urban & Schwarzenberg, 1978; *Interchange* 10 (2), 1979-80 (special issue on sex-role stereotypes); and Rosemarie Nave-Herz, 'Das Angebot weiblicher Identifikationsmodelle in Lesebücher', *Materialien zur Politische Bildung*, nr. 4, 1978 pp. 93-99.

8. A very interesting study of the mechanism at work in education which has the effect of keeping lower class students in their place is Paul Willis, *Learning to Labour, How Working Class Kids Get Working Class Jobs*, Farnborough, Hants: Saxon House, 1977.

9. For various studies on this point, see Ali Wacker (ed.), *Die Entwicklung des Gesellschaftsverständnisses bei Kindern*, Frankfurt and New York: Campus Verlag, 1976.

10. Wacker, ibid.; Willis, op. cit.

11. The kind of simplifications that result from using a positivistic approach are demonstrated by R. Freeman Butts, who asserts that the urge to promote civic education through the schools increases in times of crisis or rapid social change. This conclusion seems to be all right, but then he goes on: 'It takes on special urgency in

two quite different kinds of social situations in which the need for social cohesion and unity is seen to be particularly acute: a) when liberal reformers see the need to mobilize disparate groups to achieve (in Robert Wiebe's words) "a new social integration, a higher form of social harmony", as in the Revolutionary Era, the Progressive Era, the New Deal, and the Great Society or b) when conservative forces see the need for social cohesion to rally round their version of the American way of life and to stave off threats to it from alien sources, as in periods of massive immigration, militant radical movements, world war, or cold war.' F. Frank Brown, *Education for Responsible Citizenship*, The Report of the National Task Force on Citizenship Education, New York: McGraw-Hill, 1977, p.47. Freeman Butts does not answer the question why liberals and conservatives are sometimes more, sometimes less interested in political education. Nor does he deal with who the liberals or conservatives are, in what ways their interests are alike, what common (class) enemies they have, etc.

12. Extreme left-wing groups reject political education totally as another hideous means to manipulate and deceive children; right-wing groups usually accuse left-wing groups of indoctrination as soon as the subject is taught. This sometimes induces authorities to remove the subject from the curriculum (as in Belgium and in some 'Länder' in Germany).

13. Ralph Miliband, *The State in Capitalist Society*, London: Quartet Books, 1969, and *Marxism and Politics*, Oxford, 1977.

14. See Murray Edelman, *The Symbolic Uses of Politics*, Urbana: University of Illinois Press, 1964.

15. This is not to say that there was no political education long before universal suffrage was introduced. (However, the need for a special subject had now become urgent, or the character of an already existing subject had to change.) On the other hand, one is astonished that after their victory groups who had fought for universal suffrage hardly put energy into the development of educational activities to prepare for rational use of the voting right. This goes for socialists as well as suffragettes.

16. Educational systems have at their disposal a huge arsenal of means to block or sabotage innovations that are not appreciated by the majority of teachers. Nazism did not fully succeed in setting education in hand, although it did its utmost. Krushchev's plans for the integration of study and practical work was a complete failure, as schools did not cooperate. In 1945 the GDR government purged education of all ex-Nazis and started with an almost completely new staff, an understandable action if a real social and educational change is deemed necessary.

17. Paul Gerbod, *Les enseignants et la politique,* Paris: Presses Universitaires de France, 1967. Every country has its own examples.

18. See H. Zeigler, *The Political Life of American Teachers*, Englewood Cliffs, NJ: Prentice-Hall, 1967; I. Lister, 'Political Education in the Classroom', paper presented to the Conference on Political Socialization and Political Education, Tutzing, 1977; Farnen, op. cit.

19. Freeman Butts, op. cit.

20. Klaus Hornung, *Etappen politischer Pädagogik in Deutschland*, Bonn: Bundeszentrale für Heimatdienst, 1962; Dietrich Hoffmann, *Politische Bildung 1890-1933, Ein Beitrag zur Geschichte der pädagogischen Theorie*, Hanover: Hermann Schroedel Verlag, 1970.

21. In nineteenth century Europe as well as in the United States, nationalism was a major important reason for introducing political education wrapped in subjects like history, civil government, the constitution, etc. Nowadays in young Third World nations we see the same tendency.

22. This view is based on what I learned from educational sociology and the political economy of education. See F. Naschold, *Schulreform als Gesellschaftskonflikt*, Frankfurt: Athenäum, 1974; H. Titze, *Die Politisierung der Erziehung*, Frankfurt: Athenäum Fischer Taschenbuch Verlag, 1973; and F. Arlt and A. Beelitz, *Führungskräfte der Wirtschaft äussern sich zur Hauptschule*, Hanover: Hermann Schroedel Verlag, 1970; Bowles and Gintis, op. cit.

23. Such groups have divergent interests such as peace education, consumer behaviour, environmental pollution, health education, vocational guidance and many more.

24. In the USA 'civil government' as a subject had this function from about 1870 till 1925, when great numbers of new immigrants had to be assimilated. West European countries, with millions of guest workers within their boundaries, are now faced with comparable problems.

25. As far as my knowledge of Dutch education goes, this average lies somewhere between thirty and fifty years.

26. In spite of years of indoctrination in the Soviet Union, youth in general is not very much interested in politics. See Ivan Volgyes, *Political Socialization in Eastern Europe, A Comparative Framework*, New York: Praeger Publishers, 1975. For the situation in the GDR, see Karl Schmitt, 'Political Education in the German Democratic Republic: Effects and System Relevance,' *International Journal of Political Education* 3 (2), 1980.

27. Thomas Landon Thorson, *The Logic of Democracy*, New York: Holt Rinehart and Winston, 1962, p. 139.

28. Childhood is also a matter of definition and it is quite possible that at some point we will find ourselves in an era in which children really have the same rights as adults. We cannot yet imagine the consequences this would have for psychological development, but it might be that their potential for abstact thinking would become far greater than we presume it to be nowadays. A system that oppresses adults in many ways is not able to treat children as equals — on the contrary.

29. Derek Heater sees four factors at work that cause the neglect of political education: 'lack of tradition; lack of teachers professionally committed to this field of work; a belief that the study of politics can only be an adult activity; and fear of indoctrination' ('A Burgeoning of Interest: Political Education in Britain', *International Journal of Political Education* 1 (4), November 1978, pp. 325-347). Reasons like these have their importance, but they are not fundamental, and function as rationalizations. The first two are valid for any new subject, the third one has been used time and again for sexual education for example, which is now accepted as a special theme, so only the fourth is typical for political education, although it has this fear in common with history and religion. In order to understand the forces that work against political education, one must compare these subjects with others recently introduced.

30. See Basil Bernstein, *Class, Codes and Control, Towards a Theory of Educational Transmissions*, Vol. 3, London and Henley: Routledge and Kegan Paul, 1975.

31. Some countries have state examinations of schoolbooks and teaching materials. In the USA for instance, many states have nominated special commissions of prominent people to do this job. See Bertil Borjeson, 'State Examination of the Objectivity of Teaching Materials in Sweden', *International Journal of Political Education* 3, (2), 1980; for an interesting analysis of the way in which materials are banned, see Ann and Roger Scott, 'Censorship and Political Education: The Queensland Experience', *International Journal of Political Education* 3 (1), 1980; and Gerd Stein, *Immer Ärger mit den Schulbüchern — Ein Beitrag zum Verhältnis zwischen Pädagogik und Politik I&II*, Stuttgart: J. Metzler, 1979.

32. Y. Agnès and G. Herzlich, 'La politique au lycée', *Le monde de l'Education*, January 1978, pp. 6-22. Notorious are the 'Berufsverbote' in the FRG of which many teachers became victims. See *Berufsverbote in the Federal Republic of Germany*, Deutsche Gesellschaft für Verhaltenstherapie e.V., Uhlandstrasse 2, 7400 Tübingen, 1978.

33. Walter Göhring, 'Standortfragen und Alternativen zur politischen Bildung in Österreich', *Die Republik*, nr. 4, 1977, pp. 4-18.

34. Rob de Vries, 'Maatschappelijke vorming in het Vlaamse rijksonderwijs: een bilan', *Persoon en Gemeenschap* 31 (5), 1979, pp. 209-219.

35. Hessische Kultusminister, *Rahmenrichtlinien für Gesellschaftslehre*, Frankfurt: Verlag Moritz Diesterweg, 1973.

36. Ingrid Haller and Hartmut Wolf, 'Von der Sprachlosigkeit einer Reform und der Sprachgewalt ihrer Gegner', pp. 157-171 in Gerd Köhler and Ernst Reuter (eds.), *Was sollen Schüler lernen? Die Kontroverse um die hessischen Rahmenrichtlinien für die Unterrichtsfächer Deutsch und Gessellschaftslehre*, Frankfurt: Fischer Taschenbuch Verlag, 1973. See also Gerd Köhler, (ed.) *Wem soll die Schule nützen?* Frankfurt: Fischer Taschenbuch Verlag, 1974.

37. Also in the 'Land' Nordrhein-Westphalen was the new curriculum plan for political education criticized for being left-wing inspired. See R. Schörken (ed.), *Curriculum 'Politik'. Von der Curriculumtheorie zur Unterrichtspraxis*, Opladen: Leske Verlag, 1974.

38. Christiane Gerhards, Malte Rauch and Samuel Schirmbeck, *Volkserziehung in Portugal, Berichte, Analysen, Dokumente,* Reinbek bei Hamburg: Rowohlt, 1976.

39. Harold Entwistle, *Political Education in a Democracy*, London: Routledge and Kegan Paul, 1971, p. 2.

40. Heater, op. cit., p. 329.

41. Ibid., pp. 341-344, ('The Conduct of Political Sixth-Form Conferences'.)

2

Civic Education in the United States

Mary Jane Turner

Political education in the United States, which in the formal school setting is called citizenship education, has always had a significant place in both the reality and rhetoric of general education. Even a casual examination of state department guidelines, school district statements of goals and objectives, and published textbooks reveals that citizenship education permeates (and, in a real sense, structures) the entire social studies curriculum. Despite this overwhelming unanimity of opinion concerning its importance, however, there is remarkably little consensus about what should be taught in the name of citizenship.[1] Private citizens and educators alike assume that *they* have a correct understanding of the term as well as the objectives that such education should achieve. Many are equally confident about what the content of citizenship instruction should be. Nonetheless, we find little agreement on even the basic question of whether citizenship education means the educating of citizens or education for citizenship.

The mere fact that there are vast differences of opinion about what constitutes proper goals or the best content in citizenship education does not mean that all of the suggested approaches are equally accepted, or that all of the approaches have been implemented to any great extent in American schools. Rather, we find that most schools and the vast majority of teachers are vigorously pursuing citizenship education goals that were specified at the time

Author's note. The author is indebted to Suzanne Helburn for her most helpful comments on the first draft of this paper.

49

of the founding of the American republic. There have been changes, of course, but these have usually been at the periphery and only in response to extensive social change.

It will be necessary if we are to develop tenable hypotheses concerning the likelihood and direction of change in political education, for us to do three things. We must, first, examine the tradition of citizenship education as it has persisted over time, considering both the nature of changes that have occurred and the social forces that seemed to evoke them; and second, we must analyze the major alternative approaches which have been proposed in terms of the degree to which they fit into or depart from the tradition. Finally, we must look at social factors present today that may be powerful enough to cause movement toward one or some of the suggested alternatives.

CITIZENSHIP EDUCATION IN THE UNITED STATES: A HISTORICAL PERSPECTIVE

From the time of the founding of the American republic, it seems that twin orthodoxies — Lockean liberalism and capitalism — have largely determined the content of citizenship education. Louis Hartz suggests that America 'has within it, as it were, a kind of self-completing mechanism, which insures the universality of the liberal idea'.[2] The undergirding value of liberalism is individualism, which carries with it the right to property and equality. These rights of the individual are explicitly protected against encroachments by the prohibitions embodied in the basic contract which created the government.

A system based upon such values demands at a minimum progress toward increasingly greater 'realization of the goals of individual freedom and self-fulfillment'[3] and a stable, consensual government and framework of procedures with which to adjudicate the two basic values that are inherently conflictual. All of these ideas presuppose a reasonably uniform program of civic education. The tradition of a right to property and, by extension to material possessions, and to equality and the need for a civil elite as well as a widespread consensus among non-elites, has, then, determined a great deal of what should be taught.

At least two opposing values have tempered this pure liberal perspective and both have to some extent influenced the rhetoric of citizenship education. The first, which is closely related to the classical Greek notion of political life, presumes that public obligations rather than private interests are the proper goals for citizens to pursue. In addition, participation in public life is thought to be an important aspect of civic duty. Thus, we find that some educators focus on educating citizens for participating in public acts, while others emphasize enhancing attributes of individualism. R. Freeman Butts states that citizenship education has been expected to simultaneously serve the conflicting purposes of diversity and unity.[4]

The second value which has intruded into the private interest/limited government notion comes from majoritarianism which is characterized by Martin Diamond as the view that 'the task of government is to uplift and aid the common man against the malefactors of great wealth.'[5] This value, like the others, is a part of the rhetoric of citizenship and can be found in most of the social science textbooks that are on the market today.

Historical analysts differ considerably in their interpretations of how these values have been supported and made real in educational programs. The mainstream historians of American education depict the schools as having been generally successful in playing a major role in expanding individual opportunity.[6] Revisionists, on the other hand, challenge this assumption and state that the basic structure of schools has been designed to maintain social order by instituting the policies of negative credentialing and manpower channeling. The larger inference that can be drawn from the revisionists is that the kinds of citizenship education programs that have been implemented have encouraged the development of passive, non-participatory citizens.[7]

A middle position and the one to which we subscribe, suggests that while there has been improvement in the quality of citizenship education over the years, the reality has never approached the rhetoric. In the early 1800s, few received any formal education beyond one or two years of instruction in basic skills. The few who did receive more advanced instruction constituted the civic elite of the time. Their education was not designed to produce a corps of theoreticians. Rather, educators were intent on developing '*a group*

*of capable, practical politicians trained to implement American
ideals.*[8] Unfortunately, neither the science of politics nor the
theories of pedagogy were sufficiently advanced to achieve this
goal. Education for the non-elites was dedicated to inculcating uncritical acceptance of traditional American values and typically emphasized civic virtue, patriotism, and Protestant devotion to duty.
The principal goal was to develop 'morally upright, God-fearing,
straight-thinking citizens.'[9]

Although this was the principal goal of civic education initially,
its purpose was largely instrumental. The notion was that
patriotism had to be developed in order for liberty to be preserved
and equality achieved. By the 1860s, the dangers of disunion coupled with massive immigration made patriotism a pre-eminent value
in its own right. Thus, great emphasis was placed on consensus-
building instruction — overt loyalty, required instruction in
English, and a variety of symbolic exercises. 'The textbooks of this
era proclaimed the benefits and the perfection of the United States
of America — made possible by its Constitution, which was
established by the will of the people.'[10]

This period was also marked by the expansion of America in
business, industry, science, and knowledge. Education began to be
viewed as an important avenue for getting ahead. Those American
students who could went abroad to study in German universities.
When they returned, they were more interested in systematic
theory, careful analysis, and scientific method. There was a general
disenchantment with the moralistic stress on political ideals as well
as the quality of content in both the collegiate and precollegiate
curricula. At the end of the century and during the early 1900s, the
National Education Association, the American Historical Association, and the American Political Science Association began recommending courses in history and civil government, which was defined as 'the science of citizenship — the relation of man, the individual, to man in organized collections — the individual in relation to the state,'[11] for both college and the relatively few non-
college bound students who were enrolled in secondary schools.[12]

In line with this new academic orientation, the National Education Association established a Commission on the Reorganization
of Secondary Education in 1913. A special committee from the
Commission published a report which recommended that courses
be developed to train citizens for active participation in the local,

state, and national communities. The report from the full Commission incorporated these recommendations, added a world community dimension, and established a sequence of study that continues to dominate the curriculum today.[13]

The textbooks of this period continued to stress the virtues of the American system, 'encouraged' students to act in ways that would benefit all, and suggested that voting was the highest civic duty. Content analyses do reflect a subtle change in emphasis regarding the preferred role of government, however. With the advent of the depression of 1929 and the expanding role of government in alleviating economic distress, big government began to be accepted and even applauded in most textbooks.

World War II, McCarthyism, and the Cold War once again plunged the schools into paroxysms of patriotism and the need to support allegiance to the country. LeAnn Meyer notes that many school programs featuring adolescent behavior and psychology, marriage and family problems, vocational interests, and personal values were also taught in the name of citizenship education.[14]

The 1960s are often referred to as the era of reform in social studies and hence, citizenship education. It was certainly a time characterized by massive expenditures of government and foundation money and a flurry of curriculum development by eminent social scientists who had never before participated so actively in precollegiate educational efforts. The reform movement as far as it relates to civic education can be characterized as a response to many social forces. Changing social conditions — increased centralized power and leadership in government, urbanization, automation, and interdependence — seemed to be making traditionally sought citizen attributes and values inappropriate. John J. Patrick in a bruising indictment written as late as 1970 stated:

> Civic education in American schools has lacked a clear focus and a tightly knit conceptual framework. Disparate topics such as consumer economics, life adjustment, occupations, health, personal grooming, and descriptions of government agencies are thrown together to form the content of instruction. Bland descriptions, superficial moralizing, and distortions of reality blight standard instructional materials.[15]

We will not discuss the elements that characterized the 'innovative' citizenship programs that were developed during the 1960s beyond noting generally that they were based upon the concepts, generalizations, and methodologies of the various social science disciplines. These will be discussed in a later section of this chapter because the model constitutes an alternative approach to citizenship education that is still being considered. Suffice it to say that the impact of these materials on the schools up to this time has been modest in relation to the monetary expenditures and the level of effort involved in encouraging their use.[16]

INSTRUCTIONAL CHARACTERISTICS OF CITIZENSHIP EDUCATION

One way to conceptualize education programs is in terms of the four main dimensions of instruction: knowledge, intellectual skills, values or attitudes, and participation skills. By examining the goals and instrumental objectives of educators as they relate to these dimensions, we can begin to develop a profile of the major characteristics of instruction over time.

As we have noted, it has always been important in the United States to maintain consensus and stability in order to support the individuals' freedom to pursue economic equality. Knowledge goals, early on, had to do with a historical mythology — one derived from an idealized society. The Constitution, the Declaration of Independence, exploits of American heroes, structure of government and so on formed the content of most textbooks. At certain times during periods of massive immigration or war, for example, citizenship education has tended to become even more nationalistic, more stridently ethnocentric. Generally, at least until the 1960s, every attempt has been made to avoid the controversial, to omit the unpleasant. In short, the knowledge component of citizenship education has relied largely on facts designed 'to build a common identity and create a shared history', elements that would maintain a stable government.

Skill objectives[17] have, for the most part, been largely ignored by political educators. The Founding Fathers were interested in developing a civic elite of trained, practical politicians who could run the government. The pedagogy of the time was not up to devising a course of study appropriate for this purpose. Worse than this, it is doubtful that citizenship skills are being taught to any great extent today. On the contrary, there seems to be a perpetually abiding faith that having students read about such things as government structures will somehow produce skilled political actors. In 1971, the Pre-Collegiate Education Committee of the American Political Science Association published its appraisal of prevailing patterns and materials used in precollegiate civic education courses. One of their findings concludes that:

> On the whole, instruction about civics and government fails to develop within students a capacity to think about political phenomena in conceptually sophisticated ways; an understanding of and skill in the process of social scientific inquiry; or a capacity to systematically analyze political decisions and values.[18]

Several of the alternative approaches concentrate on developing the skills necessary to be effective citizens.

The dimension of attitudes is one in which political educators have tended to concentrate, usually pulling from the basic tenets of democratic theory those aspects that have best matched prevailing values and norms. Equality of opportunity, for example, has always had a higher value than has justice. Majority rule has been preferred to minority rights. Freedom from governmental interference remains an important value but has conflicted over time with the notion that big government has an important role in protecting the 'little' man. Patriotism and love of country have consistently been a part of traditional civic education.

It is interesting that the rhetoric of citizenship education has always supported the idea of public good, a value diametrically opposed to the idea that citizens should be free to pursue their private interests unmolested. This conflict has not gone unnoticed by thoughtful educators and many of the new approaches contain objectives and methodologies that students can use in balancing the two interests. For example, there is now an interest in providing opportunities for students to engage in social perspective taking.

Like intellectual skills, skills of participation have also been largely ignored or poorly treated in traditional civic education programs. It has always been assumed that it is important that citizens participate, particularly in the act of voting. In addition, students are exhorted and otherwise encouraged to engage in activities which will result in community improvement 'when they are older'. The gradual extension of suffrage, first to non-property holders, then

to women, Blacks and other minority groups, and finally to eighteen year-old youths underscores the great value that Americans
place on the privilege of voting. Unfortunately, however, education
for participation is largely in the values domain and few programs
systematically teach the *skills* of participation — how to influence
public policy making, how to make decisions that bear on civic
matters, how to evaluate the quality of public policy using a set of
sensible criteria, how to communicate preferences and so on.

A final note on participation has to do with the fact that willingness to participate is related intimately to a sense of personal efficacy. There has been an increasingly growing interest in providing
experiences which are explicitly designed to improve self-concept
and sense of personal worth. There are few elementary-level social
studies textbooks that do not include some self-concept improvement opportunities.

FACTORS CONTRIBUTING TO TRADITIONAL
CITIZENSHIP EDUCATION

If we presume (and we are convinced that the evidence strongly
substantiates it) that civic education has not changed markedly in
the 200 years that the United States has been a nation, what factors
can be identified that have contributed to this situation? We believe
there are at least three.

The first has to do with the values that undergird the American
form of democracy. The need for a stable government, capable of
mediating between the conflicting values of individual freedom to
excel and the public good, has demanded a program of civic education based upon unquestioned patriotism, loyalty to government,
and nationalism. These national norms have, unquestionably,
changed over time but only at the periphery and never at the core.

A second factor has to do with the training or lack of training of
teachers. The typical social studies degree program is heavily
history oriented. There is nothing that leads us to believe that
citizenship education programs have ever achieved success in
developing competent, able citizen participants. There is some
evidence that quality may be declining still further. For example,
Martin Chancey, in a study of 22 high schools in and around
Cleveland, Ohio, found among other things:

a general downgrading of the importance of politics in our schools, reflected in an inadequate training of government teachers and in the time actually devoted to this study. Ohio law calls for one year combined study of American history and government. A majority of teachers actually devote only 10-15 percent of classroom time to government and the rest to history. Many teachers have training in history; few, if any, in political science. In all too many instances, a government teacher's sole background is physical ed....Most teachers rely almost exclusively on textbooks, most of which are dull, outdated, onesided, and reactionary.[19]

The implications of programs in which such a heavy concentration of history is required are strikingly evident. First of all, it is perfectly reasonable to assume that teachers with this kind of background would tend to consider human activity in a narrative, sequential, and descriptive fashion rather than in an analytical and predictive way.[20] In the second place, a background in history does not necessarily prepare a teacher to deal with the most value-laden aspect of the curriculum — the civic education courses. The evidence indicates that most civics and government courses are taught in a formal, idealized, descriptive, and bookish way. Significant issues, inherent conflicts, and political controversies are studiously avoided. Harmon Zeigler, in a study entitled *The Political World of the High School Teacher*, concluded that teachers tend to be unpolitical especially in terms of their views of the classroom as a forum for expressing political opinions or discussing controversial issues.[21]

In addition to collegiate preparation, the kind of political education that teachers provide in the classroom is, no doubt, also structured by the kind of education they themselves experienced during their precollegiate years. Barr, Barth, and Shermis point out that the first 12 years of most teachers' school education are probably characterized by:

isolated and fragmentary bits of information about past events; the structure and function of governmental institutions; and names, places, and events, often interspersed with covert or overt indoctrination designed to promote loyalty to acceptable cultural values and particular economic institutions.[22]

These authors point out that local community values (which we would add tend to be traditional and backward-looking) also are influential in determining what teachers teach and do in the classroom.[23]

If teachers are unprepared by their college backgrounds which are characterized by a preponderance of history courses and if they repeat their own precollegiate political education experience, what do they use to help them structure their own classroom instructional programs? The answer is, of course, the textbooks, and given the time constraints and psychological predispositions under which they operate, they will choose the ones that are most familiar and that contain value positions with which they are comfortable.[24]

Let us explore this point in more detail. The content that is most comfortable for teachers is drawn from chronological history or from legalistic, structural government. The methodology is read, discuss, and answer factual questions. Furthermore, even if teachers are willing to try new approaches which are always more time consuming, they are typically constrained by class schedules. Most secondary teachers teach at least five classes per day, five days a week. A few teach six per day. The majority of these are responsible for two or more courses. Those who repeat the same course throughout the day often have a slow class or an advanced class along with the average classes. This means that only the most fortunate of teachers have as few as two preparations per day. This figures to be ten preparations per week. The rest of the teachers are responsible for 15 or more, often in different disciplines. These teachers just do not have the luxury of being able to seek out resource materials or teaching approaches beyond what is available in the typical textbook.

It is probably not necessary to do much more than point out that textbooks tend to be traditional and non-controversial. They have not, in general, been responsive to academics or other critics who have pointed out flaws in their content and/or pedagogy.[25]

In sum, most citizenship education in America at both the elementary and secondary levels can be characterized as traditional, rooted in the values of the past, and supported by methodologies that are comfortable and easy for already overburdened teachers to implement. It is equally true that although there have always been critics of this tradition, there are today probably more alternatives, more suggested approaches, more new things being tried in the schools, and stronger calls for reform than have ever been present in the past.

In order to provide a perspective about the extent to which the new approaches are divergent from the traditional, we will first characterize both the traditional programs and the new approaches in terms of political socialization literature and then examine in more detail the dimensions of some of the better known new approaches. We will also provide information about which of the new approaches seem to be the most widely used and why.

IS IT POLITICAL SOCIALIZATION OR POLITICAL EDUCATION?

We find much in the general political socialization literature that suggests that the schools as primary socializing agents of young people have the obligation of providing instruction by which students will learn to adopt and internalize the norms, values, attitudes, and behaviors accepted and practiced by the ongoing system.[26] This view of political education with its status-quo, system maintenance bias has been subjected to the same kinds of criticisms as has the conceptualization in the political socialization literature that emphasizes systemic survival.[27] It is largely descriptive of traditional citizenship education in the United States.

Educators like John J. Patrick, on the other hand, suggest that political or citizenship education is not the same as political socialization. Rather, political education is the broader term and involves fostering the competence to think critically and independently, which could lead to rejection of established beliefs and practices.[28] Political socialization for Patrick is only that 'facet of political education, which pertains to learning experiences aimed at shaping human potentialities to support the socio-cultural order.'[29]

These two polarities, it seems to us, describe the parameters of citizenship education in America: at the one end of the continuum we find political socialization/traditional political instruction and at the other, political education/some new approaches to political instruction. Other new approaches fall somewhere on the continuum depending upon whether they are intended to do a better job of achieving old goals or whether they are designed to foster new competencies while sustaining old values.

The knowledge, intellectual skills, attitudes, and participation skills that are selected to operationalize the various approaches can also be thought of as tending toward one end of the continuum or the other. For example, those who believe the preferred goal of political education is to socialize students into uncritically accepting the norms and beliefs of the system, would select knowledge objectives — facts and descriptive information — that emphasize the strong parts of America's heritage and ignore the less attractive aspects. Those who believe the function of citizenship has to do with teaching how to think critically might select concepts, generalizations, and generic organizers from the social science disciplines as a more appropriate knowledge base. Other might select concepts from jurisprudence or content from law or other disciplines.

The domain of skills objectives is similarly dichotomized. Most do insist that instruction in basic skills of reading, writing, and communicating should be included in all citizenship education courses but this tends to be the only commonality. Political 'socializers' prefer strategies that will eventually train future citizens in what to think. Education from the other end of the continuum emphasizes strategies which teach students how to think. These skills include questioning, information gathering, classifying, comparing and contrasting, inferring, analyzing, hypothesizing, evaluating, and even intuiting — all of the intellectual skills.

The values domain is an interesting one because most political educators, regardless of their preferences about the goals of instruction, believe their methodology will eventually produce students who will select as their own values those that are grounded in democratic principles. On the one hand, transmitters of values tend to tell citizens what these values are and exhort them to make them their own. In a very real sense, this approach leaves all of the final decisions about what are 'good' or appropriate values to the society and not to the thinking, independent individual. Compliance is a much valued manifestation of proper civic behavior. On the other hand, those who push for independent thinking are not as relativistic as their criticizers have professed and most subscribe to the notion that a preference for democratic values follows a rational decisioning process.

A final difference in selecting educational objectives to achieve disparate political instructional goals has to do with participation. Participation has, of course, both a skill and an affective component. Political 'socializers' focus on affect and try, primarily by exhortation, to encourage students to participate in political processes *in the future*. Generally, great reliance is placed on the act of voting as a preferred method of demonstrating participatory zeal.

Political 'educators', for the most part, believe that explicit instruction should be provided in the skills of participation. They believe that unless one learns how to play a variety of roles in the political arena and how to influence public policy, the understandings and intellectual skills which may have been attained are meaningless for the polity. They also recognize that in addition to having the competence to act, there must also be a commitment to act. These educators include learning experiences in which students grapple with the consequences of non-participation to themselves and others.[30]

Let us now turn to a careful examination of twelve new approaches to citizenship education that are sufficiently distinguishable from traditional programs that they are useful for analytical purposes. Eight of the twelve have been identified by Fred M. Newmann, one of the most knowledgeable analysts on the American scene.[31] Three others are often referred to in the literature. The last, the basic citizenship competencies approach, is of quite recent vintage and was developed as part of a knowledge interpretation project conducted at the Mershon Center, Ohio State University, and the Social Science Education Consortium.[32]

Our analysis will proceed along two fronts: (1) we will characterize each approach in terms of the political socialization/political education dichotomy and indicate where it falls on a political socialization/political education continuum. This will yield some insights into likelihood of institutionalization since we hypothesize that those programs that foster the competence to think critically and independently (educate) are less likely to be institutionalized than will those that teach students to adopt and internalize the norms, values, attitudes, and behavior accepted and practiced by the ongoing system (socialize). (2) At the same time, we will be discussing other systemic and contextual factors such as social forces that bear on institutionalization and may, in fact, help determine what will happen to American political education. We will, then, place each approach on a likelihood of institutionalization continuum. The completed continua are included here, however, for easy reference.

Political Socialization/Education Continuum

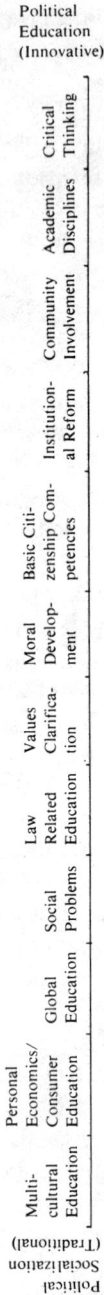

Political Education
(Innovative)

| Multi-cultural Education | Personal Economics/ Consumer Education | Global Education | Social Problems | Law Related Education | Values Clarifica-tion | Moral Develop-ment | Basic Citi-zenship Com-petencies | Institution-al Reform | Community Involvement | Academic Disciplines | Critical Thinking |

Political Socialization (Traditional)

Likelihood of Institutionalization

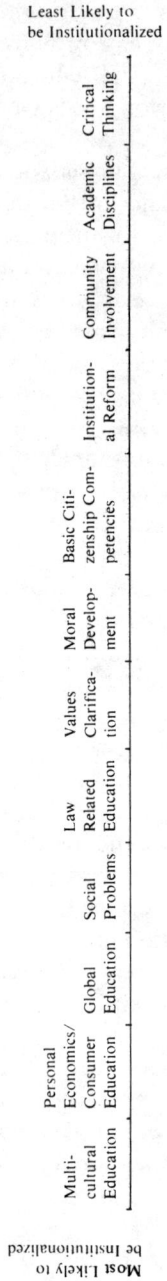

Least Likely to be Institutionalized

| Multi-cultural Education | Personal Economics/ Consumer Education | Global Education | Social Problems | Law Related Education | Values Clarifica-tion | Moral Develop-ment | Basic Citi-zenship Com-petencies | Institution-al Reform | Community Involvement | Academic Disciplines | Critical Thinking |

Most Likely to be Institutionalized

NEW APPROACHES TO POLITICAL EDUCATION

Of the twelve approaches, five—social problems, multicultural education, personal economics/consumer education, global education, and law-related education—tend to be content related. The other approaches—academic disciplines (history and the social sciences), critical thinking, values clarification, moral development, community involvement, institutional school reform, and citizenship competencies—feature strategies which transcend particular contents.

(1) Social Problems

The social problems approach draws its content from persistent and pressing social problems — poverty, racism, drug abuse, pollution, crime, discrimination and so on. The methodology that is suggested is eclectic but the strategies generally are chosen for their usefulness in helping students think about and consider alternative solutions to critical problems which affect all citizens.

In its pure form, the social problems approach is sharply divergent from the traditional approach. Controversial topics are deliberately selected; no attempt is made to gloss over past or present inadequacies in public policy; the real rather than the ideal is featured. In the skills domain, students are often provided with opportunities to hypothesize about solutions to problems, analyze causes, seek out and organize pertinent information and so on. There is seldom a preferred value position suggested although students may be required to clarify or analyze their own values. Participatory skills are not necessarily included in the social problems approach.

Social problems will probably never become the core political education curriculum. It is quite removed from what is typically taught — for many school districts and teachers perhaps frighteningly so. With modification, however, the approach is sometimes used in an institutionalized course called problems of democracy. When it is used here, the controversial aspects of the approach tend to be avoided and teachers often overlay their own 'preferred' values on the content. Thus, modified, the approach could be infused into ongoing courses when it is desirable to address special issues that seem particularly relevant. Based only upon the characteristics of the approach, social problems is relatively neutral on the socialization/education continuum. It introduces new and controversial topics but does not necessarily teach students to participate thoughtfully. We would place it in position four on this continuum. Even with typical adaptations and despite the fact that it is used in some courses, we believe that five other approaches are more likely to be institutionalized because many teachers will prefer not to focus on social problems.

(2) Multicultural Education

Like social problems, multicultural education is not a serious contender for replacing traditional citizenship education. The concern of multicultural educators is almost exclusively in the knowledge and values domains. These persons point out and many agree that it is as important to include the black, the chicano, the native American, and the Asian experience in the course content as it is the White experience. The notion that there is a single set of traits that are somehow uniquely American or that there ever has been a 'melting pot' is being called into serious question by most minority groups as well as women.

In addition, these groups in their quest for individual improvement (a typical American value) are insisting that all citizens honor other democratic values such as respect for diversity and human dignity and pluralism. We do not expect multicultural education to replace traditional citizenship education. Rather, we believe it will be incorporated into traditional programs enhancing both the knowledge and value domains of such programs.[33]

We have placed this approach in the first position on the socialization/education continuum because it is congruent with American values that have considerable vitality. In addition, the approach is attractive because it serves to support groups that might otherwise become alienated and unstable elements in the total population. The approach is also the most likely to be institutionalized in our opinion.

(3) Personal Economics/Consumer Education

This approach has objectives that are most closely related to the knowledge and skill domains.[34] The major goal of most of the consumer materials is to provide students with the necessary knowledge and skills to protect themselves and their interests in market situations. Because much of the market is impacted by private or public bureaucratic institutions, the programs teach how to operate effectively in these settings.

Consumer education is a limited content area. At best, it can only be considered a subset of citizenship. Some of the skills, for example, that students learn can be broadly applicable to the public domain. There is nothing inherently risky about this content except as it relates to challenging bureaucratic organizations nor is a major goal teaching students to think independently. We place it in second position on the socialization/education continuum and fourth on the institutionalization because the content is likely to be incorporated into the traditional.

(4) Global Education

Global education can mean several things. For some, it is primarily knowledge based, in effect, an expansion of the base of what it is important for students to know about. Newmann includes global education in the social problems category and makes the case that the approach is primarily concerned with 'consciousness raising'.[35] This clearly speaks to the attitudes/values domain. Some of the programs also focus on the growing interdependence of mankind which suggests that global education is both a content and a contextual problem. Richard C. Remy makes the following observation in this regard:

> Despite growing attention to the globalization of the human condition, we are only beginning to appreciate the impact of this change on our lives as citizens and on the task of citizenship education. At a minimum, it means people now confront the tasks and responsibilities of citizenship in a global or internationalized society . . . It may involve for the first time in human history not only an awareness of physically proximate neighbors but a capacity on the part of all citizens to perceive and understand local/global linkages.[36]

We believe that an increasing 'globalization' of citizenship education is not only a desirable but also a probable direction of the future. It must be admitted that there is growing disenchantment with bigness in the United States — big business, big government, and complex bureaucracies that seem to defy understanding or control. Thus, there is a renewed interest in grassroots citizenship and local action. Despite this, for self-interested reasons if not for ethical, Americans and American schools will recognize the importance of expanding political education to include global issues and topics. Global education is, therefore, in the number three position on the institutionalization continuum. It has a broader content or knowledge base, but the values which are integral to the approach merely represent a modification of old values in the direction of maintenance of the polity.

(5) Law-Related Education

For many, law-related education is considered to be an important subset or category of political education. For others, it is thought to be broad enough to constitute its core. However it is viewed, it is an approach that is finding its way into many classrooms all over America. There are countless reasons for this, not the least of which are aggressive support by the American Bar Association and massive subsidization by the Law Enforcement Assistance Agency.

Also important in its acceptance is the fact that the content is comfortable for traditional teachers who implicitly understand that civic education is deficient without some grounding in the law. The knowledge base is the American legal system, the Constitution, and the rights inhering in the Bill of Rights, none of which have been taught particularly well in the past. The Constitution, for example, is typically addressed from a historical perspective rather than from the perspective that it is a living, dynamic document intimately related to the lives and concerns of every citizen. Teachers seem to recognize that legal education 'gets at' old content in new and more relevant ways. This gives law-related education considerable legitimacy.

Because the approach is relatively new, however, considerable attention is being paid to the skills domain. Most materials provide opportunities for students to analyze and evaluate. Games, simulations, role plays, mock trials and case studies are among the multiple strategies incorporated into the learning packages. In this regard, legal education is different from what is traditionally taught.

Despite the incorporation of new and untraditional strategies, we believe that legal education will continue to be a vital part of political education. It is not clear exactly what form this will take. The same is true for global education and consumer economic programs. All of these approaches are presently 'add ons' to the core social studies curriculum. They have an elective or mini-course status. Over time, districts that are experiencing economic recession generally return to the 'basics', dropping or limiting the elective program.

One alternative would be to infuse the new content areas and concerns into ongoing and generally accepted courses, a direction multicultural education seems to be going. A second is to 'rethink' the social studies curriculum pattern, modifying it to include the new areas. This would involve restructuring a pattern that has persisted since 1916. The third would be to let the new approaches compete with each other and with offerings that are already a part of the tradition. This third alternative generally describes the present process and has never produced significant or meaningful improvement of curriculum. Whatever happens, we believe law-related education will continue to impact upon political education. It is number two on the institutional continuum and number five on the socialization/education because of the added skills component it embodies.

(6) Academic Disciplines (History and Social Sciences)

This approach to citizenship education is the one that was conceptualized and advocated during the new social studies movement. It is dependent upon using concepts, generalizations, and methodologies from the academic disciplines as organizers for content. The presumption is, of course, that once these conceptual skills are internalized, any discrete set of facts can be analyzed in making citizenship decisions.

The knowledge base in this approach is the powerful concepts and generalizations from the disciplines. The skills component involves teaching students how to analyze and problem solve using sound social science principles of investigation. Many of the programs that were developed during the 1960s also incorporated group process skills and were predicated upon the idea that systematic inquiry will result in a preference for democratic values.[37]

On the surface, it would seem that this approach would be the easiest of all to implement because precollegiate teachers, particularly at the secondary level, are trained in the disciplines. The problem here is that few teachers have adequate expertise in their disciplines to adequately translate the methodology for their precollegiate students. This approach may be used by a few teachers but unless massive amounts of money are invested in inservice and preservice education programs, it is not likely to have extensive impact on political education. Because the approach is predicated upon teaching students to think, it very nearly equates with Patrick's definition of education. It ranks eleventh of the socialization/education scale; however, because it is discipline-related and because other approaches are even more risky, it is the eighth most likely to be institutionalized in our opinion.

(7) Critical Thinking

The ability to think critically has always been considered a fundamental need for citizens. Textbooks at the turn of the century admonished students to 'think' critically about this or that. Unfortunately, no directions or helpful hints were provided to assist students in proceeding with this complex task.

Conceptualizing an approach relying upon teaching how to think was undertaken in the 1960s and there are today several conceptions and typologies.[38] The thinking process which is generally advocated is in some regard similar to the inquiry process of the social scientists but also includes some special intellectual operations peculiar to civic problems. There is no knowledge base beyond the critical thinking skills which students are expected to apply. Like the academic disciplines approach, it is anticipated that rigorous application of skills will lead to a preference for democratic values.

There are probably fewer teachers using this than are using the academic disciplines approach. Most have not been trained in the methodology and there are few textbooks available which are dependent upon it. We do not expect that it will change the quality of political education in any significant way. It ranks tenth on the institutionalization scale and twelfth on the socialization/education continuum.

(8) Values Clarification

Values clarification is a strategy that extends over many more issues than civic. In one sense, the intent of the approach is to give students a systematic way of thinking about their own value positions. Thus, it spans both the skills and the attitudes domains. In its ideal form, values clarification is relativistic and non-judgmental. Any value position is supportable as long as students understand the consequences of their values, are willing to state them to others, and consistently choose the same values across issues.

It is obvious that values clarification could not constitute the total political education curriculum. Furthermore, it is doubtful that the ideal form will ever make serious inroads on traditional programs. Few parents, teachers, and administrators feel easy about the non-judgmental nature of the approach.

The approach does have a skills component which means that it fosters personal assessment of values. Thus, we believe, it should rank at least sixth on the socialization/education scale. Because of its controversial nature, however, it is eleventh on the institutionalization continuum.

(9) Moral Development

This approach is based upon the theories of Lawrence Kohlberg who believes that moral development is a cognitive process with higher stages being more desirable and ethical than lower. Although the teaching strategy which Kohlberg proposes for helping students to attain the higher levels is useful with any content in which there are human dilemmas, it is operationalized in political education by confronting students with civic dilemmas and asking them to choose solutions and discuss them with their peers. Kohlberg believes that interaction with peers at higher and lower stages will push students to the higher, more principled types of reasoning.

Kohlberg's higher stages are concerned with a social contract, liberty, equality, justice, and human dignity — all values that traditional teachers can comfortably embrace. On the other hand, many teachers have not demonstrated that they are eager to pursue a rigorous examination of underlying value positions. Because of these factors, we believe the approach is the seventh most likely to be institutionalized. As it relies on a cognitive, developmental scheme, it is also ranked number seven on the socialization/education continuum.[39]

(10) Community Involvement

This approach to citizenship education evolved partially in response to widespread criticism of school practice which emphasizes verbal discussion about, but in isolation from, the 'real' world. It is also a reaction to the traditional idea that political education has to do with training students to do something in the future — when they are adult citizens.

Community involvement programs advocate putting students out into the community where they learn by doing. In addition, many such programs provide structured opportunities for students to think about and reflect upon what they see or do in the community as well as experiences in which they can become adept at participating.

There are also a few educators who advocate a middle ground between the strictly cognitive and social action extremes. One well-known model[40] views the school as a micro-political system that operates according to the fundamental principles of political behavior found in all political systems. Concepts, principles, and methodologies from political science are used to guide students in their systematic observation and analysis of the political life of the school. In addition, the students' political knowledge is put to work as they participate in the schools' ongoing political system as observers, supporters, advocates, facilitators, or organizers.

Community involvement has much to recommend it. If it is properly developed as in the Gillespie/Lazarus model, students receive instruction in all of the instructional domains. If not, there are some real problems with the approach. It is not enough to merely turn students loose in the community to observe and act. They need to be carefully prepared for the experience and debriefed following it. Many teachers also complain they are acting as managers rather than teachers when the students are away from school. In addition, elementary and junior high school students often cannot be included in programs of this type. The second model seems to have more promise although it can also be viewed as risky by administrators. Because of this, we do not believe that it is likely to replace traditional programs. It ranks ninth on the institutionalization continuum. The approach does not include instructional goals from all four domains. It is intended to educate rather than socialize. We place it tenth on this scale.

(11) Institutional School Reform

The people who advocate reforming the school are concerned that the 'hidden curriculum' which includes the organizational design and general quality of school life may have more impact on political education than the academic program. They believe that the knowledge, skills, and attitudes required of participating, responsible citizens cannot be taught in authoritarian institutions by autocratic teachers. For them, students are citizens who should be allowed to participate in a meaningful way in making decisions about school governance and policies. This does not presume that students should have unilateral power but rather that they should be allowed to participate as other citizens do.

This approach has not been nor is likely to be widely adopted in American schools. It is perceived as risky by educators and is typically not understood by parents who tend to remember their own educational experiences as somewhat more perfect than they really were. Those who believe in strict discipline and a hierarchically arranged authority structure cannot comfortably expect students to take major responsibility for their own educational development. Institutional reform is least likely of all the approaches to be institutionalized. Its ranking on the socialization/education continuum is somewhat more problematic. There is only modest evidence that indicates that students will become more competent just as a function of participating. There also needs to be additional programmatic support. It is probably true that schools that include students in the decision-making process are also likely to provide structured learning experiences. Short of more evidence in this regard, however, we can only rank institutional reform in ninth position on the socialization/education scale.

(12) Basic Citizenship Competencies

This last is the most recent of the approaches to be proposed. The developers, first of all, recognized that the term citizenship has many meanings and countless value connotations. Therefore, they have defined the term narrowly enough so that it is useful for making instructional decisions and broadly enough to encompass political interactions that occur in all settings. Second, as they believed that political education goes on in many contexts, they have developed products for academics, school administrators, content specialists and teachers, leaders in voluntary organizations, parents, and legislators and other policy makers which rely on a common vocabulary and a set of common understandings.[41] Third, they identified seven basic citizenship competencies which all persons need in order to discharge their responsibilities as citizens and protect and promote their own interests. These competencies are linked to capacities which can be used by educators in designing learning experiences for young people.

The working definition that is proposed is: citizenship involves the rights, responsibilites, and tasks associated with governing the various groups to which a person belongs. It is exercised by young and old alike and involves a range of decisions, judgements, and tasks related to making rules, distributing resources, and setting goals for groups.[42]

The seven competencies are:
1. Competence in acquiring and processing information about political decisions;
2. Competence in assessing one's involvement and stake in political situations, issues, decisions, and policies;
3. Competence in making thoughtful decisions regarding group governance and problems of citizenship;

4. Competence in developing and using standards such as justice, ethics, morality, and practicality to make judgements of people, institutions, policies, and decisions;
5. Competence in communicating ideas to other citizens, decision makers, leaders, and officials;
6. Competence in cooperating and working with others in groups and organizations to achieve mutual goals;
7. Competence in working with bureaucratically organized institutions in order to promote and protect one's interests and values.

This approach seems to have several advantages that speak both to the likelihood of institutionalization and to the development of political skills. Its focus is entirely on the skills domain, leaving to the local communities the selection of the knowledge and attitude components that seem most appropriate to them. This characteristic minimizes the risk of imposing radically different or basically controversial themes. Because it is a skill-based approach, however, it demands that learning opportunities be developed and sequenced throughout the instructional cycle during which students can learn, practice using, and think about the various competencies that are involved. The intellectual skills and participation skills that are included can be practiced in either real or simulated settings, whichever seems preferrable to the teacher or school administrator.

In sum, the approach allows for content to be selected at the local level by the persons most familiar with local norms and values. It provides, however, a structured way to assess the quality of classroom programs, compare curriculum materials, and set instructional goals. The approach is eighth on the socialization/education scale and fifth on the institutional scale.

The fit between the socialization/education and the likelihood of institutionalization is obviously not perfect. We would submit, however, that it largely substantiates our earlier hypothesis. Approaches that depart radically from the accepted norms are less likely to be implemented than are those that have characteristics which are perceived by users as similar to those which are already being used.

THE SOCIAL FORCES THAT COULD CHANGE POLITICAL EDUCATION PROGRAMS AND SPECULATIONS ABOUT THE FUTURE

We noted earlier that political education in the United States has been remarkably stable. Curriculum patterns, content, and methodology have changed but little in the 200 years of our nationhood. The modest changes that have occurred have usually been in response to the pressures of war, immigration, urbanization, and so on.

What is the social context today that would indicate we can perhaps expect modification of the political education tradition? There can be no doubt that citizenship is being exercised in an increasingly globalized environment. Global interdependence is a condition we must deal with, not a theory about other nations' problems. Citizenship education has traditionally been concerned with promoting nationalism. Today, for the first time in human history, it must include teaching all citizens to perceive and understand local/global linkages. As education in the past has responded to pressures from the outside, we believe that globalization will force schools to, at least, amend the ethnocentric bias of most instruction.

A second 'fact of life' with which we are faced today is the increasing complexity of society and the resultant alienation. Citizens feel powerless to effect change, to confront the bigness of governmental as well as private institutions. There are two effects that this situation may cause. We may, first of all, find a renewed interest in community citizenship — civic action to bring about change at the local level. Secondly, I believe we will find a renewed resurgence of interest group activity. The more that citizens feel cut off, the more they will turn to like-minded others in order to bring organized pressure and reform. These people will all need the skills of organizing, influencing, leading, following, and advocating.

Inherent in interest group advocacy is the problem of fragmentation and instability. Thus, I would anticipate that students will be asked to evaluate their own and others' decisions in terms of their consequences to themselves, to others, and to the nation-state. Furthermore, I would expect they will be encouraged to act within the framework of already existing avenues to effect change. Both law-related education and moral education may have salience in this regard.

The knowledge explosion itself is of great concern to educators. Where it was once possible to 'cover' the history of the United States, it is now impossible. One solution might be to continue to teach selectively only those attractive pieces of history that keep alive the myth, the ideal. Another is to focus on skills which students can use to analyze whatever knowledge and facts that are made available to them. Using skills and methodologies derived from the academic disciplines or from the various critical thinking typologies would seem to require extensive retraining of teachers. Retraining would not be as critical in the basic competency approach which also is intended to develop independent thinkers because it does not demand restructuring of all of the instructional domains. How the problem is handled is almost impossible to predict but it will certainly be a focus of consideration for some time to come.

Yet another cause of concern is the data emerging from such sources as the National Assessment of Educational Progress and the various national opinion polls. We are told, for example, that both students and adults are abysmally ignorant about civic matters. This kind of statement taken by itself might not produce any change or revision in political education. We have had similar reports prepared and published from very early times. One report entitled 'What Do Students Know About American Government Before Taking College Courses in Political Science?' presented at the second annual meeting of the American Political Science Association concluded that students entering college were very deficient 'in the simplest rudiments' of both American government and history.[43] The report was published in 1906.

Because it is coupled with other forces, it is clear that educators will be forced to consider the problem and propose solutions. What is not so clear is the extent to which the solutions will be implemented in the classroom settings nor which solutions will find the most favor with practitioners.

Other pressures which we anticipate making a difference are coming from ethnic groups and women who have reacted to the stereotypic and biased presentation of content in traditional textbooks and programs. Publishers have already responded and we see few texts today that are blatantly racist or sexist. There is still a need for inservice and preservice training in this area but we believe school districts will continue to act to remove bias.

Rising crime rates and school vandalism as well as demonstrated ignorance about law and the legal system makes this content an attractive one for many educators. As we stated earlier, because of the symbiotic relationship between law and citizenship, it is fairly easy for teachers to deal with. We cannot be sure exactly how the content will be integrated into the school curriculum. We can be reasonably sure it will be integrated.

Many citizens and many educators have noted a decline in morality and feel that schools should introduce courses or programs designed to raise the 'ethical quotient' of students. Traditional citizenship education has always had a strong interest in American values but the new emphasis is considerably broader and more universal. In addition, we see materials that are structured around social perspective taking, concern for the rights of others, human dignity, and so on.

We would anticipate that these values will continue to be taught in many classrooms. Values that cluster around more controversial issues such as evolution, abortion, euthanasia, and so on will not, on the other hand, be included in typical programs.

Finally, we find the number of new initiatives that have been mounted on behalf of improved political education within the past five years encouraging. A report prepared by the Citizen Education Staff of the United States Office of Education documents fifteen that involve the federal government, many state governments, private foundations, not-for-profit educational organizations, professional associations, and other groups.[44]

There is evidence that labor, business, voluntary groups, and religious organizations are taking a self-conscious look at their practices and in some cases are engaging in dialogue with educators in the formal school setting in order to try to better understand how the various social sectors can complement and contribute to the efforts of all.[45]

Based upon all of this, we project that political education practices in the United States will improve and that we will see more marked changes than have ever occurred in our history.

NOTES

1. Developmental theorists further confound the issue by raising questions about *when* such instruction should be provided. See for example, James S. Eckenrod, 'Thinking About Interdependence, Conflict, Communication, and Change' in *Global Perspectives: A Humanistic Influence on the Curriculum*, New York: Center for Global Perspectives, 1976.

2. Louis Hartz, *The Liberal Tradition in America: An Interpretation of American Political Thought Since the Revolution*, New York: Harcourt, Brace, and World, Inc., 1955, p.6.

3. Kenneth M. and Patricia Dolbeare, *American Ideologies: The Competing Political Beliefs of the 1970's*, Chicago: Markham Publishing Company, 1971, p.67.

4. R. Freeman Butts, 'Education for Citizenship: The Oldest, Newest Innovation in the Schools', *Vital Issues 26*, No. 8, p. 1.

5. Martin Diamond, 'The American Heritage and the Quarrel Among the Heirs', *News for Teachers of Political Science*, No. 16, Winter 1978, p. 10.

6. See for example, R. Freeman Butts, *Public Education in the United States: From Revolution to Reform*, New York: Holt, Rinehart & Winston, 1978; and Ralph W. Tyler, *Perspectives on American Education*, Chicago: Science Research Associates, 1976.

7. See Michael B. Katz, *Class, Bureaucracy, and Schools: The Illusion of Educational Change in America*, New York: Praeger, 1971; Colin Greer, *The Great School Legend: A Revisionist's Interpretation of American Public Education*, New York: Viking, 1973; and Joel Spring, *The Sorting Machine: National Educational Policy Since 1945*, New York: David McKay, 1976.

8. Bernard Crick, *The American Science of Politics: Its Origins and Conditions*, Berkeley, California: University of California Press, 1959, p.3 (emphasis in the original).

9. Albert Somit and Joseph Tanenhaus, *The Development of American Political Science*, Boston: Allyn and Bacon, Inc., 1967, pp. 1-15.

10. LeAnn Meyer, *The Citizenship Education Issue: Problems and Programs*, Denver: Education Commission of the States, February 1979, p. 3.

11. Russell J. Farnen and Robert M. Bjork, *The Teaching of Government*, Nashville, Tennessee: George Peabody College for Teachers, unpublished paper, nd., p.3.

12. See, for example, National Education Association, *Report of the Committee of Ten on Secondary Social Studies*, New York: National Education Association, 1894; and Byron G. Massialis and C. Benjamin Cox, *Inquiry in Social Studies*, New York: McGraw-Hill Book Company, 1966.

13. US Bureau of Education, *The Social Studies in Secondary Education*, Bulletin 1916, No. 28, Washington, DC: Government Printing Office, 1916. A recent status report is Richard E. Gross, 'The Status of Social Studies in the Public Schools in the United States: Facts and Impressions of a National Survey', *Social Education*, March 1977.

14. Meyer, op. cit., p.6.

15. John J. Patrick, 'The Reconstruction of Civics Education in American Schools', p.1 in Mary Jane Turner, *Materials for Civics, Government, and Problems of Democracy: Political Science in the New Social Studies*, Boulder, Colorado: Social Science Education Consortium, Inc., 1971.

16. A more detailed account of the history of citizenship education can be found in Mary Jane Nickelson Turner, *Political Education in the United States: History, Status, Critical Analysis and An Alternative Model*, unpublished doctoral dissertation, Boulder, Colorado, 1978; and R. Freeman Butts, 'Historical Perspective on Civic Education in the United States' in *Education for Responsible Citizenship*, New York: McGraw-Hill Book Company, 1977.

17. Several typologies of skill objectives have been developed, including those from the Basic Citizenship Competencies Project and the experimental Utah State Social Studies Project. Other educators equate intellectual skills, decision-making skills, and critical thinking skills with citizenship skills.

18. *Political Studies* 4 (3), Summer 1972, p.443.

19. Martin Chancey, 'A Study on the Teaching of Politics in Secondary Schools in N.E. Ohio', *DEA News*, No. 6, December 1975, p.3.

20. See Massialis and Cox, op. cit., for an analysis of this issue.

21. Harmon Zeigler, *The Political World of the High School Teacher*, Eugene, Oregon: The Center for the Advanced Study of Educational Administration, University of Oregon, 1966, p.156.

22. Robert D. Barr, James L. Barth, and S. Samuel Shermis, *Defining the Social Studies*: Bulletin 51, Washington, DC: National Council for the Social Studies, 1977, p.3.

23. Ibid., pp.3-4.

24. We cannot explore this generalization in any detail here. There are, however, excellent studies which support it. See, for example, Carole L. Hahn, *Relationships Between Potential Adopters' Perceptions of New Social Studies Materials and Their Adoption of These Materials*, unpublished doctoral dissertation, Bloomington, Indiana: University of Indiana, 1974.

25. There are many analyses of the content of most textbooks. Those which discuss political education texts are *Political Studies*, op. cit., and Mary Jane Nickelson Turner, op. cit. An excellent group of articles on American history texts which include reasons why the market system forces publishers to avoid controversial and innovative products are Frances Fitzgerald, 'Onward and Upward with the Arts — Rewriting American History', *New Yorker*, 26 February, 1979, pp.41-77; 5 March 1979, pp.40-91; and 12 March 1979, pp.48-106.

26. Roberta S. Sigel (ed.), *Learning About Politics: A Reader in Political Socialization*, New York, Random House, 1970. This definition of citizenship education closely parallels the definition of the process of political socialization found on p. XII.

27. See David Easton and Jack Dennis, *Children in the Political System* (New York: McGraw-Hill, 1969) for an elaboration of this point. Unfortunately, no alternative conceptions to correct this bias are provided.

28. John J. Patrick, 'Political Socialization and Political Education in Schools', p.192 in Stanley Allen Renshon (ed.), *Handbook of Political Socialization: Theory and Research*, New York: The Free Press, 1977.

29. Ibid. Lee H. Ehman disagrees with Patrick and characterizes political education as the subpart of political socialization having to do with both direct and indirect instruction in the schools. See Lee H. Ehman, 'Implications for Teaching Citizenship', *Social Education* 43 (7), November-December 1979, pp. 594-95. Although we agree with Ehman, Patrick's definition is useful in considering the range of political education instruction.

30. Insights about the objectives of social studies education can be found in Barr, Berth, and Shermis, op. cit., *Social Education* 41 (3), March 1977; Irving Morrissett, 'Citizenship, Social Studies, and the Academician', an unpublished critique of *Defining the Social Studies*; and John J. Patrick, 'Political Socialization and Political Education in Schools' in Renshon, op. cit.

31. Fred M. Newmann, in 'Building a Rationale for Civic Education' in James P. Shaver, (ed.), *Building Rationales for Citizenship Education*: Bulletin 52, Washington, DC: National Council for the Social Studies, 1977.

32. This approach is described in Richard C. Remy, *The Handbook of Basic Citizenship Competencies*, Columbus, Ohio: Mershon Center, Ohio State University, 1978; and Mary Jane Turner, *Guide to Basic Citizenship Competencies: Recommendations to Compare Curriculum Materials, Assess Classroom Instruction, and Set Goals*, Boulder, Colorado: Social Science Education Consortium, Inc., 1978.

33. Part of this hypothesis is based on the observation that most textbook publishing companies, encouraged by minority interest group pressure, have become more even handed in their treatment of all racial and ethnic groups as well as women. Thus, the instructional materials available to school districts, for the most part, are doing a better job in this area.

34. Some observers, like R. Freeman Butts, question whether or not this approach should properly be categorized as citizenship education. One of the problems with which analysts of political education are confronted is the lack of a commonly understood and accepted definition. LeAnn Meyer, for example, basing her understanding of the scope of the field, offers the following as approaches commonly associated with political education: academic disciplines (history and political science), social problems, critical thinking/decision making, values clarification and skills/concrete values, ethics/moral development, community involvement/action skills/community education, law related education, economics/free enterprise education, global perspectives education, family-related education, multiethnic education/pluralism, personal development and social skills/prosocial behavioral training. We will address the problem of ambiguity and offer what we believe is a sensible working definition of political education which is consistent with the general literature in a later section of this chapter.

35. Fred M. Newmann, op. cit., p.6.

36. Richard C. Remy, op. cit., pp. 73-74.

37. This approach has been attacked as being value neutral. It is said that true social scientists value only the process of inquiry regardless of where it leads. John J. Patrick in 'Main Themes in Political Education in American Secondary Schools', unpublished paper prepared for a Conference on Political Education in the Federal Republic of Germany and the United States of America at Indiana University, Bloomington, Indiana, 15-19 September 1975. We would argue that while this is true in the abstract sense, school programs using this approach have clearly reflected a commitment to preferred values.

38. See, for example, H. Berlak, 'The Teaching of Thinking', *School Review* 73 (1), 1965; J. Fair and F.R. Shaftel, (eds.), *Effective Thinking in the Social Studies*, Washington, DC: National Council for the Social Studies, 1967; and D.W. Oliver and James P. Shaver, *Teaching Public Issues in High School Social Studies*, Reading: Addison-Wesley, 1974.

39. Kohlberg has many detractors who do not agree that there is empirical evidence sufficient to validate his cognitive structure. We are not willing to enter into this debate and are basing our ranking on the fact that a systematic, educational strategy is involved.

40. Judith A. Gillespie and Stuart Lazarus, *Comparing Political Experiences*, Englewood Cliffs, New Jersey: Prentice-Hall Publishing Company, 1979.

41. These products are: *Handbook of Basic Citizenship Competencies; Principals and Citizenship Education: A Guide for Effective Leadership; Guide to Basic Citizenship Competencies: Recommendations to Compare Curriculum Materials, Assess Classroom Instruction, and Set Goals; The Community and Citizenship: A Guide for Planning and Leadership; Developing your Child's Citizenship Competencies: A Parent's Guide*; and *Executive Summary*.

42. If this definition were widely accepted by educators, only those approaches and programs that have to do with group governance would in the future be categorized as political education approaches.

43. Full report published in *Proceedings of the American Political Science Association*, Vol. II, 1905 and in the *Journal of Pedagogy*, June 1906.

44. Elizabeth A. Farquhar and Karen S. Dawson, *Citizen Education Today: Developing Civic Competencies*, Washington, DC: Office of Education, US Department of Health, Education, and Welfare, 1979, pp. 150-153.

45. See pp. 171-173 of ibid. for a series of publications documenting the phenomenon.

Political Education:
Developments in Britain

Robert Stradling

Until recently in Britain very few people received any kind of explicit and formal political education before leaving school. Admittedly in some schools the subject of politics has been offered in the form of examination courses for 16-18 year olds but these have usually been provided for a minority of students, never more than 3-4 percent of that age group. In an equally small number of schools some political or civic education has been provided for the less able 14-16 year olds, but this has tended to be given a low priority and regarded as 'minority-time' work.

It is doubtful whether many such courses provided an adequate political education. Too often civics and citizenship training for the less able seems to have been concerned with social adjustment and what John White has called 'instruction in obedience';[1] while the examination-based syllabuses for the older pupils have been little more than simplified versions of the degree courses offered by university departments of politics. The purpose of such syllabuses is not wholly clear. They are too academic in form, too specialized in content and politics is too narrowly defined to be of much value in preparing the young to take an active interest and get involved in the everyday world of politics, and yet many university academics doubt their value as a means of induction or preparation for the study of politics in higher education.

If the majority of school students experienced any kind of political education then they did so indirectly and in an unsystematic and piecemeal fashion, either through the more established subjects such as history, geography, and social studies or through the 'hidden curriculum' of the school: its authority structure, ethos and characteristic styles of teaching. There is no doubt that in this sense both the formal and informal aspects of the typical school curriculum have contributed to the political learning of successive generations. Clearly schools are agents of political socialization, sometimes intentionally and sometimes unwittingly, but much of this political learning can be essentially 'miseducative'. Any discussion of political education which does not attempt to distinguish it from political socialization can only confuse rather than clarify the situation. Like Harold Entwistle, I find it necessary to assert that being educated is not simply to be learning and that political education is concerned with helping the student to move 'towards a better informed, rational and sensitive perspective upon the universe.'[2] That is not to say that political education only takes place through formal teaching but it does mean that the informal aspects of the curriculum are only politically educative if they intentionally contribute to the development of this 'rational and sensitive perspective'.

In this more limited sense of the term political education has been sadly neglected for much of this century in Britain. From time to time, and usually coinciding with periods of international or national crisis, some politicians and educationalists have expressed an interest in the possibility of including civic or political education in the school curriculum. In 1918 the publisher Victor Gollancz with David Somervell proposed the substitution of political for classical education in the curriculum and avowed that 'it is only necessary that the vital issues should be honestly raised; the young and free mind may be confidently reckoned on to do the rest.'[3] However, few schools took up their suggestion. We then find a period of relative inactivity until the early 1930s when certain prominent social scientists, mostly Fabians, including G.D.H. Cole, Harold Laski, William Beveridge and Barbara Wootton founded the Association for Education in Citizenship. Disturbed by the rise of fascism and totalitarianism in Europe, the Association sought to ensure that young people in Britain would at least receive some preparation for citizenship in a liberal democracy. Their stated objective was 'to advance the study of and training in citizenship especially through political science and economics.' Few schools would seem to have attempted to implement their ideas and citizenship remained a fringe subject in the curriculum, possibly because the AEC's proposal was in direct opposition to the official line at that time.[4]

However, attitudes to political education changed decisively, if temporarily, during the Second World War. In order to counteract the influence of German propaganda some youth organizations and many schools and colleges initiated political education programmes in a variety of forms, while the Directorate of Army Education introduced politics into its education programme in 1940. From 1945 onwards there was some attempt to build on these wartime initiatives but public interest declined and teachers received little support from official quarters or from the universities and examining boards. Indeed it is perhaps indicative of the post-war neglect of political education that the first, and still the most systematic, historical account of these wartime developments was written by a German academic, Klaus Schleicher, and only a brief summary of his work has appeared in English.[5]

By the mid-1950s and 60s the scene, as Derek Heater has observed, was one of pervasive stagnation: 'Scything through luxuriant growth of officially promoted educational literature of recent years, one reaps a pitifully lean harvest of references to political education.'[6] In addition he points to the lack of books and literature offering advice to teachers on political education, the absence of a professional association and journal for teachers of politics, and, indeed, the lack of any proper teacher training facilities in any of the colleges or university departments of education.

The reasons why political education has been so neglected in Britain throughout this century are many and varied and it may seem a rather negative approach in a chapter on developments to dwell on them at any length but, as I shall attempt to show later, political education still does not have a well-established and defensible place in the school curriculum and its future is far from certain. To understand why this should be so it is important to examine current developments within their historical context. Indeed a modern Rip van Winkle, waking up after a fifty-year sleep, would find people in Britain rehearsing the same kinds of arguments for and against political education which he would have heard in 1930.

The lack of official support for political education has been well documented. One review of official attitudes and pronouncements concludes that developments, such as they are, have been in spite of rather than because of the guidance provided in the offical reports of the education departments of successive governments. The reviewer sums up official attitudes as follows: 'Throughout the greater part of the first three quarters of this century references to civic or political education have been cautious, vague and occasionally downright hostile.'[7] In part this lack of official support reflects a complacent belief in the evolutionary development and adaptability of the British political system. Until the mid-1960s it was customary for social scientists to classify Britain as an homogeneous and relatively stable society.[8] In such circumstances the provision of political education for each new generation does not seem to be of primary importance.

Coupled with this complacency has been the widely held view that political education was not a legitimate activity for schools to be engaged in. I can best illustrate this by quoting part of a leader from a national daily newspaper on the report of a survey on the political awareness of teenagers which I conducted on behalf of the Hansard Society.[9] The report indicated widespread ignorance of basic political information and misunderstandings about the main issues of the day, particularly those dividing the major political parties. In summarizing the report's findings *The Daily Telegraph* draws the following conclusions:

> Happy is the country whose youth have not the faintest idea what their rulers or would-be-rulers claim as 'the correct line' on this or that. Better by far the detailed ignorance met by the Hansard Society's researchers than the extravagant knowledge of government policy which children of other lands would have displayed — a knowledge which would have been derived from enforced attention to little red books or to the megalomaniacal chatter of a Castro, a Gaddafi, a Nyerere . . . horrified surveys of this kind never seem to understand that, in a healthy and free society, politics should not be regarded as especially important. Very many of the greatest achievements of mankind have had nothing to do with politicians — indeed, have happened in spite of them. There are many gaps to worry about in the knowledge of our school leavers. Their ignorance of, say Tory policy on incomes, is not one of them. Won't they soon be voters? Well, it is surprising how much they will discover in their first couple of years of adulthood.[10]

It would be all too easy for an advocate of political education to dismiss lightly such views as atypical and representative only of the reactionary backwoodsmen of British conservatism. I have no hesitation in labelling such views as reactionary and conservative but, unfortunately, they are far from atypical. Underpinning this editorial are certain assumptions about both politics and political education which have been and still are widely held in Britain. First we have the implicit assumption that in the realm of politics 'ignorance is bliss'. It is perhaps hardly surprising to find such a view espoused by some politicians and administrators but it has also been supported by some political scientists, particularly in the 1960s, on the grounds that active, informed participation on a large scale would only create an overload in the political system and make it highly unstable.[11]

Linked with this endorsement of political ignorance and apathy is an extremely limited conception of politics. One is reminded here of Lord Hailsham's reflection that 'Conservatives do not believe that political struggle is the most important thing in life . . . the simplest among them prefer fox hunting — the wisest religion.'[12] Although few of his political colleagues or the people who vote for them might conceive of Conservatism in quite the same terms — indeed, the Conservative Party continues to seek power while the churches are almost empty and the fox population goes forth and multiplies — nevertheless the restricted concept of politics and the tendency to devalue it as a human activity underlying the quotations from Hailsham and *The Daily Telegraph* also characterize the views and opinions of many others in Britain. Politics is widely held to be a somewhat dubious activity engaged in by political parties and from which the ordinary individual is excluded except during periodic elections. Given such a view it is hardly surprising that the idea of including political education in the school curriculum has received little public support in the past.

The Daily Telegraph's fear of pupil indoctrination is also shared by many people, although associating political education with 'enforced attention to little red books' is rather idiosyncratic and a red herring in every sense. For many parents, head teachers and administrators the main danger is not that the state will seek to indoctrinate the young through the medium of the school but that some individual teachers will seek to inculcate their own particular brand of political beliefs to the total exclusion of alternative viewpoints.

This fear of indoctrination is sufficiently widespread and strongly held that it needs to be taken seriously by advocates of political education. Unfortunately research on classroom practices in this and related areas of the curriculum is still thin on the ground and much of the debate about the potential risks of indoctrination tends to be conducted in a vacuum. Nevertheless, some salient points have emerged. Even in schools where provision for political education is not made there have presumably been opportunities for the dedicated adherents of a particular ideology to propagate their views informally in general discussion or through other subject areas such as history, geography or English. And yet there is no evidence of teachers being cautioned, suspended or dismissed on these grounds. To my knowledge the only teacher in recent years to fall foul of the authorities was a religious education teacher who taught the Book of Genesis as a factual account of the beginning of the world. The limited amount of research on political education in English schools has not as yet unearthed any examples of teachers attempting to indoctrinate their students politically. Professor Ian Lister, Director of the Political Education Research Unit at the University of York, has observed a lack of coherent political thought — of any persuasion — in much classroom teaching and notes that:

> Ideologies (such as Conservatism, Liberalism, Socialism, Marxism) remain relatively untouched. Even in sessions that promise to consider ideology, ideology often seems to disappear (explanations being offered purely in terms of self interest and material goods).[13]

Professor Lister and his team also found that students could accurately assess their teachers' value positions and make allowances for them. He concluded that if political education teachers worry about whether or not they should make their position explicit then they are worrying unnecessarily. 'This particular teachers' dilemma seems to us to be a bogus problem.'[14] Notwithstanding such findings the debate on the potential risks of political education continues and researchers will have to produce more and harder evidence if they are successfully to allay the fears of some parents and headteachers.

The fourth and final assumption underpinning the quoted editorial which also receives widespread credence is that 'it is surprising how much they [school leavers] will discover in their first couple of years of adulthood.' On the evidence available from opinion polls and surveys of the British electorate there is no factual justification for such a view. The Hansard Society's survey, which drew comparisons between the political knowledge of adults and the young, gives one little cause for optimism here.

Undoubtedly political complacency and public doubts about the appropriateness and consequences of political education have inhibited its development but due weight also needs to be given to wholly educational factors. As noted earlier in this chapter there have been various attempts in this century to introduce political education into the curriculum but each innovation failed to establish itself. Consistent official support could have increased the chances of success in each case but the educational system is a decentralized one. It is a national system in so far as it has been created by act of parliament and subject to regulation by central government but government has so far chosen to confine its actions to matters of finance, building allocation and teacher supply and has chosen not to exercise power in matters of curriculum and pedagogy. The control of curriculum policy and development is devolved through the 108 local education authorities. The situation is summarized by the government publication *The Educational System of England and Wales* as follows:

> Legally the curriculum is the responsibility of Local Education Authorities and school governors; in practice, decisions about its content and about teaching methods, timetabling and selection of textbooks are usually left to the headteachers and their staff.[15]

The autonomy regarding curriculum content which this devolution apparently gives to teaching staff might seem to enhance the chances of curriculum innovations which do not have official support. Most innovations get taken up by some schools and, if these schools receive support in the form of in-service training and resources from their local authorities, then the innovations are likely to be successfully institutionalized. But the result usually is a localized or regional pattern of provision. A small group of local education authorities will become well known for supporting a particular curriculum development but it will not necessarily be taken up elsewhere. In this respect the autonomy of individual schools can inhibit the impact and take-up of certain innovations. However, it should also be acknowledged here that administrators, educationalists and the teachers' unions engage in a good deal of myth-making concerning the extent of the British teachers' autonomy. In many schools the freedom of the teachers means the freedom of the head and his deputies or heads of departments to determine the school's curriculum, but even their freedom is circumscribed by the need to tailor their curriculum to the requirements of the examination boards. As the Schools Council working party on the Whole Curriculum observed: 'The examination dictates the curriculum and cannot do otherwise; it confines experiment, limits free choice of subjects, hampers treatment of subjects, encourages wrong values in the classroom.'[16] The result is that many schools are reluctant to change their curriculum unless the examinations will change; examining boards are hesitant about endorsing changes until they are sure that standards will not be impaired; while publishers are often reluctant to put new materials on the market unless they are linked to examinations.

From the point of view of political education it might seem that the solution would be to get it examined and to some extent this is exactly what has happened. All but one of the examining boards for the General Certificate of Education now offer syllabuses in government and politics, and some of the boards for the Certificate of Secondary Education also offer syllabuses or validate syllabuses submitted to them by schools. However, the restricted concept of assessment on which these examinations are based usually leads to courses which focus essentially on descriptive knowledge. Advocates of wider and more instrumental forms of political education find such courses highly unsatisfactory and, unless the criteria for assessment were to be enlarged, would prefer political education not to be linked to examinations in this way. In this they are probably swimming against the tide of an educational tradition which gives much greater priority to progressive selection for higher education than to preparation for adult life and assumes that those qualities of mind characteristic of 'the educated person' can only be developed through acquiring an understanding of forms of knowledge and academic disciplines. As one writer has observed, this tradition, in emphasizing forms rather than content (and knowledge rather than skills and attitudes) has a conservative effect on the curriculum, tending to encourage the retention of existing school subjects and to discourage the introduction of new subject areas and content.[17]

The pervasiveness of this tradition is exemplified by the reaction to calls for political education of Terry Casey, general secretary of one of the leading teachers' unions:

> The situation will not be put right by any ad hoc addition of political or economic education, not at a time when we are all agreed that the curriculum has been overloaded. If we taught more about the Roman Republic it might give them a better political education than something called Civics.[18]

In spite of this prevailing tradition and in spite of the other constraints operating on and within the educational system to inhibit the growth of political education, the situation is changing. Recent developments have prompted one educationalist to observe that 'after a decade of quiet gestation, the political education movement has now become a force to be reckoned with. Political education has emerged as one of the major educational talking points of the past 18 months.'[19]

Whether there is sufficent consensus amongst all the supporters of political education for them to be said to constitute a 'movement' is open to question. They may all be agreed that the school curriculum should make provision for political education but there is far less agreement about the kind of education which should be offered. Not all politicians, for example, might agree with Margaret Jackson who, when Under Secretary at the Department of Education and Science in the last Labour government, described politics as 'the highest form of education'. Her own party's *Green Paper on Education in Schools*, published in July 1977, adopted a line which probably attracts wider political support. There were only two passing references to political education and in each case it was associated with the twin objectives of generating support for the political system and the mixed economy:

> In addition to their responsibility for the academic curriculum, schools must prepare their pupils for the transition to adult and working life. Young people need to be equipped with a basic understanding of the functioning of our democratic political system, of the mixed economy and the industrial activities, especially manufacturing, which create our national wealth.[20]

The current Labour spokesman on education, Neil Kinnock, has adopted a broader view arguing that political education in schools is one of the few ways in which ordinary people can learn about their rights and how to organize themselves.[21]

For Conservatives, Norman St. John Stevas, when Opposition spokesman on education, welcomed moves to introduce political education in schools but wanted the major political parties to draw up an agreed policy for the teaching of the subject. A Conservative party study group on youth policy was set up in the autumn of 1977 and recommended that curriculum guidelines issued by central government should include political education among the 'core' to be provided by every secondary school and that if local authorities failed to respond 'a reserve power should be taken to compel them to do so.'[22] It is very doubtful whether such a policy would receive the wholehearted endorsement of the entire Conservative party.

It is with some justification that cynics have attributed the political parties' interest in political education to their declining membership. Over the last twenty years the overall membership figures for the three main political parties have declined by over a third and, in spite of the minimum voting age being lowered to eighteen in 1968, the proportion of young people in the parties has fallen at an even faster rate. If this trend had coincided with a period of widespread political quiescence and apathy then perhaps the parties would have been less concerned, particularly since the two largest ones are by no means wholly dependent on the financial support of their local constituency associations. In fact, however, this has been a period of increased political activity but instead of being content to work through the more traditional channels of influence such as the Member of Parliament and the political party, an increasing number of people have joined pressure groups. During this period we have also seen increasing support for political parties and groupings outside the mainstream of British politics. The extreme right-wing National Front, for example, which proposes repatriation of all coloured immigrants, recruits much of its support from white, working-class 16-19 year-olds in inner city areas. In 1977 the National Front initiated a recruitment drive in London schools which led in turn to counter moves by such groups as the Anti-Nazi League and SKAN (School Kids Against the Nazis) and by left-wing groups such as the Socialist Workers Party who also attempted to recruit support in schools. In response to such developments Shirley Williams, the minister for education, in a speech at the Commonwealth Institute said 'It seems to me crucially important that we should try to edge young people away from the margins of politics and into the mainstream.'[23] On the same occasion she also announced that her department would be funding two political education projects aimed at developing the political awareness and competence of young people. However, because of the government's reluctance to appear to be controlling the curriculum the grants were awarded to two youth organizations — the British Youth Council and the National Association of Youth Clubs — for work outside schools.

To some observers this rise of extremist groups and parties is just one more symptom of a major long-term political crisis in Britain. In the 1970s a spate of books appeared advocating less government, reform of existing political institutions or radical change. Typical of this mood was a BBC publication, edited by Professor Anthony King, with contributions from politicians and social scientists, entitled *Why is Britain Becoming Harder to Govern?* The editor summed up the raison d'être of the book as follows:

> It was once thought that Britain was an unusually easy country to govern, its politicians wise, its parties responsible, its administration efficient, its people docile. Now we wonder whether Britain is not perhaps an unusually difficult country to govern, its problems intractable, its people bloody-minded. What has happened? What has gone wrong?[24]

In some quarters there is a growing belief that the increasingly complex policies of modern government (on, for example, industrial relations, employment, inflation, state intervention in industry, the European Community, etc.) are not being implemented effectively because the electorate is insufficiently well-informed. They were not short of evidence. Countless opinion polls and academic surveys in the late 1960s and early 70s showed that a large proportion of the electorate lacked basic information about the political process, the main issues of the day and the policies advocated by the different political parties, and did not even know who their political representatives were. Indeed there was even evidence that many electors advocated the implementation of policies which had in fact already been in operation for several years. Ignoring the possibility that the failure of certain government policies in the 1970s might be due to their own inadequacy or to a failure of communication on their part some leading politicians seemed to see political education as one possible panacea for some of their problems.

A recent collection of discussion documents on the school curriculum for 11 to 16 year-olds produced by Her Majesty's Inspectorate of Schools reflects a similar concern with the future health of our political system. In a paper on the role of the educational system in society they note that schools have multiple obligations and purposes and must service both society and the individual. They further assert that: 'The 1980s may well be years of even greater political and economic tension than the present day, at home as well as abroad. If so, the greater will be the need for a basic political and economic education for all.'[25]

However, this concern of politicians and administrators about an impending or existing political crisis alone cannot account for the current interest in political education. Renewed interest also reflects a wider educational trend which can, I think, be traced back to the late 1960s. Then some educationalists were drawing attention to the drop-out rates from schools as an indictment of the educational system. A growing dissatisfaction was attributed to the widely held belief amongst young people, particularly the less able, that much of the school curriculum was irrelevant to their everyday lives and needs. This led to calls for a more open and flexible curriculum giving greater emphasis to the social dimension of education in its broadest sense and to preparation for life after school. It was increasingly recognized that courses needed to be seen as satisfying in themselves and not simply parts of some great design for initiating a small minority of pupils into the academic disciplines of higher education. The result of this change of emphasis was a plethora of curriculum development projects funded by the Schools Council, a semi-official body established in 1965 to stimulate and promote curricular innovations. Within a short time project teams were engaged in developing guidelines for teachers and classroom materials in social, moral and health education, industrial studies, careers education and guidance, and so forth. These developments received an added impetus when it was decided in 1968 to raise the school leaving age from 15 to 16 leaving many schools with the problem of how to construct a curriculum for school leavers who had anticipated that by the age of 15 they would be earning their livings rather than still sitting in classrooms.

To some extent political education has come in on the coat tails of this general curricular movement and has undoubtedly benefited from it. The very fact that people had to consider the implications of a notion such as 'preparation for life' has brought political education into focus but it has also meant that claims for political education are now being scrutinized from an educational as well as a political perspective. It is extremely unlikely that a new subject area would establish itself within the school curriculum simply because of political pressures given the educational climate and the devolved responsibility for decisions on curriculum content. A social and political education which acknowledges the school's responsibility for educating autonomous and rational individuals is more likely to find favour amongst educationalists than an approach concerned solely with socializing 'virtuous' citizens. Nevertheless, a tension exists between these two types of objective — the political and the educational — which is by no means yet resolved. It is a tension which is all too apparent in the working papers of Her Majesty's Inspectorate. The paper on 'Political Competence', for example, which is written by two HMIs with responsibility for history and political education, outlines the concepts and knowledge necessary for pupils to analyze political issues, and the skills and attitudes necessary to enable them to think and act for themselves as autonomous citizens, and yet clearly they also see political education as a bastion in defence of democracy. Quoting Edmund Burke — 'The only thing necessary for the triumph of evil is for good men to do nothing' — they go on to argue that 'it is not enough for political education to talk in terms of the virtues of democratic society; in addition we must provide intellectual weapons to resist those who oppose it.'[26] To what extent teachers can resolve the potential tension between demands on them to produce good citizens and autonomous individuals remains to be seen.

Political pressure, a changing educational climate, and positive support for political education from the DES have produced the right conditions for curriculum development but the main impetus has come through the work of the Hansard Society for Parliamentary Government and the Politics Association.

The Hansard Society was founded in 1944 to promote interest in and knowledge of parliamentary government. In the early 1970s the

society underwent a significant shift of emphasis away from its pro-
motional work and towards research, including research and
development in the area of political education. In 1969 the society
organized a conference of teachers of politics which in turn led to
the formation of a professional body — The Politics Association —
intended specifically to provide a service for teachers in secondary
and further education. To this end the association now publishes its
own journal, books, guides to teaching materials and information
sheets; has established local branches to stimulate grassroots activities and organizes in-service training courses and conferences
for teachers.

In its first ten years the association has met with mixed success. It
originally hoped to attract over 1,000 members but membership has
always fallen well below this target and is still falling. Also some of
the branches have failed to generate much local activity or support,
but perhaps its most signal failure to date lies in the area of political
education for the less able student. The association's executive
committee has sought to stimulate an interest at this level but the
membership is solidly entrenched in teaching the more academic,
examination-based syllabuses. One consequence of this has been
that other teachers' associations have stepped into the breach.
Thus, for example, three other subject associations have devoted
whole issues of their journal to political education and two — the
Association for the Teaching of the Social Sciences and the
Association for Liberal Education — have organized in-service
training courses and workshops in this field which have not been
restricted solely to their members.

In spite of these difficulties which may in time prove to be
nothing more than teething troubles, the Politics Association has
made a significant contribution to political education in this country. Its journal, *Teaching Politics*, under the editorship of Derek
Heater has achieved a circulation far wider than the association's
membership and done much to foster curriculum development. In
conjunction with its sister organization the Hansard Society, the
Politics Association has also gained public recognition as an
authority on matters relating to political education and both bodies
have become prime movers of curriculum development.

In 1974 a grant from the Nuffield Foundation of £40,000 for a
period of three years enabled the Hansard Society, jointly with the
Politics Association, to launch the Programme for Political Educa-

tion consisting of curriculum development schemes and evaluation of innovations aimed at enhancing the political literacy of young people in secondary and further education.

The monitoring and evaluation of innovatory schemes was conducted by an independent research unit at the University of York, under the direction of Professor Ian Lister. The responsibility for curriculum development was in the hands of a working party of educationalists and practising teachers and serviced by a central team of two full-time development officers based at the Hansard Society. In their first discussion document, issued in July 1974, the working party stated its aims and objectives and indicated the kind of political education which it thought to be most appropriate:

> We want to get away from the idea of a 'politics syllabus' which is a progressive simplification of a university discipline. Rather we plan to build from bottom up by examining early perceptions of politics in non-academic contexts and streams, and to elaborate a growing process of political literacy through whatever discipline (in most of which the influence of 'political science' on the teacher is obviously only a very small factor).[27]

The concept of political literacy which underpins the thinking in the work of the Programme for Political Education is discussed in detail elsewhere in this book, so, for the most part, I shall confine myself to a consideration of the project's strategies for curriculum development and innovation.[28] It is sufficient here simply to note some of the main characteristics of the political literacy approach. These are:

1. a very broad definition of politics. The concept is not restricted to affairs of state or to the activities of political parties and pressure groups but refers also to group behaviour at school, in the workplace, trade unions, within the local community and in most other activities of everyday life;

2. an inductive approach to the teaching of politics through political issues. That is to say, an understanding of the political process is thought to be best acquired through considering what happens when institutions and other groups deal with those problems arising when people with differing interests and beliefs disagree about what should be done, why and how;

3. an emphasis on the development of concepts and conceptual frameworks for understanding political activities;

4. emphasis is also given to the acquisition of practical knowledge
   and politically relevant skills (i.e. for communicating one's own
   ideas and beliefs, influencing others and participating in the
   making of decisions).[29]

In determining their curriculum strategy the Programme for
Political Education had to come to terms with the fact that the
typical school timetable is already overcrowded. One possible approach was to seek to convince head teachers that political education had a stronger claim to a slot on the timetable than some other
well-established subjects. Another approach involved
demonstrating to schools how political education could be introduced or infiltrated into other subjects. Initially they opted for a
combination of the two:

> From the beginning we intended to advance in two ways: a massive frontal attack
> combined with permeation and infiltration aimed at specified targets behind the
> lines. The frontal attack was to be a generalized programme or outline of cur-
> riculum development for local adaptation as a two-year course and the permea-
> tion was a strategy of infusing political literacy into the curriculum through other
> subject disciplines (for example, we said 'history, English, geography, social
> studies, sociology and economics') and we intended to monitor the progress of
> the advance by Hansard producing materials, both for the big push and the in-
> filtrations, getting schools to try them out, and then for York to monitor and
> assess the results.[30]

To this end the working party concentrated its efforts on producing guidelines for curriculum development whilst also setting up
groups of teachers representing different subject areas to produce
draft syllabuses and materials showing how these guidelines could
be put into practice. It was intended that these materials and
syllabuses should be regarded as 'exemplars' which individual
teachers could adapt and develop in relation to their own particular
situation and to meet the particular requirements of their own
students. It was not intended that teachers should simply and un-
thinkingly adopt a new and 'teacher-proof' approach.

In this respect the PPE differed markedly from earlier Nuffield-
funded curriculum development projects (and some Schools Councils projects) which had adopted what Donald Schon has termed
the 'centre-periphery' model;[31] that is, a central project team of experts deciding on the structure of the subject and the relevant content to be learned, then negotiating with educationalists and media

experts to translate these ideas into standard courses with accompanying texts and classroom materials. The centre-periphery model has not proved particularly successful in Britain. Many of the curriculum innovations which were developed in this way, in virtual isolation from the teaching profession itself, seem to have had little or no significant impact on classroom practice. By the mid-1970s an increasing number of development projects were adopting a strategy of curriculum re-interpretation in which practising teachers were involved in every stage of curriculum development and made the key decisions regarding what was to be taught and how.

In most instances such projects adopted the strategy because it was thought to be the most appropriate approach to curriculum innovation and consequently the one most likely to have a significant impact upon the nation's schools and classrooms. But, as a participant observer at most of the working party meetings of the PPE, it is my impression that at the outset they (we) did not see the full implications of adopting this strategy. It was not adopted because it was thought to be the most appropriate one for introducing and sustaining an innovation. It was adopted because the analysis of issues was central to the political literacy approach and the project believed that issues should be discussed which touch upon or are closely analogous to the experience of a particular group of pupils. Consequently there seemed little hope of developing a ready-made package which would be universally applicable. It was thought essential that teachers should take, at least as a starting point, issues which were local and had some relevance to students' direct experience. This strategy was also adopted because it was believed that it would be both intellectually and morally wrong to assume that there is a consensus in society about political values 'to the extent that a single model curriculum could or should be instituted and taught.' It was not until the third year in the project's life that much attention was given to the twin problems of project diffusion and consolidation of innovations. Then funding was obtained from the Schools Council to enable the PPE to establish a few locally-based groups of teachers, working on a voluntary basis and with the support of their schools and local education authorities, to develop political education courses and to modify existing subjects and multi-disciplinary programmes.

Unquestionably the project encountered its fair share of problems and failures. Some of the teachers' groups failed to produce materials in sufficient time for them to be evaluated by the research unit; other groups broke up after a few meetings without proving productive. The programme also encountered problems with its strategy of infiltrating existing subjects. The development officer concluded from his observations of courses in schools cooperating with the project 'that political literacy teaching is only really successful where it is done through courses which have been constructed with exclusively political literacy objectives.'[32]

This raises a difficult problem which is not confined to the political literacy approach to political education. All head teachers contemplating the introduction of political education into the curriculum are faced with the necessity of choosing between political education courses and the infusion approach. If they have sufficient space on the timetable and the trained staff and resources available then the former may seem to be the most attractive and desirable option. Even so, on the evidence so far available, few head teachers as yet would be willing to devote sufficient resources to the introduction of a course for all pupils, regardless of ability. Some introduce it as a course for the less able streams; others as an examination course in the academic study of government for the more able students. In either case such courses will be optional and for a minority of students and, as such, would be regarded as undesirable by most proponents of political education.

Nevertheless, as the Programme for Political Education found, there are considerable problems with the alternative infusion approach. Essentially it is found in two forms within our schools and colleges. Sometimes politics appears as a module or unit of lessons inserted into a single subject or, more often, a multi-disciplinary course. In other instances, politics is integrated into single subject and inter-disciplinary courses, that is, teachers attempt to bring out the political dimension of the subject matter of other disciplines. The problem with the modular form of infusion is that it is little more than a scaled-down — and watered-down — version of the full course. It is more limited in scope, of course, and because the teachers are usually non-specialists they tend to fall back on set texts and materials and concentrate on the transmission of knowledge rather than the development of skills and conceptual understanding. The integrated form of infusion offers more scope and, in the case of inter-disciplinary courses, it may provide students with a more realistic picture of human behaviour than either full courses in politics or modules, given that most aspects of human activity are seldom totally political in nature. On the other hand, some teachers adopting the integrated form of infusion seem curiously prone to indulge in reductionism. Instead of their teaching being broadened to take account of new aims and objectives the objectives of political education are 'reduced' until they virtually coincide with the existing objectives of the original subject specialism or course. In my experience it is subject specialists, particularly historians, who are most likely to fall into this trap. Those teachers trained to teach mutli- or inter-disciplinary courses in, for example, the social sciences, social studies, or general studies in further education tend to be more flexible.

The solution to this problem lies, I suspect, in the development of appropriate courses in teacher training establishments. It would seem in Britain that when a new subject area begins to stake a claim for itself in the school curriculum the first response of teacher training colleges is to ignore it in the hope that it will go away. Then with some reluctance the philosophical issues raised by the new subject will be discussed in courses on educational theory and the philosophy of education, and then finally an academic course on the structure and content of the new subject will be instituted. But, with few exceptions, it is training in the *teaching* of this subject area which is ignored and yet this is precisely what is most needed in the case of political education. The concern should be less with training subject specialists and more with producing flexible and versatile teachers.

There is a virtual consensus amongst the supporters of political education that it should not be confined simply to the transmission of political information and that it should be provided for all students within a given school regardless of their ability. However, this means that teachers cannot rely solely on directive teaching or 'chalk and talk' but need to be skilled in organizing group exercises, projects, games and simulations, and in enabling enquiry-based learning to flourish. Furthermore they need to be versatile in their use of language to cope with mixed ability classes. It is, for example, a continual source of surprise to me that so many teachers and student teachers treat political concepts (and presumably concepts basic to other disciplines) as if they were 'labels' to be learned rather than ideas and generalizations to be understood. As a result they are either unable or unwilling to find suitable analogies and the differential language which would enable them to explain these concepts to their students. Unless initial and in-service teacher training takes account of these factors the problem of infusing political education into the curriculum will remain intractable.

It is not yet possible to estimate with any degree of certainty the extent to which political education is being introduced into British schools or in what form. The Curriculum Review Unit, under the co-direction of the present writer and Alex Porter, former development officer in the Programme for Political Education, has been commissioned by the Department of Education and Science to study and assess innovations in political education from 1979-82 and to look at the implications of different approaches both for the future provision of political education in secondary and further education and for the provision of teacher training schemes in this area. Until the CRU has collected more data one can only speculate about the nature and extent of provision. For what it is worth my guess would be that comparatively few schools offer political education courses for students below the age of 16. Of these by far the majority are likely to concentrate on the structure and function of political institutions, parties and groups combined with some emphasis on the rights and duties of the citizen. Only a few schools as yet have adopted the political literacy approach, or something similar, to the extent of developing a complete teaching programme. This approach is more commonly infused into humanities and social studies courses whilst a political science approach is sometimes adopted both in modular and integrated forms in social science courses for the 14 to 16 year-olds. Political education through single subjects such as history and English for the most part remains purely incidental.[33]

What then are the future prospects for political education in Britain? Tapper and Salter have argued that the political education movement has arrived on the scene at the end of a great wave of curriculum innovation and may have 'missed the boat'.[34] Notwithstanding the fact that Tapper and Salter are labouring under the misconception that the political education movement is calling for 'the explicit teaching of politics as a school discipline in its own right', there may be some validity in what they say.[35] When the Programme for Political Education got underway in 1974 there were already signs of educational retrenchment. Britain was already sliding into a new economic depression, educational budgets were being reduced, some teacher training establishments were being closed down, and newly trained teachers were facing unemployment. These were hardly ideal circumstances in which to argue the case for yet another innovation in the school curriculum requiring a reallocation of resources in its favour. The circumstances in 1980 would seem to be even worse. With inflation at 17 percent and a government in power claiming to have a mandate to cut public expenditure, political education will have to struggle hard for survival. The PPE can claim some modest victories and breakthroughs but the curriculum in many schools remains remarkably similar to that of twenty years ago.

However, it may be unfair simply to point to the small number of schools introducing political literacy courses or courses with a political literacy component and use this as a yardstick for success or failure. A Schools Council working paper on curriculum dissemination has expressed the view that the success of a particular dissemination exercise should not necessarily be measured by the degree of take-up:

> We believe that dissemination has been successful when teachers understand the project's ideas and materials sufficiently well to use them in school if they choose to do so. We are concerned with communicating understanding to the point at which informed choices can be made and sustained.[36]

Alex Porter, on behalf of the PPE, echoes this view when he argues that from his contact with teachers, advisers and people responsible for in-service training, there is now much greater awareness of the importance of political education and, above all, the concept of political literacy is now widely known and regarded by teachers as influential on what they are doing in the classroom.[37] For a project which opted more for an infusion approach than a full frontal attack on the curriculum this would seem to be as much as they could hope for. The pebble has been dropped into the pool and they must now wait for the ripples to spread.

There are other indications of favourable prospects. At the level of initial teacher training there have been considerable developments over the last ten years. In 1968 Derek Heater conducted a survey of teacher training establishments and found only two colleges offering anything which approached a systematic course in political studies and no college offered a post-graduate certificate course in the teaching of politics. In 1975 Tom Brennan, on behalf of the PPE, conducted a similar survey and found relevant courses in 37 institutions. Since then 13 of the colleges have merged and another 5 have been closed down, but even so, from the initial returns of a survey conducted by the Curriculum Review Unit this year it would appear that the number of colleges providing some form of politics or political education programme is still increasing.

There is also evidence of growing support now from local education authorities. Approximately one in four local authorities supports the introduction of political education. In some cases this support takes the form of in-service training and back-up for teachers from full-time advisory staff. In other instances it takes the form of resources for local curriculum development groups and in yet other instances the LEAs are offering little more than moral support. To readers from countries which have a more centralized educational system this kind of development may seem far from adequate, but with a devolved system such as we have in Britain it is a significant achievement to have as many as 25 local authorities involved in and supporting a given innovation at any particular time.

However, whether or not the present degree of diversity in the content of the curriculum, both between schools and for students within schools, will continue to persist is a matter of some conjecture at the time of writing. In 1977 the Labour government initiated what came to be known as 'The Great Debate' on education. Following on from and arising out of this debate the government issued a circular to all local education authorities seeking information about their policies and practices in curricular matters. A report on this was published in November 1979 revealing that many local authorities have no view about what should constitute an essential framework for the curriculum.[38]

The new Conservative government's response to this report was to invite Her Majesty's Inspectorate of Schools to draw up a draft policy document suggesting the form a framework for the curriculum might take and the ground it should cover. In advance of the publication of this policy document, the secretaries of state for education have already indicated their belief that 'a good deal of support has been found for the idea of identifying a "core" or essential part of the curriculum which should be followed by all pupils according to their ability.'[39] They suggest that the essential elements or core would consist of English, mathematics, science, a modern European language, religious education and physical education. Whilst these are held to be the core subjects they also express the view that within the optional subjects offered by schools greater concern should be given to the broad area of preparation for adult and working life, including social education, moral education, vocational guidance and 'preparation for a participatory role in adult society'. At one stage or another, according to the ministers, these subject areas should 'find a place in the education of every pupil.' The Inspectorate's policy document, when it was subsequently issued, outlined a similar framework for a common curriculum except in so far that it made out a case for including the area of 'preparation for adult and working life' within the common core. In so doing they drew attention to the problems which might arise if this area was seen by schools as simply a compendium of competing options:

> difficult decisions may arise in relation to social and political education. Schools do quite commonly now offer pupils a choice from history, geography, economics or some form of combined social or environmental studies, and there clearly are some overlapping interests and skills which pupils could be expected to derive from them. It is, however, questionable whether, in view of the way these subjects have developed over recent years, young people will derive enough of what they need to know and understand from a choice of only one of these.[40]

It remains to be seen just exactly how narrowly or broadly the government will interpret the idea of a common core. One thing is certain; it will be under strong pressure from one quarter to include a core of knowledge and skills for the citizen which draws on social studies, economics, politics and law. It is equally certain that the government will also be under strong pressure from the National Union of Teachers, and other teachers' unions, to preserve the existing arrangements concerning decisions on the content of the curriculum, even though a recent opinion poll indicated widespread support among teachers for a compulsory core.[41]

The situation as it now stands leaves supporters of political education in a curious even paradoxical position. If the Department of Education and Science should decide eventually that political education should be included in a national core curriculum then this would seem to represent the fulfilment of all they have been working for. On the other hand, one is still left with the nagging suspicion that any political education which this, or any other government, would wish to introduce might prove to be precisely the kind of political education which we have been arguing so strongly against.

NOTES

1. J. White, 'Instruction in Obedience', *New Society*, 2 May 1968.

2. H. Entwistle, 'Education and the Concept of Political Socialization', *Teaching Politics* 3 (2), 1974.

3. V. Gollancz and D. Somervell, *Political Education at a Public School*, London: Collins, 1918.

4. For a history of the AEC see D. Lawton and B. Dufour, *New Social Studies*, London: Heinemann, 1973.

5. K. Schleicher, *Politische Bildung in England 1939-1965*, Heidelberg: Quelle and Meyer, 1970. A brief account in English of his work appears in the *Bulletin of the General Studies Association* 12, 1968, pp. 9-15.

6. D. Heater, 'A Burgeoning of Interest: Political Education in Britain', *International Journal of Political Education* 1, 1977-78, p. 327.

7. T. Brennan in the unpublished evaluation report of the PPE, York, 1977.

8. See e.g., G.A. Almond and S. Verba, *The Civic Culture*, Princeton: Princeton University Press, 1963.

9. R. Stradling, *The Political Awareness of the School Leaver*, London: Hansard Society, 1977.

10. *The Daily Telegraph,* Friday, 12 August 1977.

11. See e.g., W.H. Morris-Jones, 'In Defence of Apathy', *Political Studies*, 11, 1964, pp. 25-37.

12. Lord Hailsham, *The Conservative Case*, Harmondsworth: Penguin, 1959.

13. I. Lister, 'The Aims and Methods of Political Education in Schools', *Teaching Politics*, 6, 1977, p. 10.

14. Op. cit., p. 66.

15. DES booklet, *The Educational System of England and Wales*, London, February 1977, pp. 18-19.

16. Schools Council, *Working Paper no.53*, London: Evans/Methuen Educational, 1975.

17. J. Beck, 'Social and Political Education: A Question of Priorities', *Cambridge Journal of Education* 8, 1978, pp. 66-77.

18. *Times Educational Supplement,* 19 August 1977.

19. G. Whitty, 'Political Education: Some Reservations', *Social Science Teacher* 8 (3), 1979, pp. 112-116.

20. DES, *Education in Schools: A Consultative Document,* London: HMSO, 1977, para. 10. 9.

21. Neil Kinnock in Whitty, op. cit.

22. *A Time For Youth,* London: Conservative Party Central Office, 1978.

23. *Times Educational Supplement,* 6 January 1978.

24. A. King (ed.), *Why is Britain Becoming Harder to Govern?,* London: BBC, 1976.

25. DES, *Curriculum 11-16: Working Papers by HMI,* London: HMSO, 1977.

26. Ibid.

27. B. Crick and A. Porter (eds.), *Political Education and Political Literacy,* London: Longman, 1978.

28. The PPE's own account of its strategy appears in Crick and Porter, ibid., ch.1.

29. Since the establishment of the PPE in 1974 the concept of political literacy has undergone considerable refinement and amendment. (See, for example, the chapter in this book on political literacy by Alex Porter.) My comments here reflect the thinking of the Political Literacy in Further Education Project which was established in 1977 as an offshoot of the PPE under the direction of myself and Mr Geoffrey Stanton, then lecturer at Garnett College and now Development Officer in the Further Education Unit at the Department of Education and Science.

30. Crick and Porter, op. cit., p. 9.

31. D. Schon, *Beyond the Stable State,* London: BBC Reith Lectures, 1971.

32. Crick and Porter, op. cit., p. 203.

33. Further details of this project can be obtained from the Curriculum Review Unit, 16 Gower Street, London WC1E 6DP.

34. T. Tapper and B. Salter, *Education and the Political Order,* London: Macmillan, 1978.

35. Ibid., p. 75.

36. Schools Council pamphlet 14: *Dissemination and In-Service Training,* London: Schools Council, 1974.

37. Interviewed on 22 November 1979.

38. DES, *Local Authority Arrangements for the School Curriculum,* London: HMSO, November 1979.

39. DES, *A Framework for the School Curriculum: Proposals for Consultation by the Secretaries of State for Education and Science,* London, January 1980.

40. DES, *A View of the Curriculum,* HMI Series: Matters for Discussion 11, January 1980.

41. *Times Educational Supplement,* 23 November 1979.

II

POLITICAL EDUCATION
AND POLITICS:
THE RELATIONSHIP

4

Political Education:
A Reflection of Society

Dieter Schmidt-Sinns

INTRODUCTORY REMARKS

The fact that there is a close interrelation between politics and political education, even general education, is undeniable. Education is a subsystem of society. The American educator Lee F. Anderson speaks of a political eco-system, part of which political education is considered to make up.[1] But whether we are inclined to follow this systems approach or not, we will find that the decision about the kind of education our children may get is a political issue. In societies where educational tradition is strong and, as a consequence, educational change is slow, education may for periods of time appear to be far from politics; but as soon as a social group attempts to introduce new structures or new goals, tradition-minded people will oppose it and the matter will become a political issue at once. So the task of proving the necessity of their goals will usually be laid upon the progressive side: tradition needs no arguments.

The close relationship of politics and political education can be studied particularly well by using the Federal Republic of Germany as an example. In its 'remade political culture'[2] we discern different didactic trends which, almost in a parallel development, correspond to similar phases of the political climate. The material illustrating our statements will therefore be taken mainly from Germany's recent history.

Educators are inclined to consider our topic from their own field. From their standpoint, politics appears to be intruding into the realm of teaching and learning. Politicians, on the other hand, have to fulfill a task comparable to teachers, if politicians want to be successful: they have to set goals, convince people that they are the right ones, and show ways of attaining them. In short, political leadership consists to a considerable extent of the art of telling people what should be done. To those who argue that the model described does not seem to be very democratic, I would readily agree. I just want to make the point that any policy needs consent, and politicians try to get as many people as possible as close to their goals as they can. This way of proceeding is a didactic one.

Education, however, has traditionally sought autonomy, an idea which necessarily goes with a trend of keeping politics out of school altogether. Good indicators for such an attitude in a country are the books or readers used in the primary levels to teach the mother tongue. How do they describe the respective society? In what kind of roles are the women shown? Do the texts transmit an ideal of countryside idyls, whereas the country's economy has proceeded far on the way to industrialization? Are the people (male and female) mentioned in the texts politically active citizens, or is politics totally excluded? Questions like these have to be asked to find out the political relevance of the curriculum, especially in the parts where it is not expected to contribute to political literacy. A 1967 study of the results of political education in the schools of the Federal Republic of Germany came to the conclusion that the effects of social studies proper were neutralized by subjects like German or even history,[3] for their hidden curriculum insinuated apolitical attitudes through the lack of political matters in German textbooks or through the teaching of mere events in history.

PARALLELS BETWEEN LEADING IDEAS IN POLITICS AND POLITICAL EDUCATION IN POSTWAR GERMANY

The fact that political and social education is closely connected with the political culture of a country is impressively illustrated by the development of political education in the Federal Republic of Germany after the Second World War. The early attention the subject was given was not caused by the foresight of German educators, but was an outcome of an urgent necessity felt after the total destruction of German political culture by the National-Socialists. After the establishment of the Federal Republic, the division of the nation, communist rule over one quarter of the former Reich, the loss of another quarter to Poland and Russia, and a very lively European unification movement were political challenges which concerned, in some way or the other, nearly every single German and demanded interpretation. The impact of these developments can be compared to the end of colonialism for the peoples in Asia and Africa and the problems connected with it.

Official measures taken in Germany were manifold: the introduction of chairs for the political and social sciences at many universities; the gradual introduction of a subject called civics, social studies or, very lately, politics in the schools of the various federal states; the foundation of 'Centres of Political Education' both in the states and for the federation in Bonn. The tasks for the Federal Centre as formulated in the official inaugurating document reflect the political situation: the office should, through measures of political education, awaken an understanding of the political process, strengthen the democratic idea and promote political participation; it should enable citizens to take a democratic standpoint towards fascist and communist totalitarianism; it should foster a peaceful understanding and cooperation with all peoples and promote European unification.[4] In the transformation of these ideas into practice, we discern several periods characterized by different didactic approaches, where certain goals stood in the foreground while others were neglected. These phases closely corresponded to the political history of the Federal Republic, though naturally overlapping in the reality of education.

The investigation of this development which is best verified empirically is a study by Thomas Ellwein and Ralf Zoll.[5] Out of 4,000 periodical articles that appeared in the years between 1948 and 1968, a random sample of 720 was selected. Of this sample the frequencies of 350 central concepts and the relationships among them were investigated.

First Period, 1948–1955/56

It is the period when people had to surmount the severest damage resulting from the National-Socialist regime and the war, physically as well as mentally. But except for an elite of mostly elder politicians, the vast majority of the population was disillusioned with politics in spite of the challenging situation mentioned above. They had grown accustomed to the idea of being the objects of politics. Economic reconstruction seemed to be the most vital task for the moment, and therefore, the necessity for cooperation was seen as one of the most urgent demands, more so as the quarrels between the democratic parties during the last years of the Weimar Republic had been one of the causes for Hitler being able to take over the political power.

In education, corresponding to those leading ideas, the concept of partnership clearly dominated, the title of one of the most widely used civic textbooks being *With One Another and For One Another*.[6] Teaching concentrated on the child's social environment, mainly the community. A more or less idealized view of political life was conveyed, concepts like power or conflict were rarely introduced; the typical civics courses aimed at social rather than political learning.

Second Period, 1955/56–about 1966

During this decade, the Federal Republic was well on the way towards consolidation. The Christian Democratic party reigned supreme with Konrad Adenauer as a father figure, although mostly in a coalition with the Free Democrats. There was no anticipation of a political change, the opposing Social Democrats gaining only between 30 and 40 percent of votes in elections.

During this rather conservative era, government courses were regarded as the core of social studies. Knowledge of state institutions and of the democratic process were held to be most important, insights and understanding based upon these concepts were taught. Leading representatives of this school were Eduard Spranger and Theodor Litt, educators who had been influential in civics instruction as early as the Weimar period. This approach has to be judged as restorative.

Third Period, since 1960

Criticism against the leading ideas in the still young democracy — both within political education proper and within political life in general — gradually came up in the early sixties and slowly gained ground together with the phasing out of the so-called 'fair-weather-democracy'. Adenauer had to resign as chancellor in 1963, and in 1967 the Social Democrats, for the first time in the Federal Republic, exerted political power as members of the government, though in a coalition with the Christian Democrats. Opposition in Parliament was left to a small party, the Free Democrats, who held less than 10 percent of the seats.

These political developments again have to be related to the approaches of political didactics during this time; one political issue even had a direct impact. In 1962, one of the secretaries of state in Adenauer's cabinet, Franz Joseph Strauss, was forced to resign because he had interfered with the freedom of the press. On his orders, the office of the magazine *Der Spiegel* had been occupied by the police and a member of its staff had been arrested in a foreign country as a reaction to a *Spiegel* article about the state of the German army. Both measures were illegal; the freedom of the press seemed to be threatened. For the first time since 1949, there was a political issue connected with democratic rights which aroused public opinion tremendously. The experience of the *Spiegel* affair caused Hermann Giesecke to consider conflict as one of the central concepts of political education. Together with other educators like Kurt Gerhard Fischer and Wolfgang Hilligen he criticized the existing civics courses as conveying an idealized 'harmony model' of democracy and thereby distorting reality.[7] More recent events in other countries, like the Vietnam War and the Watergate affair in the United States, have shown how conflict situations may promote political participation.

This sketchy picture of some of the main streams of political education in Germany is not meant as a historical description; they serve as some examples for my general thesis.[8] Other trends could also be mentioned, such as the concept of totalitarianism which was equally applied to the Nazi regime and to communist rule. The way it was taught, in history as well as in social studies, partly distorted reality and functioned as an ideology itself: the National-Socialist movement thus appeared as an extraordinary power which had overwhelmed and totally gripped a whole society; the roots of their thinking and the relation of their goals to German policy early in this century were neglected. Communists and National-Socialists were fitted into the same pattern so that a crude anticommunism gained ground, in public opinion and in textbooks and teaching alike.[9] In all, it was the political climate that, in the Federal Republic more than elsewhere, led to the formation of didactic camps which often argued against one another more fiercely than political parties.

POLITICAL SOCIALIZATION AS A TASK OF SOCIETY

In order to find out the requirements and necessary limits, the advantages and the dangers of the existing relation between politics and political education inside and outside school, we have to analyze more precisely the process of political socialization. Every society is bound to integrate the individual in the course of a process which, strictly speaking, lasts from birth to death. This is done through a variety of social institutions and groups as agents for transmitting an ideology as a frame of thinking. In traditional societies, myths, taboos, and a rather strictly fixed set of customs regulate behaviour. The same is more or less true, although not generally admitted, even for modern societies: religions, ideologies, political beliefs, and behavioural patterns which need no explanation regulate thinking, attitudes and behaviour throughout the world.

The development and conveyance of such a framework of ideas and expected behaviour is vital for every society, once natural, but nowadays highly precarious. Jürgen Habermas pointed out that the inability to produce sense is a token of the crisis of 'late capitalist societies'. A value pattern and the belief that life is worth living, once a natural outcome of socialization, have become 'scarce resources' so that the individual may in vain seek for his or her identity: 'The most important function of society is nomization. The anthropological presuppostion for this is a human craving for meaning that appears to have the force of instinct. Men are congenitally compelled to impose a meaningful order upon reality. This order, however, presupposes the social enterprise of ordering world construction.'[10] That 'ordering world construction' presupposes a sound political socialization.

As in traditional societies, this process also in developed industrial societies is still partly unintentional and uncontrolled by the state, especially as long as it operates through the family and the peer group. The part the mass media play heavily depends on the organization of the respective state; the introduction of television and the way it is controlled by the government will always have a strong impact on the socialization of the population. The classical socializing agent, however, the institution through which the state is capable of exerting immediate influence, has always been the school.

State control over teaching in schools is no doubt legitimate; for a good many populations in the third world the schools (and later on the army) even have to serve as the main integrating force for a growing nation. We remember that Nigeria, in the late sixties, was on the brink of breaking into two or three territories which would probably have meant nations. Accordingly, Nigerian authorities (together with ten other African countries in a more or less comparable situation) 'redefined the role of the school as a politicizing agent in the transition from colonialism to nationhood.'[11] They agreed that 'while every school discipline must provide social education, Social Studies have a unique role in giving the new generation of Nigerians a firm base in national consciousness through a study of man, and of himself as an individual member of a young but growing country.' 'Nigerianizing the child' was set as one of the central goals.[12]

For educators of the countries which passed their periods of growing into a nation during the nineteenth and early twentieth centuries, nationalism as a goal of political learning will now raise certain doubts, but for a society threatened by tribalism, national integration ought to rank high within the taxonomy of educational aims.

The state takes measures to influence political thought even where a special subject for political or social studies does not exist. History and the teaching of the national language are the usual means of transmitting the ideology desired. In 1889, Emperor William II issued an order to the Prussian ministry of state, in which he pointed out that it was one of the main tasks of the school 'to lay the basis for a sound conception of the political and social reality by teaching the fear of God and love of the country.' 'Besides,' he goes on, 'school has to strive for convincing the young generation that the doctrines of the Social Democrats not only contradict the divine order and Christian morality, but are also impracticable and in their consequences detrimental to the individual and the community alike.'[13] In our times, the followers of communist theories in many countries are treated as the Social Democrats were then.

Thus, the entire educational system is not only a subsystem of society, but it has even to be regarded 'as an institution stabilizing political power, as an instrument of government of the ruling forces in a society.'[14] 'The school implants religions, national and moral ideals into the young mind, and thus seeks to adapt it to the actual state of society and to make it governable for the respective supreme power.'[15]

In the early seventies, some German reformers cherished the hope to bring about social change through innovations within the educational system, the struggle for the introduction of comprehensive schools being one of the main issues. This endeavour, as far as we can see today, totally failed. Rolf Schmiederer had stated already in 1971 that it was an illusion to consider the educational system as a means of social revolution. Although one of the most decided democratic socialist reformers in the Federal Republic, he emphasized that we cannot but recognize the fact that 'in a society, the educational system in fact serves the goal of conserving civilization as it is.'[16] That is why political education, basically, has to be affirmative: no social system will ever intend its own supplanting.

But the educational system not only depends upon the leading social forces, it also exerts feedback into society. Taken literally, the model as depicted would not allow any social change. Reality shows that this is not true. We will have to consider below, therefore, how change actually takes place.

POLITICS AND POLITICAL EDUCATION
IN A DEMOCRATIC SOCIETY

We have discussed so far how society and the state exert influence. The issue becomes much more complicated when we recall that in modern pluralistic societies different social groups, such as political parties, churches, trade unions or employers' associations, legitimately attempt to realize their educational goals. During the harsh didactic arguments in the mid-seventies, a German educator, Felix von Cube, even saw the school 'between God and Marx'.[17] He pointed out that both Marxist and Christian goals were 'confessional' ones; both creeds trying to implant certain beliefs into the pupil, their goals are incapable of scientific proof or refutation. Thus, von Cube reminds us of the fact that every curriculum is based upon value decisions like the democratic citizen, the good Muslim or the socialist worker; normally it is based even on a whole set of values and beliefs. Traditional authorities like religious communities tend to take their values for granted. But they are not, even if they are in accordance with the beliefs of a large majority.

In an undemocratic system with one-party rule, political education officially creates no problem, although there may occur a competition for the souls of the young generation between opposite camps like the Communist party and the Roman Catholic church in Poland. But this essay is restricting the issue to political education in pluralistic societies, because from the theoretical point of view it is in this context that the core of the problem can best be developed.

We pointed out earlier that every society attempts to integrate its members and to provide them with a social identity. The political and the religious culture as well as traditions and beliefs help in this task. Within this framework, there ought to be room for opposition groups with alternative value systems in order to allow social change. The protection of minorities which represent differing issue-solutions is one of the basic features of modern democracies. This element has to be fostered also in political education which does not mean less than an intentional introducing of ideas which may restrict, counterbalance and after some time even subdue the existing societal forces. One might argue that the expectation that a social group should promote opposition to itself is an illusion. But if opponents are deprived of the space they need for growing, the political system will lose its learning capacity; its reactions to new challenges — take the ecological issues of the present as an example — will set in too slowly or be lacking altogether. Paralysis instead of evolution will be the result, a revolution may become the last way out of the crisis. We have to assess the means in political education which may help to improve the social learning capacity.

In the Federal Republic of Germany, educational variety is guaranteed by eleven ministries of education in eleven cultural territories. Although an advantage in the sense of the aims mentioned above, the problems implied with the system cannot be overlooked: the variety of schooling in the different *Länder* has disadvantages for the students whose families are obliged to move across the boundaries during their school life-time. Another issue connected with cultural federalism, but relevant for all countries with more or less centralized school systems, is that of party influence on the curriculum. (The issue is a general one but will be particularly felt in political education.) Is the introduction of a new curriculum through new official guidelines after taking over government for the next four or five years legitimate? On the other hand, how can educational change take place if not through decisions by political representatives? The job can no longer be left to educational administrators as was the case traditionally.

The political struggle between the parties, teacher organizations and parents' organizations about the comprehensive school and the guidelines in social studies, history and occasionally German led to educational decisions in Germany being brought within the purview of the law (*Verrechtlichung*): the Federal Supreme Court had to deal with the case. In 1975 the judges proclaimed that the parents were not entitled to decide upon the organizational structure of the school and the goals and contents of learning; the Parliaments were requested to take the fundamental decisions concerning the school system themselves and not to leave them to the administration. This way of proceeding is no doubt more democratic than the traditional custom of regulation by administrative orders, as long as the educational goals are clearly distinguishable from the political ones in the argument between the political parties.

The media for exerting political influence on education are official guidelines and curricula, textbooks, and the teachers themselves. Guidelines officially ordered exist in some states, in others not; their absence alone does not secure the liberality of the system. This can be judged only by using a precise analysis of the goals overt or implicit in the curriculum, the hidden ones naturally being more dangerous. That is why the demand of clearly defining one's goals is one of the most beneficial results of modern curriculum theory for political education.

Clearly political education requires safeguards against indoctrination, from whatever side it may come; the openness of the curriculum is among the vital demands. The teachers need freedom in their teaching, the students need freedom in their participation. The idea of making students reach attitudinal goals in equal step is absurd.

Some remarks on the concept of political education may be useful here. The terminological combination of education and politics at first glance opens up uneasy feelings for the English-speaking reader. The term appears to be close to 'propaganda' or 'political indoctrination'. The German equivalent 'politische Bildung' is less menacing, the background of 'Bildung', more than 'education' embracing all the traditions of classical learning and the fine arts. 'Politische Erziehung', as political education could possibly be translated, would not sound well in German ears either. 'Political literacy', a term some British prefer, is closer to 'Bildung', but refers only to an achieved goal, not the process of approaching it as 'Bildung' does. Apart from these difficulties the concept of 'political' ought to be a very broad one as relating to public affairs or society, a meaning that can be referred far back to classical Greece, political then meaning all affairs related to the community or city-state, the 'polis'.[18]

For the progress of democratic teaching, curriculum theory, as it became known world-wide in connection with the new social studies, was only partly helpful. Taken seriously, goals and objectives, contents and teaching aids up to the final evaluation, form a closed model of learning which may easily be abused. Political literacy, that is the ability of the citizen to judge political issues independently and to behave according to his interests and understanding, is a result of personal experience more than that of teaching contents, knowledge of and insight into the political process admittedly being among the conditions. But such learning processes require a certain independence, and their results cannot be evaluated in the same way as the attainment of a goal in maths or sports, mainly because the vital goals in political education are attitudinal. On the other hand, one of the rare results of political socialization research we may be sure of is the fact that an open school climate and the opportunity for the students to exert influence on classroom proceedings has a democratizing effect on the young people. Most societal groups trying to influence the curriculum are not aware of the fact 'that it is not who teaches or what is taught, as much as it is how the teaching is carried out, that makes an impact on student political orientations.'[19]

We have discovered a whole range of obstacles to a streamlined political education: the influence of different social groups and organizations; regional variations, either maintained through cultural federalism or, generally, through the different schools themselves; transparency of curriculum decisions and openness of the curriculum itself; finally the wide differences introduced by thousands of teachers teaching social studies or socializing politically by their modes of teaching and behaviour. If we add all the other socializing agents, like mass media, the family and the peer group, there is no doubt that intentional political education can have but a very relative impact.

CONCLUSION

The relations between society, politics and teaching and the function of the academic disciplines in the didactic process can be visualized in the figure.

Teaching is in the centre. Social reality — the constitution, existing laws, the economic system etc. included — influences political decisions both directly and as interpreted through the social sciences. In the political process, goals are determined. The content of teaching is found in a process of demands and offers between teaching and the academic disciplines. In the didactic process which is constituted by curriculum development and evaluation, goals and contents are related to one another, objectives are defined, media and teaching aids fixed. It is the exclusive feature of political education that the social sciences refer to it in a double manner: they filter social reality for the goal defining process and they constitute the learning objects.

THE DIDACTIC PROCESS

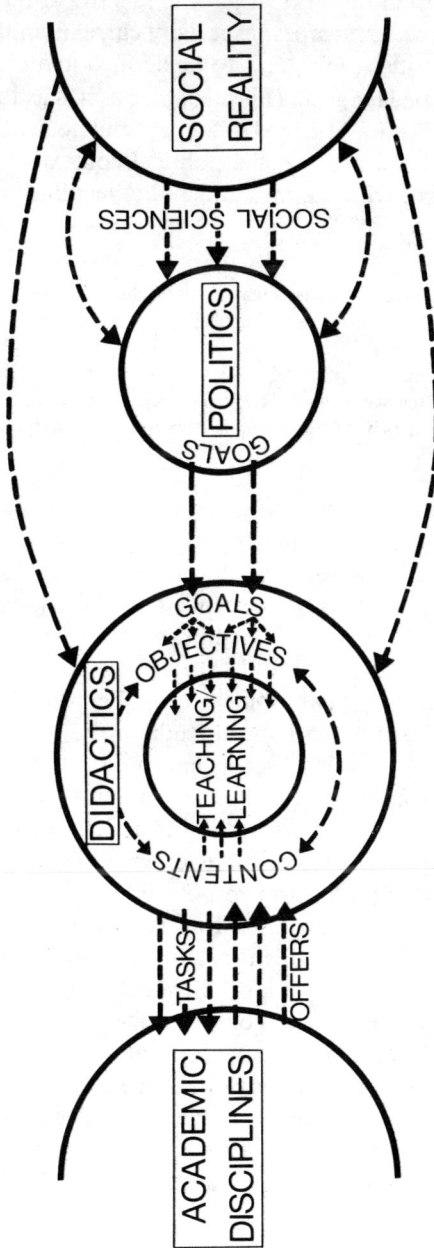

SOCIAL REALITY

SOCIAL SCIENCES

POLITICS

GOALS

GOALS

OBJECTIVES

DIDACTICS

TEACHING/
LEARNING

CONTENTS

TASKS

OFFERS

ACADEMIC
DISCIPLINES

Some additional remarks about the identification of goals seem appropriate here. Educators, especially curriculum developers, are inclined to consider their goals to be defined in a didactic process, that means by pedagogics. This idea, true as it is as far as objectives are concerned, is doubtful regarding general goals: these are determined socially and are set in a political context. Again we quote Felix von Cube, who claims, under the headline 'Goals are Personal Value-Decisions':

> Thus, science makes statements which can be checked about what there *is*, but it cannot make statements concerning what there *ought to be* . . . The postulate of educating young people to become a good Christian or a Socialist is neither true nor false. One can accept or refuse such goals, but one cannot prove them right or wrong. No science whatever can tell if Religion or Latin should be taught at school or not, if private ownership of the means of production should be permitted or not . . .[20]

As convincing as this reasoning may be, we would not like to follow von Cube with the idea that this is true for any educational aim. Lower down in the taxonomy, objectives will have to be fixed in the process of curriculum development, that is in relation to goals *and* possible contents, as is indicated in the diagram.

This model, which no doubt means a simplification of highly complex procedures, yet in some way applies to reality, makes clear that political learning and social studies are not determined in an arbitrary way. Education, according to Saul B. Robinson, has to convey qualifications enabling the learner to master future life situations.[21] This future-orientation is a claim more indispensable for political education than for any other subject, for those who are students today will take over responsibilities in political life up to about the year 2030! Education for the twenty-first century cannot be progressive enough, which means that future issues have to be taken up in order to create a problem consciousness: disarmament and the military-industrial complex, the vast field of economic growth/energy/ecology, equal opportunities for the third world countries are among the main global issues. Thus, a future-oriented political education has in a double sense to be global: it has to prepare for a global society as well as to reach every citizen in the world — which again is a political demand.

What conclusions are there to be drawn from these reflections? The first is very plain: political education, generally speaking, will not be more nor less democratic than the corresponding society. But on a second glance we will perceive the relatively strong impact of the school systems; that is why the comprehensive school in most countries is such a fiercely disputed issue. It is being disputed as a socializing agent, not as a place of learning. In all, pluralistic societies seem to be rather secure from indoctrination. The individual is exposed to such a number of various competing agents that there are chances of personal choice and change of attitudes and behaviour, and that means freedom. Early socialization, however, may prove more manifest.

'Totalitarian' societies are totalitarian only to a certain extent, even the computer-aided power of the modern state is not unlimited. The individual needs privacy, and people will strive for it somehow in whatever environment they may live — before and after '1984'. For this reason free societies are both more agreeable and more efficient.

Allow me to conclude with some very personal remarks. The author of this chapter was socialized in an unfree society for the first eleven years of his life: he grew up in a National-Socialist family, attended a school of the same kind, never entered a church, and became a member of the NS-youth organization at the age of ten as was usual then. In spite of this consistent political education he grew up to become a democrat, a process of change which must have happened to millions of Germans after 1945. Man is the being most capable of learning.

NOTES

1. L.F. Anderson, 'An Ecological Approach to the Study of the Context of Political Education', paper presented at a conference in Bloomington, Indiana (September 1975, Social Studies Development Center) and published in German as 'Politische Bildung im Regelkreis', in *Politische Bildung in den Vereinigten Staaten*, Bonn: Bundeszentrale für politische Bildung, Schriftenreihe v.115, 1977, p.157.

2. C. Foster (1978) in a book review, *International Journal of Political Education* 1 (2), p. 189.

3. M. Teschner, *Politik und Gesellschaft im Unterricht*, Frankfurt: Europäische Verlagsanstalt, 1968, p.8.

4. Inaugurative document, issued by the Ministry of the Interior, 1952.

5. T. Ellwein and R. Zoll, 'Politische Bildung und empirische Sozialforschung', *Materialien zur politischen Bildung* 1 (1), 1973, p.34.

6. D. Seitzer, *Miteinander — Füreinander*, Stuttgart: Klett Verlag, 12th ed., 1967. The theoretical foundations of the concept were laid by F. Oetinger alias T. Wilhelm in a book *Partnerschaft. Die Aufgabe der politischen Erziehung*, which was first published under a slightly different title in 1951. In teaching, its ideas were often simplified and distorted. For a sound judgement see H. Giesecke, *Didaktik der politischen Bildung*, München: Juventa, 1972, p.20 ff.

7. Giesecke, ibid., p.29.

8. For a history of political education in postwar West Germany see R. Schmiederer, *Zwischen Affirmation und Reformismus*, Frankfurt: Europäische Verlagsanstalt, 1972.

9. Konferenz der Kultusminister der Länder der Bundesrepublik Deutschland, Richtlinien für die Behandlung des Totalitarismus im Unterricht, 1962.

10. P. Berger, *The Sacred Canopy*, New York, 1967, p.22, quoted from J. Habermas, *Legitimationsprobleme im Spätkapitalismus*, Frankfurt: Suhrkamp, 1973, p. 162.

11. F.A. Adeyoyin, 'The Role of the School as a Politicizing Agent Through Citizenship Education', *International Journal of Political Education* 2 (2), 1979, p. 163.

12. Ibid., p. 162. For the situation in India see the recent essay by A.R. Kamat, 'Education, Politics and the Political Content of Education', *International Journal of Political Education* 2 (3), 1979, p. 273. We are very much in accordance with the general approach of this author.

13. Quoted from D. Hoffmann, *Politische Bildung 1890-1933*, Hannover: Schroedel Verlag, 1970, p. 65. This, like all the other quotations from German in this chapter, has been translated by the author.

14. 'Das Bildungssystem ist auch eine Institution zur Herrschaftserhaltung und Herrschaftsstabilisierung, es ist ein Herrschaftsinstrument der bestimmenden Kräfte in der Gesellschaft'. R. Schmiederer, *Zur Kritik der Politischen Bildung*, Frankfurt: Europäische Verlagsanstalt, 1971, p.9.

15. T. Geiger, Demokratie ohne Dogma (München, 1963), p. 310, quoted from Schmiederer, ibid., p.9.

16. Ibid., p. 10.

17. F. von Cube, 'Schule zwischen Gott und Marx. Konfessionelle Lernziele in einer pluralistischen Gesellschaft', *Aus Politik und Zeitgeschichte, Beilage zur Wochenzeitung Das Parlament*, B 25/1974.

18. From the perspective of the American curriculum theory, the terminological problem has been discussed by H. Mehlinger in *Politische Bildung in den Vereinigten Staaten. Verfahren der Curriculumentwicklung*, Bonn: Bundeszentrale für politische Bildung, Schriftenreihe v. 115, 1977, p. 19 ff.

19. L. Ehman, 'Die Funktion der Schule im politischen Sozialisationsprozess', *Politische Sozialisation in entwickelten Industriegesellschaften*, Bonn: Bundeszentrale für politische Bildung, Schriftenreihe v. 132, 1979, p. 260.

20. F. von Cube, 'Grundsätzliche Probleme des Curriculums: Zielsetzung und Zielerreichung', *Lernziele und Stoffauswahl im politischen Unterricht*, Bonn: Bundeszentrale für politische Bildung, Schriftenreihe v. 93, 1972, p.9.

21. S.B. Robinsohn, *Bildungsreform als Revision des Curriculum*, Neuwied: Luchterhand, 1972, p. 45.

5

The Politics of Political Competence Education

Robert Weissberg

It is probably fair to say that most scholars concerned with the political content of education accept the following general argument:

1. Schools — formally and informally — have an impact on shaping people's attitudes and behavior. This includes political orientations and skills.
2. In all societies, but especially in a democratic society, schools have a special obligation to train citizens in 'civic competence'.
3. The existing educational system, perhaps due to lack of proper technique or resources, has done a less than adequate job in the area of civic competence.
4. Therefore, a major goal of research is to formulate and help implement programs that will improve the quality of citizenship education.

This general argument is so deeply imbedded in people's thinking that the debate over civic competence tends to focus on the specific of what should be taught and with what techniques. Many important issues associated with using the educational system to promote greater civic competence are rarely — if ever — explicitly raised. They are 'givens' beyond the scope of research or discussion.

The basic contention of this paper is that the quest of greater civic competency through educational change raises several issues that deserve much greater scrutiny. Promoting civic virtue involves far more than formulating lists of desirable traits and suggesting programs to implement these traits. There are important questions regarding the purpose of what is to be taught, whether some type of instructions are possible, and whether increased promotion of some conceptions of civic competence is desirable. We shall not claim that heightened civic competence is not worth pursuing; obviously, nobody is opposed to the schools training 'good' citizens. Rather the purpose of this paper will be to explore certain important problems not adequately examined in most discussions of how the educational systems can or should promote good citizenship.

Our analysis will be divided into three sections. First, we shall consider the use of the term 'civic competence' (or 'good citizenship') as employed by several researchers. The key point in this section will be that definitions of 'political competence' are not politically neutral. To advance a conception of 'good political training' is also to advance a particular brand of politics. The ideological character of such conceptions has important implications for both the political system and for explanations of why such programs are resisted.

Second, we shall review some of the literature that deals with the school's amenability to being used as a vehicle for civic training reforms. Our contention will be that while the school may have an impact, it does not follow that the school's impact can be systematically controlled for any particular purpose. This will be demonstrated by examining political socialization studies dealing with attempts to implement political attitude and behavior change among students, and by making some observations regarding school politics.

Finally, we shall explore some of the possible unforseen consequences of instituting a massive effort to increase civic competence by using the school systems. Our analysis will focus on what might occur in the schools themselves and broader consequences for society as a whole. It is entirely possible, for example, that success in achieving higher levels of political participation may help further numerous social and economic inequalities, a situation probably not desired by those who advocate training citizens to be more politically active.

THE POLITICAL CONTENT OF
POLITICAL COMPETENCE

While it may be proper to speak of political competence or good citizenship as a universal goal, it should be apparent that the specific content of such competence must vary across political systems. To be sure, all standards of competence may require certain basic traits, e.g., reasoning ability, but the content must make allowances for the rules and expectations of a particular political setting. To claim otherwise would be to maintain, for example, that a competent US citizen could quickly adjust to political life in the Soviet Union. Political competence may be likened to athletic ability — though all sports require some coordination, a good baseball player is not necessarily a good hockey player.

Given the absence of a universal standard of political competence, the next question is: How does one derive a conception of 'good citizenship'? The answer is that one must begin with a political system whether existent or as a future goal, and then deduce attributes necessary for a citizen who could operate effectively in such a system. What is crucial to understand is that there is an unavoidable link between a particular conception of civic competence and the institutional rules, power distributions, and accepted methods of participation that define a political system. Thus, to the extent to which a conception of comptence is inconsistent (intentionally or unintentionally) with the existing political system, this conception is a call for political change. Put most bluntly, underlying every program of increasing civic competence there is a political ideology.

To show the political character of conceptions of civic competence, let us briefly review some notions that have been put forth by different researchers. We make no claim that these conceptions represent either the full range of proposals or that they reflect a general consensus on the subject. They do, however, seem to mirror widely held values in the field. Moreover, even if these conceptions are atypical, this does not invalidate our analysis. Recall that our purpose here is to show a connection between political values and conceptions of competence, not to catalog all conceptions of competence that could be found.

Perhaps the most comprehensive formulation of 'good citizenship' is the one offered by Fred M. Newmann (1975) in his book,

Education for Citizen Action. For Newmann political competence is the ability to exert influence in public affairs. Public affairs is broadly defined — it encompasses both national politics and closer to home institutions such as schools and social groups. To achieve this goal of training to exert influence, Newmann offers a 'model' which is comprised of three broad groups of skills. The components of this model of competency derive from the author's 'synthesis of literature in social science, education, and social activism and from my personal experience in curriculum development, teaching, and citizen action' (p. 76).

The first part of the model involves formulating policy goals. Such formulation requires 'principled moral deliberation and responsible social research.' In other words would-be activists should base their goal not on whims or irrational prejudice, but on some set of ethical principles that could be supported by empirical evidence (but, individuals who did select goals based on impulse or some non-moral criterion would not be excluded from political activity). One example of this goal formulation offered is someone who adopts the positions of 'we ought to legalize abortion' which is defended by evidence showing that unwanted children lead a life of suffering.

The second element of the model involves working to achieve these ethically and empirically based goals. Such action requires several specific skills. One must have a knowledge of the political-legal process and this includes both its formal aspects (e.g., how a bill becomes law) and informal mechanisms (e.g., how to build alliances). Next, one must effectively advocate one's cause. Such advocacy shows that 'proposed actions, policies, or candidates are consistent with principles of justice and human dignity and that they constitute the most reasonable choices among possible alternatives' (p. 88). Advocacy also calls for 'creating messages that specific audiences want to see and hear and building slogans, symbols, and images that elicit feelings of identification and enthusiasm, not simply cognitive assent' (p. 88). A third skill necessary to achieving one's goals is a knowledge of how groups operate: things like knowing how to listen, how to ask for help, and how to give criticism. Finally, a competent citizen must have what Newmann calls 'organization-administration-management skills'. These comprise things such as raising money, managing communications with the media, or organizing a demonstration.

Finally, Newmann posits that effectiveness requires a capacity to resolve several psycho-philosophic concerns that might prevent a competent individual from acting. The emphasis here is not so much training for activism, but removing barriers that may foster apathy among those with the proper training. Among other things, good citizens would be confident of their positions (but not be dogmatic), sensitive to the needs of others, know what goals are obtainable, and be able to use personal power.

A second attempt to define civic competence in a comprehensive and systematic manner can be found in the Civic Competence in a Free Society program developed by the Mershon Center. Like Newmann's approach, the approach of the Mershon project is rooted in the goal of political participation. As Remy and Turner in their report (1979) put it:

> We have defined citizenship competence as the quality of a person's participation individually or with others in processes related to group governance such as making decisions, protecting one's interest, or communicating effectively with group leaders.

Moreover, in a democratic society the actions of citizens do not violate human rights and are consistent with liberty and justice.

How is such competence to be achieved? Remy and Turner say that proper political training would entail education in seven major areas:

1. Acquiring and using information. This involves everything from how to gather diverse types of information (e.g., books, maps, government documents) to knowing how to evaluate and organize such information.
2. Assessing one's involvement in political situations and policies. A competent citizen would perceive the implications of a situation for themselves and others and identify their rights and obligations in the situation.
3. Making decisions. Alternative goals would be formulated and these goals are analyzed in terms of one's values.
4. Making judgments. A competent citizen must be able to develop and use standards based on conceptions of justice, ethics, morality, and practicality in judging institutions, policies, and decisions.
5. Communicating ideas. This requires both developing reasons for one's point of view and being able to advocate this view to diverse audiences — from friends to government officials.
6. Cooperating and working with others to achieve mutual goals. A competent citizen could take different group roles, tolerate ambiguity, manage group disagreement, interact democratically with others, and be able to work with people of diverse backgrounds.

7. Work effectively with bureaucracies. One's goals and interests must be recognized, a strategy of influence developed, support encouraged, and one must learn the appropriate grievance procedures for the organization.

The third, and final, conception of civic competence we shall examine is offered by Robert E. Cleary in his *Political Education in the American Democracy* (1971). The primary purpose of political education to Clearly 'is to contribute to the fullest possible development of the individual by giving him (or her) every opportunity to develop his (or her) ability to think logically and to analyze problem situations in a rational manner' (p. 111). Moreover, such individual level training is essential for the existence of democratic government since democracy depends on rational, thinking citizens who can analyze problems in terms of underlying values and specific goals.

The development of individual analytic ability depends on several factors. Exposure to controversy allows students to develop arguments and to make decisions. Moreover, students must acquire 'an intelligent understanding of the diverse values of their society . . .' (p. 115). Values — even democratic values — are not to be transmitted through rote learning and indoctrination since such methods are inconsistent with democracy and freedom. Indoctrination is not even justified for inculcating allegiance to the political system.

Though each of these conceptions of civic competence places varying emphases on different traits, all three share a certain perspective and set of assumptions about how the political system functions and what values have priority. For purposes of simplicity, we shall use the shorthand label 'rational-activist competency' to refer to these three conceptions. We should also add that several other conceptions of civic competence not described here likewise share similar perspectives and premises (in fact, this 'rational-activist' perspective appears to dominate the contemporary civic competence literature). The topic that we now turn to is what might be deemed the political ideology underlying these conceptions of civic competence.

Each of these conceptions claims to derive from a commitment to 'democracy'. And by 'democracy' the authors seem to mean a form of government characterized by widespread direct participation and informed debate. This is explicit in Newmann (competence is defined as the ability to exert influence in public affairs) and strongly implied in the other two conceptions (such skills as communicating ideas and analyzing problem situations are unnecessary unless citizens will use these skills in taking some form of action). Moreover, democracy seems to be not only the preferred way of running government, but democracy should also apply to institutions such as schools and social groups. In short, a good citizen is a democratically disposed citizen, and this means lots of involvement.

A second feature of these rational-activist conceptions is that they allow, even encourage, each individual acting independently to formulate his/her own political values and goals. Constraints are supplied by ethical or moral principles, reason, or logic, but they are self-imposed. Political rules and values are to be challenged, not accepted on the basis of some higher authority or mere custom. Group decisions, moreover, are based on a 'one person, one opinion' rule and majority rule rather than some form of authoritarian leadership.

Finally, and perhaps most importantly, all three conceptions downplay such traits as loyalty, patriotism, obedience to authority, and deference as components of good citizenship. As Cleary puts it:

> The writer explicitly rejects the argument that political education should aim at the indoctrination of desirable values in children, even a value as fundamental as the need for system support. Systemic needs should certainly be taken into account in any classroom discussion . . . but the teacher should not advocate system support as the goal of the discussion. (p. 116.)

To be sure, traits such as national loyalty are not rejected as harmful; rather they are secondary to more 'rational-activist' traits. If patriotism and the like are to develop, they should flow from conscious choices, not blind indoctrination.

It should be clear that the political process implied by these conceptions of 'good citizenship' is not consistent with existing US institutions and political values. Take, for example, the activist definition of democracy. The present US political system, while legally permitting extensive citizen involvement, is not designed to handle massive and continual political participation. In fact, the basic institutional structure, which remains intact, was originally intended to thwart large-scale citizen political involvement. Once we move beyond voting and campaign-related activity, there is little institutional capacity to deal with millions of sophisticated activists advancing their personal political values. Such institutional capacity is probably even less evident in private organizations such as corporations and social groups. Perhaps an institution like Congress could develop mechanisms for dealing with, say, a twentyfold increase in citizen involvement, but this would produce a different institution, not just the same Congress with more constituency pressure. Similar transformations would occur in almost all governmental and private structures.[1]

Permitting individuals to formulate their own political goals, constrained only by personal moral or ethical principles, is likewise an idea that runs contrary to existing practices. Only at the most abstract level does the existing system allow every conceivable idea to be debated in public. Censorship and pressure to conform abound in contemporary political and social life. Moreover, this type of individualism would most certainly lead to a challenge to the status quo by widening the scope of political conflict. Preferences that are currently 'out of bounds' or 'unthinkable' could be defended on the grounds that each individual, acting according to his/her own sense of ethics, justice, or whatever, can legitimately demand any conceivable policy. A public debate on crime, for example, might entail dozens of alternatives ranging from the decriminalization of all crime to multilating criminals as a means of reducing crime. Reaching a consensus under such conditions might be very difficult. In addition, the fact that goals are rooted in abstract principles may make conflict much more intense than if values were only casually held.

The emphasis on 'rational' understanding and justification in these conceptions of civic virtue would likewise challenge present-day politics. In particular, many well-established US institutions and customs are difficult to justify on rational or principled grounds. For example, the power of the courts to declare legislative or executive actions unconstitutional (judicial review), though a key element in existing politics, would probably be deemed a commonly abused and anti-majoritarian rule under close scrutiny. An even more devastating analysis can be made of such traditions as the US Senate, appointing US judges for life, a federal system of government and many other practices currently accepted with no debate. In other words, there is no reason to suppose that well developed analytical skills will be limited to specific policy choices within certain institutional constraints; eventually the basic rules and institutions themselves will likely be scrutinized and called into question.

Perhaps the sharpest disjuncture between the rational-activist conceptions of competence we examined and current practice occurs in the general area of national loyalty. Traditionally, allegiance to the US government has been one of the key purposes of citizenship education (and frequently the only goal of such education). The conceptions of competence we have described do not reject such loyalty; rather, it is not the primary goal and, if it is to be achieved, it is to be accomplished more through reason than indoctrination. The political consequences of this hit-or-miss approach to the inculcation of national loyalty would be considerable for the present system.

To appreciate the importance of instilling national loyalty as the primary political allegiance of citizens, one need only examine what happens when such political loyalty is not pervasive. In nations such as Northern Ireland, Lebanon, and India the co-existence of deep religious loyalty with political loyalty has frequently resulted in extensive violent conflict. Ethnic loyalties can also contribute to domestic violence as witnessed by civil conflict in Nigeria, Iraq, and many parts of southeast Asia. Even Canada has seen sharp conflict between English- and French-speaking citizens due to the absence of an extensive and deeply imbedded Canadian identity.

Of course we cannot assert that a failure to inculcate national loyalty will automatically generate more civil strife. However, given the ethnic, racial, religious, and regional diversity of the United States the absence of such an over-riding loyalty would make such conflict more likely. Without deeply-rooted nationalistic attachments we might see, for example, demands for black self-rule, greater political autonomy for Spanish-speaking communities, or even calls for the establishment of separate areas where religious bodies would be politically sovereign. Even if such demands were unsuccessful, their presence on the political agenda would constitute a major change in current politics.

The de-emphasis or complete neglect of traits like obedience to authority could also encourage far-reaching political changes. Instead of citizens routinely obeying laws, paying taxes and otherwise doing what they are told, the exercise of government authority itself will become part of the political debate. For example, citizens might refuse to pay portions of their taxes on the grounds that they do not approve of how some of the money is to be spent. The government would then have to convince these citizens — rationally or by physical force — of the merits of supporting policies they opposed. Here again, this constitutes a significant departure from present practices.

In describing some of the potential consequences of instituting a different notion of civic competence, we are not criticizing these rational-activist conceptions as undesirable or as inherently unworkable. It would be presumptuous for us to assert that it is wrong for, say, each citizen to decide on their own what values they will pursue or whether national loyalty should be unquestioningly accepted. Our basic argument is merely that imbedded in these notions of civic education are significant political changes. Advocates of these conceptions are thus, intentionally or unintentionally, calling for a different type of political system, not the same political system run better by virtue of greater citizen competency. One might desire the political changes implied by these conceptions of competence, but to advocate them on the ground of 'competence' is somewhat misleading.

CONSTRAINTS ON INCREASING
RATIONAL-ACTIVIST POLITICAL COMPETENCE

Any attempt to promote a new form of civic virtue must sooner or later confront the question of how this is to be accomplished. This involves far more than drawing up lists of desirable traits and projects designed to foster these traits. Even the best designed program will amount to little if people refuse to adopt it or it is implemented too late in the learning process. Especially where what is to be transmitted will generate widespread controversy, and almost anything new associated with 'political education' is controversial, the implementation process is crucial. The purpose of this section will be to consider some of the problems likely to be found in an attempt to increase the rational-activist type of political competence.

Perhaps the best place to begin in considering the re-education of a citizenry is the extent to which the political socialization process can be systematically controlled to bring about the desired changes. Societies differ substantially in this regard. In totalitarian systems such as the Soviet Union the central authority can control almost all the messages received by almost all young children. Political learning is conveyed in state-supported nurseries, in the classroom, through state-run social groups, in the state-controlled mass media, and even in sports activity. At the other extreme we can imagine a nomadic society in which political learning is the almost exclusive domain of autonomous family units well beyond the reach of a central authority.

The situation in the United States (and probably most Western European nations as well) is much closer to decentralized control than manipulation of the sort possible in an authoritarian regime. Certainly the family, perhaps the most important of all socializing agents, is beyond the reach of any interest trying to develop new skills and orientations among children. The mass media are likewise a poor channel of influence given both their commercial and fragmented character (imagine trying to influence the content of hundreds of TV programs, children's books, movies, and the like). Social organizations such as the Girl Scouts or the Little League are also not readily available as mechanisms of political education. Informally organized groups are even less useful for moulding citizens into 'good citizens'. To be sure, the mass media and social organizations may play a vital role in the political education of citizens, but their decentralized nature makes them poor resources for controlled, systematic change.

In terms of its potential as a conduit for political re-education, the school stands as the most amenable institution. Schools not only possess a long history of explicit political indoctrination, but exercising influence through the educational system appears far easier than programs directed at millions of separate families, social organizations, and friendship groups. It also seems likely that considerable sympathy exists among professional educators for the rational-activist concept of good citizenship. The question now becomes: Can the schools be used to implement the programs associated with this notion of civic comptency? To answer this question, let us briefly state some facts about the US educational system and previous attempts to use the educational process to bring about political change.

THE EDUCATIONAL SYSTEM AND
POLITICAL CHANGE

Any would-be reformer seeking to use the educational process to advance a goal should keep the following four points in mind. First, while it may be convenient to speak of 'the school' or 'the educational system', at least in the United States education is highly decentralized. In 1972, for example, there were some 17,238 public school districts (*U.S. Statistical Abstract,* 1978: 297). As our experiences with the implementation of school racial integration and the banning of classroom religious observances suggests, monitoring and enforcing rules across thousands of units can be a bureaucratic nightmare. The problem of access become even more troublesome if we orient our goals to the individual school or classroom. It is perhaps only in comparison with millions of families or idiosyncratic mass media consumption that the educational system appears to provide centralized access and control.

Second, curriculum content in US public schools can be, and frequently is, ensnarled in political conflict. In recent years, for example, civil rights organizations, feminist groups, patriotic groups, religious and morality-oriented groups, and others have at one time or another vigorously intervened in school politics on questions regarding classroom instruction. Such intervention has even been felt by textbook publishers. The significance of this fact, especially in view of the liberal or even radical character of rational-activist civic competence, is that attempts at implementing a new political curriculum will certainly be vigorously challenged. It is politically unrealistic to believe that a brand of political education that lacked a heavy dose of nationalistic indoctrination and respect for authority would not generate intense political opposition from groups like the American Legion or ad hoc conservative groups. Such opposition would have to be overcome, not explained away by characterizing it as 'unenlightened'.

Third, the survival of a particular educational program depends heavily on the satisfaction or at least acquiescence of the community. Regardless of how 'good' a program is for students, the political system, or even world peace, it will have a difficult future if it does not please parents and others who ultimately pay for schooling. Imagine a situation in which elementary and high school students began challenging the local political status quo (e.g., showed that illegal pressures had been put on school board members to retain an unscrupulous but victorious football coach). What if children began seriously questioning widespread traditional values? Perhaps such behavior can be educationally justified as 'healthy', but politically it is asking for trouble from challenged citizens and parents. Even the mere discussion of sensitive local political issues might threaten many people.[2]

Fourth, we must recognize that there is an almost inherent tension between a program calling on students to deal critically with their environment and the need to maintain order in a school. In fact, we may face a paradox here. If students come to school well-socialized into accepting the authority of teachers, then, with the maintenance of order resolved, training in rational-activist civic competence is possible. However, if such obedience has not been established, then the teacher is forced to emphasize discipline at the expense of such things as learning how to handle controversy, acquiring communication skills, and resolving various problems of group participation. To put this argument in its most extreme form: before students can be taught to be rational-activists, they first must be passive acceptors of unquestioned authority and values. Such acceptance is an inherent feature of schooling, regardless of what is taught.

THE USE OF THE EDUCATIONAL SYSTEM TO PROMOTE POLITICAL CHANGE

Thus far we have outlined some of the major obstacles faced by those who seek to implement political competence based on activism and analytical thinking. Assuming for the moment that access is permitted, what are the chances of success? Can pre-adults be transformed from poorly informed, largely apathetic citizens to activists who can correctly analyze and communicate complex political phenomena? While the answer to the question cannot be conclusively given until much additional research is conducted, a clue to a likely answer can be gained by examining the successes of previous attempts to change political behavior and orientations.

On the basis of several studies using different methods the prognosis for any significant changes towards greater activism and analytical ability seems pessimistic. Consider the following sampling of research findings on the impact of civics course content:

● Edgar Litt (1963) examined the impact of the high school civics in three socio-economically different towns in the Boston metropolitan area. In no community was this course associated with increased support for political participation. In the higher status community, where both community leaders and the textbook endorsed these themes, there was a modest increase in support for the ideas of politics as a process (as opposed to mechanistic institutions) and politics as group conflict. No such change occurred in the other two communities where these ideas received less community and textbook support. Litt concludes by suggesting that participatory behavior may be deeply rooted in non-school learning and the learning of attitudes about politics may depend on outside reenforcement.

● Langton and Jennings (1968) in 1965 examined the impact of the civics course in 97 schools selected in a national sample. Among the relevant (for our purposes) traits examined were political knowledge and sophistication, political interest, following politics in the mass media, discussing politics, sense of political efficacy, and defining good citizenship in terms of participation. To assess the net contribution of the civic courses, seven variables were held constant in the analysis (e.g., sex, quality of the school, parental education, and so on). Jennings and Langton find: 1. there is little difference in impact between traditional American government courses and more topical 'problem' courses; 2. the impact of the civics courses was positive but differences were slight, almost trivial; 3. the very small impact of the exposure declined with time; and 4. the orientations, goals, and student evaluation of teachers made little difference. However, among blacks the civics course does have a greater impact (though not always positive) perhaps due to the lack of redundancy.

● Albert Somit and others in the mid 1950s explored the impact of the introductory college course on student orientations towards the political process and individual political participation. Over a three-year period students were assigned either to the traditional course, which emphasized factual learning, or a more participation directed course that involved exposure to real life politics and political personalities. With one small exception, there were no differences in outcomes between the two types of introductory courses.

These three studies focused on the content of the educational process. A different dimension relevant for civic education might be described as the structure of the learning environment. By structure we mean such factors as the exercise of classroom authority, openness of classroom debate, level of controversy accepted, and degree of student participation. To what extent can the manipulation of these factors encourage the traits associated with the rational-activist conception of civic competence?

● Almond and Verba (1963: 352-60) in their five-nation study of adults done in 1959 found that those recalling having taken part in classroom discussions or complained about unfair treatment from teachers were somewhat more likely to believe that they could influence government. However, this relationship seemed to hold largely among the less well-educated. For those from better educated families, the existence of non-authoritarian school environments had no marginal impact.

● Ehman (1969) in his study conducted in Detroit focused on the willingness of teachers to discuss controversial issues and the openness of classroom discussions as intervening factors in political learning. The study finds that these structural factors have an impact on outcomes of civics courses, but this is a complex relationship. Overall, no clear and strong relationships hold between classroom structure and the presence of controversy and increases in support for political participation, a heightened sense of political efficacy, and reduced cynicism about politics.

These studies constitute only a sampling of studies on the impact of schooling on political attitudes. Moreover, much more research needs to be done, especially research on the results of political education at the grade school level. Nevertheless, this brief review does suggest a note of caution for those who hope to re-educate citizens politically by changing course content or classroom structure. Changes have sometimes occurred, but even then, their magnitude is frequently modest and not always in the predicted direction. Major, controllable changes might be possible, but they require techniques and understandings not yet developed.

SOME POSSIBLE UNFORESEEN CONSEQUENCES OF INCREASED COMPETENCE

Our analysis suggests that a major effort to train citizens to a rational-activist competency will generate both political resistance and problems of implementation. Nevertheless, it would be presumptuous to claim that success is impossible. In this section we shall consider some of the possible unforeseen consequences of such success. Obviously, our analysis is highly tentative, yet a reasonable argument can be made that such speculation is necessary as part of an informed debate on the subject. At a minimum, we hope to broaden analysis beyond issues of program content and implementation strategies.

Perhaps the most basic and difficult issue to resolve associated with an attempt to increase citizen participation and analytical ability concerns the relationship between the political character of a people and the character of a political system. Essentially, advocates of rational-activist competency have assumed a very simple, additive relationship between individual-level traits (e.g., respect for the opinion of others) and the operation of the political system (e.g., freedom for citizens holding unpopular opinions). The assumption is one of simple aggregation: two hundred million politically active, democratically-oriented citizens result in an activist democracy. This assumption is not only questionable, but it also ignores the complex relationship between political and non-political factors.

Several writers (Lipset, 1960, ch. 2; Moore, 1966, ch. 7) have suggested that the existence of a democratic political system (defined in terms of competition for power and the existence of certain rights) depends on certain economic and social prerequisites. Among such possible factors are a reasonably high level of economic development, widespread literacy, the absence of strong overlapping economic and ethnic cleavages, and norms limiting violent conflict. These factors might be viewed as the foundations of a democratic political order. It is crucial to realize, however, that such conditions may depend on non-democratic or even authoritarian practices. For example, large-scale industrial enterprises typically require hundreds of citizens who unquestioningly accept the power of others over their lives. Similarly, compulsory education typically requires millions of students to remain in school contrary to the desires of many teachers, parents, and the students themselves.

The point we are suggesting here is that we cannot consider possible changes in political learning apart from other elements. It is at least conceivable that the successful implementation of higher levels of activism, greater awareness of one's own self-interest, and so on will adversely affect economic performance which ultimately might reduce politics to civil strife, not some form of participation-oriented democracy. Keep in mind that the ancient Athenean model of direct citizen participation ultimately rested in a system of slavery, political exclusion, and military power. Bringing everyone into public debate would not have made Athenean democracy 'better' or more participatory; it probably would have meant the end of Athens.

A second issue worthy of greater attention concerns the substantive policy results of greater rational-activist competence. Examination of the illustrations used by authors of what more competent citizens are likely to do suggests that competence is believed to be associated with liberal or 'enlightened' policies (e.g., help solve an environmental pollution problem). Advocates of such competence appear to feel that, along with competency training, young adults will also acquire a respect for the rights of others, human dignity, community service and other 'virtuous' traits (there is some uncertainty, however, on whether such values should be explicitly inculcated or whether they will emerge more or less without coercion).

There is, however, no logical relationship between being a rational-activist citizen and endorsing what most professional educators would deem 'enlightened preferences'. It is entirely possible that a fully competent citizen might work for the suppression of unpopular ideas, racial segregation, and overseas military aggression. In fact, given the anti-democratic, repressive attitudes among many pre-adults (especially those from working class backgrounds) increased participation might result in a more authoritarian politics (see, for example, data in Zellman and Sears, 1971). Moreover, it is possible that greater political activity and awareness could lead to greater frustration which in turn might result in greater alienation and violence (remember, the larger the number of participants, the larger the number of losers). We are *not* claiming that authoritarian politics or violence will result from increased rational-activist political competence; rather, there is some evidence to suggest that greater political involvement need not result in the 'enlightened' policies that advocates of greater competence assume and probably desire.

Finally, and somewhat paradoxically, increased rational-activist competence if widely implemented might exacerbate social and economic inequality. Observers of current politics (for example, Dahl, 1961, ch. 24) note that groups lacking in power and resources can frequently win over well-established interests (e.g., the Southern blacks' quest for racial equality). The principal reason is differences in effectiveness of resource mobilization and skills: a few resources well managed can sometimes defeat a clumsy, inept giant. Such occasional victories prevent the complete domination of society by the powerful. What if, however, resources were effectively employed by all interests? The possible edge gained by the effective use of limited resources against the powerful would be diminished. Political outcomes would simply reflect political power and, as a result, the weak would lose consistently instead of just much of the time.[3]

CONCLUSION

The arguments made in this essay are not based on any new research or complex twists of logic. If anything, they derive from a few simple observations, some straightforward textual analyses and a few fairly well-known research findings. The conclusion from all of this seems obvious; attempts to produce what we have called the rational-activist conception of political competence are likely to encounter political resistance and severe problems of implementation. And keep in mind that we have completely avoided the important question of whether this set of behavior and orientations can be learned by most citizens. We are not asserting that it is doomed forever. Our claim is that success is unlikely.

The fact that this conception of citizen competence is so vigorously advanced in the face of so many clear obstacles raises some interesting questions. At the risk of sounding as if I were questioning the motives of its advocates (I am not), let me briefly discuss what might be two reasons for this advancement. The first reason concerns the conception of 'competence' and view of the US political systems held by some advocates; the second explanation focuses on the political ideology of certain advocates.

Regarding the first possible explanation, it is fair to say that advocates of rational-activist comptency begin by viewing civic competency as a skill on which people can be arrayed on a continuum. That is, in the sense that we can talk about competent and incompetent drivers, swimmers, or mechanics, so we can talk about competent and incompetent citizens. This approach is perfectly valid so long as we are talking about the execution of certain tasks (e.g., the difference between a well-written and an incoherent letter to a public official). Competency training would thus take the political values or goals of an individual as a given and teach people the best means of achieving this goal. This would even apply to goals deemed objectionable to most people (e.g., the best way of ridding a neighborhood of blacks). Political education is thus fundamentally no different from, say, teaching children how to cross the street without getting hit by a car.

The problem occurs when competency is subtly transformed from a task specific attribute to a more general orientation to politics. In particular, a competent citizen becomes an active, questioning citizen who supports a political system characterized by freedom, equality, justice, and other 'enlightened' traits. To be passive, inarticulate, unable to work with others in groups, willing to accept strong leadership, in favor of repression policies, and willing to use violence makes one an 'incompetent' citizen. This transformation falsely equates the development of a skill level with a particular definition of good citizenship or civic virtue.

The equating of a good, competent citizen with a rational-activist citizen only makes sense if the existing politics *depends* on such virtues. If this were the case, we could claim that such rational-activist training was as appropriate as, say, training auto mechanics in how to use automobile tools. The fact of the matter is that the existing system hardly depends on, or even requires, such competence. US politics would not necessarily be run 'better' if more citizens were rational-activist type competent citizens. It is not even clear that the political system would be any more democratic or characterized by less group hostility, repression, or inequality. To exaggerate only a little, it appears that advocates of rational-activist competence mistakenly sees the US political system as a large-scale direct democracy where citizens are responsible for making a wide range of policy decisions. Therefore, it then follows that citizens must be 'good' at such involvement.

A second possible reason for the vigorous advancement of a rational-activist conception of good citizenship in the face of severe obstacles is rooted in the political values of the researcher. Specifically, it appears that such advocacy is but another way of advancing what are generally deemed liberal political values. Perhaps it is hoped that competent citizens will 'naturally' favor environmental protection laws, more freedom of speech, limits on the use of military force, racial equality and greater concern for less well-off citizens by virtue of their reliance on reasoning and abstract principles of justice and democracy. At a minimum, it is probably hoped that millions of rational-activist citizens will at least 'shake-up' the social and economic status quo.

Of course, there is nothing inherently improper about saying 'I personally desire more liberal policies and thus also favor educating children in ways that will increase the likelihood of such policies.' Instead, however, researchers usually imply that the educational changes they advocate are politically neutral. While such a statement may be perfectly sincere, it is difficult to envision a continuation of numerous existing policies if such advocates were successful. Only in the very limited sense of not being perfectly predictable in its consequences can the rational-activist notion of good citizenship be deemed politically neutral.

In sum, the basic argument of this paper can be stated as (1) conception of rational-activist 'good citizenship' as appropriate citizenship training is, in effect, a call for a different type of politics, not present-day politics done 'better'; (2) implementing such a conception of civic virtue will face considerable resistance and, based on past research findings, such efforts will not yield immediate, striking results; and (3) even if successful, the creation of an active, rational citizenry need not result in a democratic political system characterized by enlightened policies. Again, let us emphasize that our purpose is not to discredit efforts at making children into good citizens; rather, we have sought to explore several issues that are rarely explicitly considered in discussions of achieving political competence.

NOTES

1. A good illustration of the institutional problems caused by increased citizen participation can be seen in the federal court system. Thanks in part to a greater citizen awarness of their legal rights, more citizens are taking the grievances to court. Between 1970 and 1976, for example, civil suits in US district courts increased from 59,284 to 130,597. This litigation explosion has frequently caused considerable delay in dispensing justice. To increase sharply the number of courts, however, might not so much result in speeding justice, but even a greater amount of litigation which would bring large-scale judicial intervention in areas previously beyond litigation. In fact, this has begun to happen in the area of university personnel policies — suits have been commonplace and university actions have changed accordingly.

2. In the early 1970s Cornell University instituted a program of 'community involvement' for some of its students. Such involvement frequently meant that students mobilized tenants to fight their landlords in court. Needless to say, landlords were not enthusiastic about the university's promotion of such involvement, and pressure was successfully exerted to end the program.

3. It is also possible that if higher status children are better able to group all the complexities of rational-activist citizenship, class differences in politics will be further exacerbated. To insure greater political equality in political conflict, higher status children, with their home and environment derived advantages, may have to be given less exposure to competency instruction.

REFERENCES

Almond, G. and Sidney Verba, *The Civic Culture*, Princeton: Princeton University Press, 1963.

Bureau of the Census, US Department of Commerce, *U.S. Statistical Abstract 1978* Washington, DC: US Government Printing Office.

Cleary, R.E., *Political Education in the American Democracy*, Scranton, Pa.: Intext Educational Publishers, 1971.

Dahl, R.A., *Who Governs?* New Haven, Conn.: Yale University Press, 1961.

Ehman, L.E., 'An Analysis of the Relationship of Selected Educational Variables with the Political Socialization of High School Students', *American Educational Research Journal* 6, 1969, pp. 559-80.

Jennings, M.K. and K.P. Langton, 'Effects of the High School Civics Curriculum' in M.K. Jennings and R.G. Miemi, *The Political Character of Adolescence*, Princeton: Princeton University Press, 1974.

Langton, K.P. and M.K. Jennings, 'Political Socialization and the High School Civics Curriculum in the United States', *American Political Science Review* 62, 1968, pp. 852-67.

Lipset, S.M., *Political Man*, Garden City, NJ: Doubleday and Co., 1960.

Litt, E., 'Civic Education, Community Norms, and Political Indoctrination', *American Sociological Review* 28, 1963, pp. 69-75.

Moore, B., *Social Origins of Dictatorship and Democracy*, Boston: Beacon Press, 1966.

Newmann, F.M., *Education for Citizen Action*, Berkeley: McCutchan Publishing Corporation, 1975.

Remy, R.C. with M.J. Turner, 'Basic Citizenship Competencies', *Mershon Center Quarterly Report* 5, Autumn 1979, pp. 2-8.

Somit, A., Joseph Tannenhaus, Walter H. Wilke, and Rita W. Cooley, 'The Effects of the Introductory Political Science Course on Student Attitudes Towards Personal Political Participation', *American Political Science Review* 52, 1958, pp. 1129-32.

Zellman, G.L. and D.O. Sears, 'Childhood Origins of Tolerance for Dissent', *Journal of Social Issues* 27, 1971, pp. 109-35.

6

Political Participation:
An Analytic Review and Proposal

Fred M. Newmann

INTRODUCTION

What should schools teach about political participation in a modern democracy? Contemporary curriculum proposals reflect three general positions, not mutually exclusive, representing different conceptions of the way an 'ideal' citizen should participate.

The prevailing model seems to be a *rational decision-maker*. The student should learn how to carry on rational debate on ethical, definitional and empirical questions related to public policy so that when choices present themselves, as at election time or when asked to contribute to a social cause, the student can make rational defensible decisions (e.g., Hunt and Metcalf, 1968; Oliver and Shaver, 1966). This approach stresses the development of cognitive abilities to process information about politics, law and social life. Students' inquiry into social issues might involve them actively in debates with peers and adults in or out of schools, but the promotion of specific action other than study and reflection is not considered a central task of education.

In contrast, the ideal of *community participant* is evident in a variety of proposals which stress the application of study and reflection in such activities as volunteer service, political advocacy and democratic self-governance in schools (e.g., National Commission on Resources for Youth, 1974; Conrad and Hedin, 1977; Newmann et al., 1977). This approach emphasizes students taking responsibility for action that affects the lives of others — to bring educational benefits to students (e.g., in cognitive or ego development), but also to make contributions to society. While programs vary in the extent to which they encourage service, advocacy and research in the community, they share a common commitment to the cultivation of participation skills that take students beyond the classroom to interact with the non-school world.

The rational decision-maker and community participant models can be applied to a variety of social issues, but attention to no issue in particular is implied. Many proposals for curriculum, however, do single out particular topics, suggesting that students' political participation concentrate on certain issues. Such programs convey an image of citizen as *critical topic specialist* on such matters as global interdependence, environmental protection, elimination of discrimination, or equitable distribution of wealth. The call for attention to such issues indicates a desire to raise the consciousness of people on problems that receive insufficient or inaccurate treatment in the traditional curriculum. Programs vary in the extent to which they promote general cognitive awareness on the topic, specific policy solutions, or direct participation by students. They convey a notion of political education based on awareness of particular topics, rather than a generalized set of cognitive or participatory skills.

A school program may reflect aspects of each approach; for example, a high school course in political science might involve students in studying the positions of local candidates and choosing who to support (rational decision-making), working on the campaign (community participant), and helping to gather information for a candidate's speech on energy conservation (critical topic specialist). At first glance each approach seems reasonable, but none has been justified by an explicit philosophy of education that adequately applies democratic theory to realities of life in today's complex culture. The rational decision-maker ideal, for example, fails to respond to citizen alienation due to apparent lack of opportunities for meaningful citizen participation in government. The community participant model supports local participatory opportunities for youth, but neglects the issue of how students can take part in the resolution of larger societal problems. The critical topic specialist approach assists in developing awareness, but offers no consistent position on the nature of democratic participation at either the local or global level.

The purpose of this paper is to organize analytic knowledge about democratic political participation in a way that helps to integrate intellectual contributions from diverse sources. This will be done through a review of conceptions of participation and of justifications offered either to promote or discourage certain forms. The review will serve as background for a proposal to conceive of participation as a balance between two levels: communal and societal. The intent is to assist educators and others in building a conception of participation that applies democratic ideals to realities of modern culture.

CONCEPTIONS OF POLITICAL PARTICIPATION

Political participation involves behavior related to affairs of 'government', but how narrowly or broadly should this be construed? One might restrict the concept to direct, intentional activities to influence the actions of formal governmental bodies; for example, political campaigning, lobbying of public officials, public demonstrations, subversion or revolution. Or one might expand the notion to include any behavior, intentional or unintentional, that affects (or attempts to affect) the allocation of values in society. Political participation under this definition could include classroom discussion of public issues, decision-making on a bowling team, a slowdown by workers, or an individual's purchase of a TV set. The narrow definition above might be rejected, because it excludes much behavior that can reasonably be considered political, for example, taking part in the governance of a church or a labor union. The broad conception might also be rejected, because it seems to embrace almost all behavior, making it impossible to distinguish political participation from other behavior. The most useful definition probably falls somewhere between these two extremes, but offering a middle range, 'compromise' definition may not be helpful. Disagreement over how broadly or narrowly to construe political activity can be grounded in ideological differences that definitions do not resolve. Instead let us simply recognize a wide range of uses, but continuously inquire as to whether any particular use serves to reinforce a given ideology or set of values.

Since the 1960s 'citizen participation' has often been used synonomously with political participation (Langton, 1978), although the former has frequently implied citizen involvement in the design and operation of public programs, while the latter has been most commonly associated with activities in electoral politics. Our analysis will suggest no distinction between 'political' and 'citizen' participation but will draw attention to other distinctions. Since each of the conceptions of participation mentioned below raises issues in the exercise of influence and the allocation of values, each relates to the 'political' realm. Since each suggests how individuals can and should relate to the governance of groups to which they belong, each conception also deals with issues of 'citizenship'. Thus, political and citizenship participation will be used synonomously, but we shall explain how different conceptions of participation suggest different implications for education.

Social scientists have identified a number of distinct forms of participation, based on both empirical and analytic research, and these can be summarized in the following categories:[1]

1. Obligatory activity — discharge of mandatory citizenship responsibilities such as paying taxes, jury duty, obeying laws.
2. Spectator activity — showing interest in public affairs by reading, contact with other media, and discussion of issues.
3. Voting — casting votes in local, state, national elections.
4. Campaigning — working for the election of candidates to office by donating money and effort (other than voting).
5. Government involvement — serving as a public official, a member of an advisory committee, or a consultant to a public program or agency.
6. Advocacy — activities initiated by citizens to affect public policy through lobbying, public advocacy, legal challenge, demonstrations, boycotts, etc.

These categories represent diverse forms of participation, but they seem to focus attention almost exclusively on interaction with formal agencies of government, reflecting the narrow end of the definitional spectrum suggested above. We should not overlook the vast amount of political activity in contexts such as the workplace, school, church, or voluntary association where people strive to protect their rights and to secure some measure of self-governance, without significant interaction with the formal governmental structure. We can, therefore, add another category of participation,

7. Participation in community organizations — working in voluntary groups that offer services to members or to others (e.g., a garden club, fraternal organization, church group, parent teachers organization, charitable organization), but which generally do not engage in public advocacy.

Since the 1960s there have been many attempts to expand citizen contact with policy-makers in both public and private institutions (Langton, 1978). Arnstein (1969) suggested that any device advertised as promoting citizen participation be scrutinized to determine whether it actually helps to shift power from traditional elites to the 'have nots'. By holding meetings with citizen groups, for example, government officials can sometimes convince citizens that their participation is not needed. Such meetings can be vehicles for therapy or manipulation of citizens, not genuine enhancement of their influence. Other participatory mechanisms such as delegating legal veto power to a citizen organization could represent a more authentic sharing of influence with common citizens. Arnstein's 'ladder of participation', progresses from 'nonparticipation' techniques of therapy and manipulation, to the 'tokenism' of informing, consultation and placation — where citizens present their views with no guarantee that they affect decisions, to 'citizen power' through partnership, delegated power and citizen control — mechanisms that assure citizen concerns having an impact on policy. The concepts in the ladder can be used to question the potency of participation in any organization, from a bowling league to a church or federal agency, in which leaders of a group are entrusted to represent the public interest of a constituency.

We can also classify political participation through function and/or motivational analysis that tries to assess the social significance of different participatory forms. Analyses of theories of participation by authors such as Pranger (1968), Scaff (1975), and Salisbury (1978) suggest three broad categories for distinguishing among participatory experiences.

Supportive forms of participation are activities required of or strongly suggested to most citizens, and seen as necessary for healthy functioning democratic procedures. These include voting, jury duty, paying taxes, obeying laws, acquiring basic knowledge about the political system, contributing to community life through voluntary service (e.g., serving on a parent-teachers' organization, participating in a clean-up of parks). Supportive forms are often construed as doing one's 'duty' in the community.

Instrumental forms of participation emphasize power in politics, the importance of citizens aggressively pursuing particular interests so as to achieve self-determination. The implied goal is not necessarily to support the system, but to use it to gain power or to influence those in power for the purpose of achieving the citizens' goals. This is done through special interest advocacy groups, political parties, or individuals bargaining and negotiating with those in power.

Participation can also be valued primarily as a vehicle for human *interaction*, offering opportunities for individuals to share experiences, to confront differing viewpoints, to develop interpersonal and collective bonds. The essential value in this perspective is the promotion of social intercourse and the individual growth likely to accrue therefrom, rather than the generation of general support for a political system or the achievement of particular policy objectives. This attitude toward the value of participation is particularly evident in proposals for intentional communities, alternative schools, and also in expressive and fellowship activities (picnics, workshops, parties) of local political parties and advocacy groups.

These categories are not mutually exclusive, and there may be difficulties in classifying any given activity (or individual experience) as only one or the other. This is due in part to the problem of accurately identifying personal intentions (For what purpose does an individual engage in an activity?) and also to the problem of accurately identifying the social function of any given activity (Does this event tend to lend support to the system, advance particular interests, or constitute open sharing among citizens?). While such distinctions may not lend themselves to facile empirical confirmation, they illustrate vastly different social meanings that may be associated with participation in its different forms.

As we encounter familiar, but all too vague claims that there is too little or too much citizen participation, these distinctions may help to identify more precise implications. Some persons may vote to show support for the system, even though they believe it will not help to attain their own policy goals. Some may advocate programs to increase voting, but oppose measures to increase participation in advocacy groups or workplace democracy. Persons committed to interactive styles may devote great energies to neighborhood work and small voluntary associations, but refuse to engage in 'power politics' with the larger system. Conversely, those urging more citizen advocacy might oppose emphasis on interactive communal organizations, fearing this might divert attention from broader national problems. Persons concerned with the apparently declining role of political parties may wish to increase involvement in the partisan political process and to decrease emphasis upon issue-oriented forms of participation. Those responsible for programs in public agencies may genuinely desire forms of citizen participation that elicit support for the agency's work, but oppose forms that diminish the autonomy of agency personnel.

If educators are to make a reasoned choice as to which form(s) of participation should be studied and/or practised in schools, they should heed Salisbury's (1975) analysis of differential costs and benefits attendant to various forms of participation, and his admonition (1978) that preference for or competence in some forms does not necessarily transfer to others. In short, we must try to recognize similarities and potential contradictions among various forms and attempt to assess how students of different backgrounds and learning styles may react differently to alternative forms. To build such analysis, we must examine the ways in which conceptions of participation have been justified.

JUSTIFICATIONS FOR PARTICIPATION

In selecting conceptions of participation to teach, we face questions of value and social philosophy: participation for what ends? Different responses to this reflect different assumptions about the nature of social justice, revealed most commonly in three dominant schools of political thought: participatory idealists, pluralist elitists, and Marxists.[2] While numerous complexities *within* these schools exist, they can be considered distinct traditions that have guided debate for decades.

156   *Political Education in Flux*

A. Three Political Traditions

Participatory idealists

The participatory idealist position assumes a reasonably small community (as large as a Greek polis or as small as an eighteenth century New England town). It assumes that all people who have citizen status participate directly in governing the community. People take the time to participate. The issues they deal with are comprehensible to virtually everyone, i.e., intelligent decisions can be made without special technical knowledge, and ´the consequences of decisions on various aspects of the community are reasonably predictable to all. In this context, the major governance problem is, 'How should we govern ourselves to resolve disputes between private interests and between private interests and the public good?' Only rarely does the community have to face the problem, 'How do we prevent outside forces from gaining control of our affairs?' Finally, deliberations in the community are guided by some reasonably clear consensual values that define the good life, the 'beloved community', and the nature of justice. Often the values derive from a shared system of religious meaning.

Writers as diverse as Mill (1958), Aristotle (1962), Rousseau (1968), Pateman (1970), Hegel and Arendt (see Stillman, 1977) have argued that participation in such a context is a critical requirement for achieving social justice and meeting human needs. To deliberate and act upon questions of the public good is a defining characteristic of the human species itself. If robbed of this opportunity, humans are denied fundamental integrity, for a critical aspect of their nature is suppressed. Because the participatory ideal concentrates upon direct citizen involvement in collective self-governance, it seems most applicable to pre-industrial societies composed of reasonably small, decentralized communities. Several theorists argue, however, that it is applicable in some form even in modern technological cultures (e.g., Walker, 1966; Bachrach, 1967; Thompson, 1970; Pateman, 1970; Benello and Roussopoulos, 1971).

Pluralist elitists

The pluralist elitist position evolved in response to modernization. As industrialization brought higher concentrations of people in small areas, specialization of labor, bureaucracy, centralization of social control in centers beyond local communities, geographic mobility, and interaction among cultural groups with different value systems, the community roots of the participatory ideal virtually disappeared. New institutions and styles of life in a modern city within a national society challenged the participatory ideal to accept a more restricted version of citizen participation, i.e., a representative system in which citizens choose their leaders periodically. In this conception communities are governed by elected elites and their appointees. Common citizens are largely excluded from direct participation in governance, because of the inefficiency that large numbers would entail, the incompetence of lay persons to comprehend modern issues and the way that modern institutions of work and leisure consume time that formerly could be devoted to participation in public affairs.

Along with this new concept of participation, elitist pluralism brought a different conception of social justice. Modernization in general and capitalism in particular held out a view of the good life that emphasized primarily two values: individual freedom to pursue the satisfaction of private wants (whether material, cultural, or psychological) and a procedure of 'fair-fighting' for resolving disputes among conflicting private wants. The presence of different racial, ethnic, and religious traditions in the US made consensus on more specific values impossible. Instead of anchoring society in a shared commitment to one god and a code of life deriving from one tradition, the social fabric would be held together by the threads of 'toleration', and procedural values which presumably would help to make combat among competing private interests fair. In this view, the citizen could participate freely whenever appropriate in pressing elites to meet private wants, but would not participate in a continual quest to achieve the public good.

The pluralist elitist conception has been defended by modern writers as diverse as Schumpeter (1956), Dahl (1956), Almond and Verba (1963), and Milbrath (1965). It is the dominant conception of participation taught in political science, civics courses, and held in the minds of most citizens. Intelligent critics demonstrate, of course, that the model's implied free market of fair competition among private interests does not actually exist; it has been destroyed by unforeseen accumulations of centralized private and public power (Dahl and Lindblom, 1976; Lowi, 1979). Nevertheless, the ideal lives on as a perceived standard for social justice;

for many continue to assume that if people have a chance to choose their leaders periodically and to press their private interests upon elites, and if elites are regulated to bargain fairly and openly among competing interests, justice will be done.

Marxists

Marx's analysis of the economic determinants of social relations presents a critical challenge to democratic theory, whether of the participatory or pluralist-elitist variety. From this perspective, one examines how a society's methods for meeting material necessities tend to affect the ways citizens treat one another and their own sense of worth. Marx explains how the structure of capitalism necessitates the alienation of people — one from another and from the fruits of one's own labor. The key to social justice and the achievement of human dignity is, therefore, an economic system based not on the exploitation of some people for the benefit of others, but upon a mutual sharing of work and material benefits. The ultimate vision of a communist society is consistent with democratic ideals of equality and self-determination, but Marxist theory emphasizes broad-scope economic restructuring as a prerequisite for political democracy; procedures such as elections or public hearings give only an illusion of participation in self-governance if they are embedded within a capitalist economy.

Since Marx did not address specific forms of participation available in twentieth-century political democracies one can only make inferences about the application of Marxist principles to modern movements. According to Evans (1972) meaningful participation in pre-communist social orders must be aimed at raising the consciousness of exploited classes, that is, developing an awareness of their own exploitation, its systemic sources, and collective commitment to massive class action. Second, participation must be oriented toward programs that demonstrate the contradictions of capitalism so as to undermine its functioning.

In a communist society, after class struggle has subsided, Marx would endorse active participation of all citizens in public affairs, although the specific nature of this is unclear. In spite of a lack of clarity on specific forms of participation, and confusion on the relationship between revolutionary elites and the common folk, Marxist writers (Miliband, 1969) provide a powerful critique by demonstrating a) the inability of certain classes to participate meaningfully in the governance of a capitalist society, b) the ways in which economic relations affect an individual's total con- sciousness and social thought, and c) the importance of individual citizens connecting their 'private' concerns to frequently obscured larger collective interests. Modern Marxist writers (Edwards, 1979) have emphasized building collective direct democracy in local set- tings, especially at the workplace, as a critical initial step in developing wider consciousness of structural issues.

B. Persistent Issues

The three dominant political traditions represent different visions of participation in democracy, but advocates within each tradition appeal to some common themes. That is, as they attempt to justify particular mechanisms for participation or to place limitations upon them, the participatory idealist, the pluralist elitist and the Marxist each speak in some way to issues of self-determination, human development and functional system requirements. In pro- moting the teaching of particular forms of participation, therefore, educators ought to consider their own positions on these issues.

Self-determination and power

One of the most familiar propositions in defense of citizen par- ticipation is the claim that people should have the right to deter- mine their own destiny. They should control their own institutions, rather than be subject to authorities and forces beyond their con- trol. A concern for power and control is evident in the rhetoric of people trying to free themselves from tyrants, colonial regimes, modern bureaucratic structures, or absentee landlords. On what grounds is it asserted that men and women should have the power to determine their own destiny? The claim is usually accepted on faith as a principle of justice or natural law, but it need not be. We can defend the right to control one's destiny through a reasoned ethical argument.

Without reviewing the complicated free will-determinism pro- blem, we can acknowledge the significance of some degree of in- dividual self-determination in making moral judgments about *per- sonal* action. Individuals should be held accountable in relation to others only to the extent that they have the power to choose and to act deliberately. To the extent that individual behavior is not self-determined, but involuntary (through coercion, physical or mental defect), it becomes impossible to consider oneself morally responsible in the sense that could be applied to those having a larger degree of power to deliberately affect the environment. While the power of self-determination offers no guarantee of moral behavior by a person, it is a logical prerequisite; without the power to affect events in a deliberate or self-conscious way, it is unreasonable to expect people to feel a sense of social responsibility.

Ethical foundations of the right to self-determination are also found in a different argument. Assuming that morality itself is based on a principle of human dignity that signifies equal respect for persons (Baier, 1965; Kohlberg and Turiel, 1971; Rawls, 1971), the right to self-determination can be seen as a political mechanism for implementing that principle. Under that principle, the claims and interests of each person must be treated impartially, that is, given equal consideration. Since it is a fact of social life, however, that some persons gain power over others, there is great risk that equal rights will be denied to the less powerful. To guard against this possibility, governance can be organized to disperse political power as equally as possible. Equal rights by all citizens to participate in governance thus minimizes inequalities of power. The sharing of powers of governance by all citizens provides no foolproof guarantee that equal rights of all will be respected, for any group can deny rights to a minority within its body. Nevertheless, affirming the principle of equal rights to self-determination should minimize the possibilities for some people exploiting others or treating them unfairly.

A recurring problem in discussion of the rights of people to control their destinies is the failure to distinguish between *individual* and *collective* rights to self-determination. The distinction is critical, because important social conflicts emerge between the two. Various collectives (religious or ethnic groups, intentional communities, nations) may struggle for the right of self-determination against the power of external authorities, but may also place constraints on the rights of self-determination of individual members within the collective. In fact, some groups are held together largely by the conviction that certain aspects of individual self-determination should be abdicated to serve some larger purpose (Kanter, 1972). Often individuals feel imprisoned by the constraints of a collective tradition, and they invoke the right of individual self-determination to challenge group norms.

The distinction is particularly notable in US history. The vision of self-determination prevailing as an ultimate value in modern affluent culture emphasizes the rights of people to make countless individual choices in ideology, lifestyle, career, forms of personal affiliation. McWilliams (1973) reminded us, however, that this sense of self-determination was not intended in the rhetoric or political philosophy of the American revolution. Rather, eighteenth century 'liberty' and self-determination referred to the right of a group of people to pursue its tradition, to govern itself without interference from an external or foreign out-group. Liberty was construed as the right of persons to participate within the limits of a particular culture that usually imposed many collective constraints on individual behavior (e.g., Puritanism).

To the extent that advocates for citizen participation base their case on the right of self-determination, a major question is whether the ultimate value is the self-determination of individuals to pursue private interest, or whether it is a more substantive concept of public good, containing principles other than individual liberty or self-determination such as economic requirements for social justice, religious notions of salvation, or other consensual definitions of the public good, which themselves help to justify collective self-determination for that society.

Just as the value of self-determination may be used to support widespread citizen participation, it may also be used to place limits upon it. Limits tend to be justified by either the 'tyranny of majority' or the 'incompetence' arguments. If, in the name of collective self-determination, a majority denies that right to minorities, as has been done through discrimination based on race or religion, then participation of the majority must be limited. Or, through lack of competence, citizen participants might make unintentional errors in public policy that could deny self-determination to the public at large; for example, mistaken calculations on pollution standards for a local water supply or failure to plan for long-term consequences of industrial expansion. The public should be protected from citizen abuse or misuse of power, it is argued, either through legal restraints from higher authorities such as state and federal governments or by delegating certain powers to more competent elites (e.g., scientists and economists).

A commitment to self-determination legitimately necessitates close attention to power relationships, but Pranger (1968) explained how an exclusive preoccupation with power can itself undermine other democratic ideals. The necessary concern for power must be balanced by a respect for interactive models of participation emphasized in the next main issue.

Humanistic development

The case for participatory democracy has been argued for centuries on grounds other than self-determination or power to control one's destiny. In addition, political participation by citizens has been justified through beneficial effects it presumably brings to individual participators, such as enhancing individual social identity (Dewey, 1929), cultivating cognitive skills (Bennett, 1975), increasing moral sensitivities (Sprinthall and Mosher, 1978; Kohlberg, 1980), or most generally allowing individuals to develop their full human potential (Mill, 1958; Aristotle, 1962; Rousseau, 1968). The principle of allowing each person to develop his or her unique potential can be defended on moral grounds: the ethical norm of equal respect for persons implies respecting the opportunity for all to express their unique talents, interests, points of view.

In analyzing authors from Aristotle to Mill to Dewey, Scaff (1975) documented the persistence of the point of view that man's individual growth and identity must be rooted in participation in social networks, not in personal isolation. For growth and productive identity to develop, however, participation must challenge the individual to confront diverse perspectives, to resolve contradictions among one's own beliefs to deal with conflicts between ideals and reality. This line of thought supports theory that endorses the developmental power of dialectic and/or synergistic interaction (Hampden-Turner, 1970; Riegal, 1975). Because political issues continually raise questions in the allocation of social values, discourse upon them requires a particular form of communication or interaction which, according to Dewey (1927, 1929) and others, offers unique opportunities for citizens to develop increased social consciousness, tolerance and respect among people.

A considerable literature (Verba, 1961; Nisbet, 1962; Oliver, 1976; Berger and Neuhaus, 1977) suggests that a sense of community is required not only for social harmony, but for individual psychological health. Stress, anxiety, alienation in modern cultures can be explained in part by the breakdown of intimate social networks, based on shared religious, ethnic, economic or residential identity, where people find reasonably stable social support. These avenues for social bonding have been weakened, but they may be augmented by interpersonal affiliations developed through political participation. As individuals participate, they are more likely to feel connected to a group that offers personal support and to a cause that offers common meaning, thereby reducing feelings of isolation and estrangement.

It has been shown that personal development rests to a large degree on a sense of competence, the sense that one can affect the environment in ways consistent with one's intentions (White, 1959; Smith, 1968). To the extent that persons hold strong preferences related to public policy and to the extent that they feel powerless to affect those preferences, they will experience a low sense of efficacy. Political participation certainly offers no assurance that each citizen can affect the world in his or her own preferred way, but participation can reduce a sense of powerlessness in two ways. First it can help to cast one's social ideals within a realistic perspective which, by facilitating modification of goals, can reduce unproductive feelings of frustration. Second, it can lead to achievement of certain ideals, thereby enhancing one's sense of efficacy.

In assessing the value of political participation to individual participators, we must not assume that all forms of participation will necessarily bring all conceivable benefits to all participators. To the contrary, one might predict psychologically harmful consequences of indiscriminately expanded participation: frustration and sense of impotence when goals are not achieved, or rather than developing increased moral sensitivity, some may acquire an amoral instrumentalism to succeed in the game of power politics. To the extent that participation itself might involve people exclusively in the quest for power, it could be seen as blocking rather than assisting personal development. Thus, educators might oppose certain forms of participation on the argument that they are irrelevant or harmful to human development. Instead of assuming that participation in general does or does not enhance development, one must examine different contexts for participation and inquire about the extent to which various benefits seem likely for particular people.

The functional system perspective

According to this third general theme, participation is evaluated in terms of its contribution to the functioning of a social system. To what extent does political participation by citizens tend to distribute goods and services in an appropriate, cost-efficient, or just manner? This issue is raised in a variety of arguments both for and against citizen participation.

In short, the argument for participation from a functional perspective is that no agency, regime or political system can operate effectively without support of its ultimate constituents. Participation helps to cultivate support; therefore, participation is necessary to the functioning of a system. To the extent that input from citizens is invited by ruling elites and responded to, citizens will presumably see the governors as exercising authority legitimately in behalf of citizens. As citizens put time and effort into public affairs, presumably they will develop commitment to the process, giving leaders a base of general support from which to operate so they need not fear subversion or revolution.

Advocates of participatory democracy cast different light on this argument by suggesting that the virtue of citizen participation is not merely to build support for a system or its elites, but to provide substantive policy guidance that will better serve the interests of the public at large. This position implies not that every citizen is more competent in making judgments than all experts in government, but that the 'truth' about what is good and bad for the public is more likely to be revealed through widespread citizen participation than by judgment of isolated elites whose sources of information are often limited by professional and political biases.

Elitist opponents of wide scope citizen participation tend to rely heavily on a functional perspective, but reach an opposite conclusion. They argue it is logistically impossible to gather all citizens' views on most matters of public significance. Even if this information could be gathered, it would merely disrupt policy-making with 'noise' and misinformation, because citizens cannot acquire adequate knowledge on the many issues that require high technical expertise (nuclear energy, monetary policy, environmental impact, foreign affairs). Marxists may view functional implications still differently, perhaps opposing electoral participation on the grounds that its primary function is to convey the symbolic illusion of self-governance. Instead, some Marxists would emphasize grass roots organization of cooperative economic efforts aimed to liberate low-income people from corporate domination.

The point here is not to resolve debate among participatory idealists, elitists and Marxists, but to illustrate their common concern with functional requirements. As with the issues of self-determination and human development, functional system requirements can also be defended from an ethical viewpoint. An argument can be made that mutual respect among persons is possible only in a society in which persons generally trust one another (and trust institutions) not to infringe upon basic rights. This cannot occur within social chaos; it demands an orderly system that offers some predictability about individual and institutional action. Such order is established through rules that remain constant from day to day, or if they change, change transpires in a framework that maintains orderly social relations. While order or a smooth functioning system offers no assurance that human rights will be respected, in a general sense it can be shown to be a necessary prerequisite. To acknowledge this, of course, is not to endorse all attempts to control human behavior in the name of 'order'. Efforts in that direction should be taken only to promote the ultimate ethical principle of equal respect for persons. While a concern for functional order does not itself prescribe a particular form of citizen participation, it does suggest that any proposals on that topic be subject to evaluation, in part, on this criterion.

Each of the dominant political traditions makes persuasive observations about the kind of participation toward which society should strive, but no single tradition has responded to each of the persisting issues well enough to end dispute regarding particular forms of participation appropriate in a large, technologically complex culture that claims to aspire to democracy. Disagreement about what kinds and how much participation to support is sustained by uncertainty on a number of empirical problems: In what situations will individuals actually benefit from increased opportunities to participate? To what extent will expanded opportunities for participation lead to increased social conflict or possibly to policies that violate democratic ideals? Can there be opportunities within a large capitalistic society for all citizens to affect public affairs in a meaningful way or will certain classes of citizens inevitably be excluded? Considerable empirical study has been devoted to political participation, but definitive answers to these questions are not available.[3] In spite of uncertainty on such matters, we must seek a conception of participation responsive to legitimate contributions from each of the political traditions that also responds to the three persisting issues.

A PROPOSAL FOR DUAL LEVEL PARTICIPATION

Let us conceive of participation on two abstract levels, communal and societal. Communal participation occurs in gróups where people work together to govern themselves on a broad range of issues, where members know each other well and understand enough about issues that they can rotate responsibilities and share tasks of governance. The group often engages in activities of fellowship, informal recreation and expression ('idle' conversation, dining together, sharing music, dance, sports) in addition to the formal tasks of governance. In contrast, societal participation is oriented primarily toward influencing external sources (e.g., a legislature or corporation) and in modern culture this seems to entail organizations that focus on a narrow range of issues, that try to build large diverse memberships whose members usually have little familiarity with one another. Influencing modern institutions often requires high levels of technical expertise (e.g., legal and scientific skills) which leads to specialized roles among members. Groups of this sort expend most resources on their formal instrumental mission rather than on expressive social activity among members. The two contexts for participation should be seen as 'ideal types', reflecting much of the qualitative difference originally suggested by Tönnies' (1963) distinction between *Gemeinschaft* and *Gesellschaft*. As ideal types, they can be defined by the criteria just mentioned, and should be viewed on a continuum, rather than as categorial variables.

The structure, functions and activities of any group may reflect a greater or lesser degree of each criterion, and these can be 'added' to gain a rough indication of the extent to which participation in a group represents communal or societal participation.

Communal	*Societal*
1. internal focus on quality of life within the group	focus on influencing agents external to thegroup
2. broad range of issues-concerns	narrow range of issues-concerns
3. high interpersonal familiarity	low interpersonal familiarity
4. low specialization of members roles	high specialization of member roles
5. balance between instrumental and expressive activity	dominance of instrumental activity

Communal participation seems most possible in local small-group settings where people can interact on a continuous face-to-face basis. Such settings as the family, neighborhood, voluntary association, church, peer group, possibly schools and some places of work can offer opportunities for people to deliberate meaningfully about their responsibilities to one another and about procedures for resolving conflicts fairly so as to achieve the public good within the limited context of the group. Though subject to larger structural constraints and also to many internal forces that can inhibit democratic governance, such settings have the potential to fulfil conditions on the communal side of the continuum. In contrast, societal participation is most likely to occur in groups whose interests extend beyond small local constituencies: public interest organizations, political parties, special interest organizations (unions, professional and trade associations). Through such groups citizens can pursue access to larger public and private structures, and participation with such groups is often characterized by qualities on the societal side of the continuum. Groups characterized primarily as communal can approximate the participatory idealist vision of direct democracy, because the low degree of role specialization allows wide participation of members in governing the group. In contrast, a group characterized primarily as societal will probably have a governance structure similar to a modern state or corporation where high specialization of roles tends to result in delegation of governance to elites.

In general we might predict that the smaller, more local and particularistic the concern of a group, the more communal participation will be evident; the larger and more universal the concerns of a group, the more societal participation will result. The quality of participation, however, cannot be predicted so easily from such a formula. A small group of people from diverse nations may work together for many years governing a private club or professional association, and this could reflect several aspects of communal participation (internal focus, low specialization, familiarity, expressive fellowship). In contrast, a local parish, normally preoccupied with serving particular parishioners, might devote major efforts to influence international organizations affecting the treatment of refugees. To accomplish this, the parish might take on (perhaps temporarily) certain features of societal participation (external influence, focus on narrow range of issues, high specialization of member roles). Furthermore, any given setting may often reflect both communal and societal qualities. In an urban neighborhood organization, members may work in small groups trying to define what is best for the neighborhood (communal). On the other hand, to preserve self-determination for the neighborhood, their organization might become involved in power struggles with national agencies, forcing the neighborhood to join with others and to organize on a large scale (societal) (Perlman, 1978).

In urging that we examine the participatory experiences with these categories in mind, we are not, therefore, recommending that each group or setting receive a definitive label. Instead we ask that experiences within any setting be examined to assess the extent to which members' activities can be described by the suggested dimensions. The more the experience of most members consistently fits one pole or the other, the more reasonable it would be to describe the group experience as communal or societal. In applying such judgments to a given group or setting, we might reach any of the following conclusions: a) most members most of the time share a communal (or societal) experience; b) most members most of the time share a mixed experience but a minority consistently shares a communal (or societal) experience; c) at certain periods most members share a communal experience, but at other times most share a societal experience; d) the nature of the group experience varies such that most members of the group are involved at both the communal and societal level, but in no predictable fashion.

While some group settings might be classified primarily in one category (e.g., Common Cause as societal, a local club for single parents as communal), we have shown that most activities cannot be so easily designated. The categories are proposed not because they provide a neat and consistent classification of all group experiences, but because they assist in assessing the potential social psychological benefits of political participation. Such assessments might yield policy implications.

One possible reason for citizen reluctance to participate in political parties, for example, may be the perception that they have so little relevance to communal participation. Citizens may see few opportunities to enhance local life through party affiliation, but find other contexts such as church or neighborhood organization more appropriate. If one wishes to build meaningful opportunities to participate in local self-governance and simultaneously to stimulate significance of political parties in the society at large, then one might attempt a restructuring of political parties such that they become more involved in communal activity. Or, one might assume that political parties must of necessity serve only the purpose of citizen representation on societal issues. If this be the case, one might expect and accept relatively low rates of party participation, based on the realization that active involvement at the societal level attracts only a small proportion of the population.

Each level of participation seems required in modern society; neither is adequate by itself. Communal participation helps to establish a sense of community amidst otherwise alienating conditions. Self-governance in communal contexts can establish social connectedness and provide firsthand experience in resolving issues of individual rights and social obligations. Such experience can be beneficial not only in stimulating democratic interaction, reducing social estrangement and enhancing individual development, but also in creating models, norms, sensitivities that citizens may then project to more abstract and distant issues of society at large.

Only through societal participation, however, can citizens exert influence upon larger corporate organizations — government agencies, legislatures, corporations, unions — that dominate so many aspects of modern culture. Yet societal participation inevitably takes on many features of corporate organizational life itself. It requires large numbers of people, many of whom do not know or interact with one another; high degrees of technical expertise (e.g., attorneys or experts on pollution); specialization and hierarchy in the organization (i.e., delegated power rather than direct democracy); a dominant posture of advocacy and instrumental goal achievement, rather than mutual sharing and fellowship; finally, goals are phrased in abstractions (reducing racial discrimination or saving the environment) rather than in particular concrete terms (get Joe Smith a job, or clean up this stream), and progress toward them comes in small, often invisible steps over long periods of time. Citizen participation at the societal level presents few opportunities for participants to function in the close-knit holistic kinds of relationships characteristic of communal activity. On the other hand, societal participation provides the only realistic opportunity for citizens to influence broader social policies.

The proposal is that education and social policy should facilitate both communal and societal participation, aiming for a general balance between the two. The virtue of communal participation is its empowering of citizens to work closely in direct self-governance to enhance their own lives. The value of societal participation rests in access to influence elites who run larger institutions. Balance between the two forms could be achieved within individuals' lives if people felt comfortable saying to themselves:

> To keep our humanity and to enhance democracy, we need opportunities to participate both as communal and as societal citizens. Sometimes I am involved in a communal role where I derive the benefits of community governance, but I should not depend upon that role to achieve such goals as world peace or redistribution of wealth. At other times, I must function in a societal role. While this does not carry the benefits of fellowship and a direct sense of collective control, this more formalized relationship is necessary for tackling larger problems amenable to solution only through more massive, centralized structures.

Cultural balance between the two forms would be achieved if high levels of citizen participation were found at each level. Many individuals might restrict their own participation to one level, some becoming almost exclusively communal, others, societal participants.

In suggesting that communal and societal forms of participation involve distinct social-psychological qualities, and that both forms are needed to enhance democracy, I have not addressed how policy aimed at enhancing both levels might affect individual loyalty to local vs. national vs. global community. There is widespread concern that parochial allegiance to local tradition obstructs possibilities for harmonious interdependence among the various parts (cities, states, regions, nations, continents) of the world. In this sense some might want to promote societal consciousness first, so that communal commitment is nested within a larger system of peace and justice. My use of communal and societal participation here is not intended to signify anything regarding an individual's preferred loyalties or frames of reference; that is another issue for debate in citizenship education (see Newmann, 1977).

The call for balance among opportunities for participation, however, is not inconsistent with the position that seeks to develop cognitive awareness and commitment that extends beyond local self-interest to aggregate national or global concerns (Butts, 1979; Rosenau, 1979). The present analysis intends no sanctification of particular interests over universal ones, but it does suggest that if universal interests can be pursued *only* through societal participation, this will have limited social psychological benefits to participants. Ideally, there should be opportunities for citizens to pursue such goals as world peace or equitable distribution of wealth through communal as well as societal activity.

Dual level participation represents a number of ideas previously mentioned. It supports the participatory idealist emphasis on direct, collective self-governance, but responds to legitimate concerns of elitists that this cannot be meaningfully extended to many arenas of decision-making in modern culture. Impersonal, corporate institutions governed by elites are here to stay, but their alienating qualities can be reduced by two general forces: societal participation by citizens to hold elites accountable, and the preservation and enhancement of opportunities for communal self-governance. The call for balance among the two levels is consistent with both liberal and conservative emphases upon pluralism, for through communal participation it encourages the strengthening of local and cultural diversity. While not grounded in Marxist theory, dual level participation is not inconsistent with it. In fact it seems to share with Marxism the values of equality and self-determination, and it supports the dialectic in Marxism between consciousness rooted in local, particularistic experience versus the need for consciousness extending to mass, or world-wide collectivities.

Dual level participation echoes the persistent human concern for self-determination, but by making a distinction between the levels at which this may be pursued in modern culture, it offers a more realistic approach than either participatory idealist or the elitist notion alone. The humanistic developmental tradition is reflected in emphasis upon opportunities for humane interaction through direct self-governance. This is not to suggest that societal participation is necessarily inhumane, for it is absolutely necessary to achieve 'humane' social policies. Yet the quality of participation within societal contexts lacks opportunities for people to discuss issues in an open, informal style. Concern for the requirements of a functional system is also evident in the dual level approach. Recognizing the fact of global interdependence, it does not pretend a nostalgic return to simple, self-sufficient communities, nor a desire for massive direct participation by all citizens in all institutions. Instead, it finds a need for balance, encouraging a continuing effort to distinguish among social services that might best be provided through local, communally structured organizations versus those that of necessity must be delivered through centralized institutions.

Conceiving participation simultaneously on two levels may be consistent with varying strands of previous theory and social argument, but this is not sufficient to establish its validity for modern culture. At least two important questions remain to be answered. One is whether the concept is psychologically feasible. Is it possible for most people to conceive of and invest themselves in two levels with possibly contradictory implications? Can an individual be committed with equal strength to one's local neighborhood, sports club or church *and* also do justice for exploited people across the state, nation or globe? This represents the classic problem of integrating particularistic and universalistic orientations. Empirical research is needed to examine the extent to which persons can use (or be taught to use) these two concepts to make sense of the ways they participate in society.

The second question is whether dual level participation is socially feasible. To the extent that large corporate institutions continually require those involved in communal participation to expend most of their energies trying to preserve autonomy against the onslaught of modern centralization, then communal participation will vanish. Berger and Neuhaus (1977) have addressed this problem, and publications of the Mediating Structures Project will hopefully shed light on how public policy might be developed so as to keep a balance between local mediating structures and modern institutions.[4] The history of modernization indicates dramatically enough the escalating dominance of institutions that allow only societal forms of participation.[5] In other words, unless people come to value and to assert themselves strongly on behalf of communal participation, there will be no chance to examine the social feasibility of balancing the two.

IMPLICATIONS FOR EDUCATORS

Prevailing conceptions of citizenship and participation focus almost exclusively at the societal level. Teaching about democracy, following from the elitist school, concentrates upon representative government in institutions entrusted to serve the large constituencies of city, state and nation. Even advocates for participatory democracy, trying to combat elitism, often concentrate on issues pursued most often through societal, rather than communal contexts (e.g. citizen control over nuclear power or equal rights amendments). The dominant focus on societal participation creates profound disillusionment for students who internalize the democratic ideal of government of, by and for the people. They soon learn that most societal institutions are run by elites, with few meaningful opportunities for citizens to participate in the making of social policy.

Teachers attempt to resolve this contradiction by pointing to devices within the constitutional tradition which allegedly make it possible to adapt the vision of participatory democracy to modern society: periodic elections, majority rule, freedom of speech and assembly, checks and balances, spearation of powers, referendum and recall. Unfortunately, such mechanisms are inadequate for generating that sense of self-determination and connectedness implied by the participatory ideal. They presuppose that individuals will be able to identify with the institutions that affect public life, but in mass, technological culture these institutions are so large, diverse and distant from immediate human concerns that most persons are likely to feel alienated from rather than connected to 'their' government.

Disillusionment might be alleviated if educators would: a) give more attention to communal participation and b) present societal participation not as a logical extension of town meeting democracy, but as a special set of challenges in gaining control over modern institutions. Effective teaching about the balance between communal and societal participation requires modification of classroom instruction and new laboratory experiences for students in the community. In this paper we cannot specify curriculum content and program details, but let us elaborate these two suggestions.

Communal activity should be studied and celebrated as an opportunity for democratic participation as legitimate and critical as voting or becoming informed on societal issues. It has long been argued that democracy and respect for human rights in the society at large can be only as healthy as relationships in face-to-face human communities, for these are the contexts that allow the most meaningful opportunities to practice self-governance. In neighborhood groups, churches, local voluntary associations, at some schools and some workplaces, we can find examples of people trying to govern their lives 'justly'. These situations should be recognized by educators and public figures as crucibles of citizenship and studied as rigorously as the formal legal-political structures of government.

Students could observe, study and participate in communal contexts to gain a sense of: 1) the ways in which such groups encourage or inhibit self-governance, 2) the groups' contribution to or violation of democratic values (other than self-governance) in the society at large (e.g. due process, free speech, equal opportunity), 3) the kinds of public policies that weaken or strengthen such groups, 4) the extent to which such groups seem constrained by forces (institutions) beyond their control, and 5) the kinds of personal satisfactions and dissatisfactions arising from participation in the groups. The main reason for increased attention to communal participation is not to indoctrinate students to value it as the only possible arena for democratic citizenship, but to evaluate its potential contribution to the three persisting requirements of self-determination, humanistic development and system maintenance raised in discussions of political participation.

Increased attention to communal participation should entail no retreat from the study of societal or global issues (institutions). Students should be taught to examine how corporations, foundations, legislatures, administrative agencies and international networks might be shaped to contribute to justice in the world, and part of this is to inquire about their relationship to communal democracy. Rather than assuming that lay participation in such organizations represents a logical extension of Aristotelian or Jeffersonian citizenship, students must examine the special complexities of decision-making in large-scale institutions. Topics such as the distribution of power, formal and informal decision-making processes, the relative influence of individuals versus organized collectives and the dynamics of bureaucracy may help students to understand differences and similarities in various contexts for citizen participation; for example, trying to alter the national distribution of wealth versus trying to preserve an ethnic heritage through a local 'fraternal' organization.

As students comprehend the disparity between 'town-meeting' models of decision-making and the ways decisions are made in societal contexts, the educator will be faced with the critical question: What power or voice do I, as an individual, have in making decisions in societal organizations? No simple answer can be offered, but the course of inquiry suggested above should illuminate contingencies (economics, collective strength, law, rational argument, and charisma) that affect individual influence in specific situations. We must find ways to help students cope with the ambiguity following from complex contingencies and help them to resolve what they may see as a major violation of the principle of self-determination. It may be jolting for students to learn (and accept) that the ideal of democratic participation was originally intended to secure neither unilateral self-determination for each individual nor protection from ambiguity. These two myths may die hard (much in the culture reinforces unbridled individualism and the desire for absolute truth), but their demise is essential for a productive understanding of democratic participation in societal contexts.

The suggested issues and themes could be developed in instructional materials on communal and societal participation for courses in history, government, sociology and political science. Expository material on conceptions of democratic participation should be illustrated by case studies of decision-making and citizen participation in communal and societal contexts. In addition, schools should help students examine actual settings for participation in their communities. Fieldwork can include both observation-study and active student participation. At the communal level students can participate in organizations run by youth (clubs, church groups, self-help centers), in school governance, and in advisory roles on adult governing bodies with small constituencies (school board, park commissions, neighborhood councils). Societal level participation should include work in electoral politics, advocacy for issue-oriented pressure groups (environment, civil rights, consumerism), or special youth advocacy projects (bike trails, teen centers).[6]

The balancing of participation in the two realms of communal activity and advocacy in large institutions will be difficult, especially in schools that persistently resist departure from the format of teacher-telling-the-truth-to-students. What lends hope is that the concern for more adequate frameworks for citizen participation is not just a curriculum problem, but a pervasive social issue. There is widespread estrangement from large institutions, some of which has been transformed into vigorous self-help movements in medical care, legal assistance, urban agriculture, neighborhood government, and revitalizing local cultural and religious institutions. Since we must continue to rely also on services that can be delivered only through centralized institutions, effective citizen organizations are needed to 'watch' them (through consumer organizations, political parties, American civil liberties union, labor unions, civil rights organizations). It is now time to recognize more critically and forcefully the potentials and limitations of participation at each level.

NOTES

1. The categories are derived from the work of Milbrath (1965), Verba and Nie (1972), Langton (1978).

2. I am indebted to Kasperson and Breitbart's (1974) outstanding summary of theories and issues in participation, which I have augmented and modified.

3. Space does not permit a review of relevant literature here, but for illustrative studies that bear on these issues, see Spiegel (1971), Verba and Nie (1972), Smith (1973), Cole (1974), Alford and Friedland (1975), Crozier et al. (1975), Sniderman (1975), Checkoway and Van Til (1978), and Salisbury (1980).

4. The project intends to produce publications showing how public policy in housing, welfare, criminal justice, education and health care might be modified to protect and to nourish local mediating structures.

5. Writers of vastly divergent ideologies seem to agree on this point; for example, Dahl and Lindblom (1976), Oliver (1976), Wright (1978).

6. The selection of non-school learning contexts typically raises many questions: What kind of productive work can youth actually do within the adult world? To what degree can we ensure that youth will learn useful skills, information, ways of approaching problems? Will youth participation raise tumultuous ethical and political issues that interfere with educational benefits? These are important issues, but in general they have been adequately treated in selected school programs and in educational literature (e.g., Conrad and Hedin, 1977; Newmann et. al., 1977).

REFERENCES

Alford, Robert R. and Roger Friedland, 'Political Participation and Public Policy', *Annual Review of Sociology* 1, 1975, pp. 429-479.

Almond, Gabriel A. and Sidney Verba, *The Civic Culture: Political Attitudes and Democracy in Five Nations,* Boston: Little Brown, 1963.

Aristotle, *The Politics of Aristotle,* E. Barker (ed.), Oxford: Oxford University Press, 1962.

Arnstein, Sherry R., 'A Ladder of Citizenship Participation', *Journal of the American Institute of Planners* 35 (4), 1969.

Bachrach, Peter, *The Theory of Democratic Elitism: A Critique,* Boston: Little Brown, 1967.

Baier, Kurt, *The Moral Point of View,* New York: Random House, 1965.

Benello, Geroge C. and Dimitrios Roussopoulos (eds.), *The Case for Participatory Democracy: Some Prospects for a Radical Society,* New York: Grossman, 1971.

Bennett, W. Lance, *The Political Mind and the Political Environment,* Lexington: Lexington Books, 1975.

Berger, Peter L. and Richard Neuhaus, *To Empower People: The Role of Mediating Structures in Public Policy,* Washington, DC: American Enterprise Institute for Public Policy Research, 1977.

Butts, F. Freeman, 'The Revival of Civic Learning', *Social Education* 43 (5), May 1979, pp. 359-364.

—— 'Historical Perspective on Civic Education in the United States in National Task Force on Citizenship Education', *Education for Responsible Citizenship,* New York: McGraw-Hill, 1977.

Checkoway, Barry and Jon Van Til, 'What Do We Know About Citizen Participation? A Selective Review of Research', in Stuart Langton (ed.), *Citizen Participation in America,* Lexington, MA: D.C. Heath, 1978.

Cole, Richard L., *Citizen Participation and the Urban Policy Process,* Lexington: D.C. Heath, 1974.

Conrad, Dan and Diane Hedin, 'Citizenship Education Through Participation' in B. Frank Brown (ed.), *Education for Responsible Citizenship,* New York: McGraw-Hill, 1977.

Crozier, Michel J., Samuel P. Huntington and Joji Watanuki, *The Crisis of Democracy: Report on the Governability of Democracies to the Trilateral Commission*, New York: New York University Press, 1975.

Dahl, Robert A., *A Preface to Democratic Theory*, Chicago: University of Chicago Press, 1956.

Dahl, Robert A. and Charles E. Lindblom, *Politics, Economics and Welfare: Planning and Politico-Economic Systems Resolved into Basic Social Processes*, Chicago: University of Chicago Press, 1976.

Dewey, John, *The Public and Its Problems*, Chicago: Swallow, 1927.

—— *Individualism Old and New*, New York: Capricorn, 1929.

Edwards, Richard, *Contested Terrain*, New York: Basic Books, 1979.

Evans, Michael, 'Karl Marx and the Concept of Political Participation', in Geraint Parry (ed.), *Participation in Politics*, Manchester, England: Manchester University Press, 1972.

Hampden-Turner, Charles, *Radical Man: The Process of Psycho-Social Development*, Cambridge: Schenkman, 1970.

Hunt, Maurice P. and Lawrence Metcalf, *Teaching High School Social Studies*, New York: Harper and Row, 1968.

Kanter, Rosabeth, M., *Commitment and Community: Communes and Utopias in Sociological Perspective*, Cambridge: Harvard University Press, 1972.

Kasperson, Roger E. and Myrna Breitbart, *Participation, Decentralization and Advocacy Planning*, Washington, DC: Association of American Geographers, Commission on College Geography, 1974.

Kohlberg, Lawrence, 'High School Democracy in Educating for a Just Society', in Ralph L. Mosher (ed.), *Moral Education: First Generation of Research and Development*, New York: Praeger, 1980.

Kohlberg, Lawrence and Eliot Turiel, 'Moral Development and Moral Education', in G. Lesser (ed.), *Psychology and Educational Practice*, Glenview, IL: Scott Foresman, 1971.

Langton, Stuart, *Citizen Participation in America*, Lexington: D.C. Heath, 1978.

Lowi, Theodore J., *The End of Liberalism: The Second Republic of the United States*, 2nd edition, New York: Norton, 1979.

McWilliams, Wilson Carey, *The Idea of Fraternity in America*, Berkeley: University of California Press, 1973.

Milbrath, Lester, *Political Participation*, Chicago: Rand McNally, 1965.

Miliband, Ralph, *The State in Capitalist Society*, New York: Basic, 1969.

Mill, John Stuart, *Considerations on Representative Government*, Indianapolis: Bobbs Merril, 1958.

National Commission on Resources for Youth, *New Roles for Youth in the School and Community*, New York: Citation, 1974.

Newmann, Fred M., 'Building a Rationale for Civic Education' in James P. Shaver (ed.), *Building Rationales for Citizenship Education*, Washington, DC: National Council for the Social Studies, 1977.

Newmann, Fred M., Thomas A. Bertocci, Ruthanne M. Landness, *Skills in Citizen Action: An English-Social Studies Program for Secondary Schools*, Skokie, IL: National Textbook Co., 1977.

Nisbet, Robert A., *Community and Power*, New York: Oxford University Press, 1962.

Oliver, Donald W. and James P. Shaver, *Teaching Public Issues in the High School*, Logan, UT; Utah State University Press, 1966.

Oliver, Donald W., *Education and Community: A Radical Critique of Innovative Schooling*, Berkeley: McCutchan, 1976.

Pateman, Carole, *Participation and Democratic Theory*, New York: Cambridge University Press, 1970.

Perlman, Janice, 'Grassroots Participation from Neighborhood to Nation', in Stuart Langton (ed.), *Citizen Participation in America*, Lexington, MA: D.C. Heath, 1978.

Pranger, Robert J., *Eclipse of Citizenship: Power and Participation in Contemporary Politics*, New York: Holt, Rinehart and Winston, 1968.

Rawls, John, *A Theory of Justice*, Cambridge: Harvard University Press, 1971.

Riegal, Klaus F. (ed.), *The Development of Dialectical Operation*, Basel, Switzerland: S. Karger, 1975. Reprinted from *Human Development* 18 (1,2,3), 1975.

Rosenau, James N., 'Toward a New Civics: Teaching and Learning in an Era of Fragmenting Loyalties and Multiplying Responsibilities'. Paper delivered to American Political Science Association, Washington, DC, 4 September 1979.

Rousseau, Jean-Jacques, *The Social Contract*, trans. M. Cranston, Baltimore: Penguin, 1968.

Salisbury, Robert H., 'Research on Political Participation', *American Journal of Political Science* 19, May 1975, pp. 323-341.

—— *Key Concepts of Citizenship: Perspectives and Dilemmas*, Washington, DC: HEW Publication no. (OE) 78-07005, 1978.

—— *Citizen Participation in the Public Schools*, Lexington, MA: D.C. Heath, 1980.

Scaff, Lawrence A., *Participation in the Western Political Tradition: A Study of Theory and Practice*, Tucson: University of Arizona Press, 1975.

Schumpeter, Joseph A., *Capitalism, Socialism and Democracy*, New York: Harper and Row, 1956.

Smith, David H. (ed.), *Voluntary Action Research: 1973*, Lexington, MA: D.C. Heath, 1973.

Smith, M. Brewster, 'Competence and Socialization' in John A. Clausen (ed.), *Socialization and Society*, Boston: Little Brown, 1968.

Sniderman, Paul M., *Democratic Personality and Politics*, Berkeley: University of California Press, 1975.

Spiegel, Hans B.C., 'Citizen Participation in Federal Programs: A Review', *Journal of Voluntary Action Research*, Monograph No. 1, 1971, pp. 4-31, reprinted in Smith (1973).

Sprinthall, Norman A. and Ralph L. Mosher, *Value Development . . . As the Aim of Education*, Schnectady, NY: Character Research Press, 1978.

Stillman, Peter G., 'Freedom as Participation: The Revolutionary Theories of Hegel and Arendt', *American Behavioral Scientist* 20 (4), March/April 1977, pp. 477-492.

Thompson, Dennis F., *The Democratic Citizen: Social Science and Democratic Theory in the Twentieth Century*, Cambridge: Cambridge University Press, 1970.

Tönnies, F., *Community and Society*, trans. and ed.ted by C.P. Loomis, New York: Harper Row, 1963.

Verba, Sidney, *Small Groups and Political Behavior: A Study of Leadership*, Princeton: Princeton University Press, 1961.

Verba, Sidney and Norman H. Nie, *Participation in America: Political Democracy and Social Equality*, New York: Harper and Row, 1972.

Walker, Jack, 'A Critique of the Elitist Theory of Democracy', *American Political Science Review* 60, June 1966, pp. 285-295.

White, Robert W., 'Motivation Reconsidered: The Concept of Competence', *Psychological Review* 66, 1959, pp. 297-333.

Wright, Erik Olin, *Class, Crisis and the State*, London: New Left Books, 1978.

7

Political Literacy

Alex Porter

The greatest obstacle to the development of political education in Britain is the confusion between political education and the teaching of politics and government. I am convinced that if political education is to make real headway in securing a place in the curriculum of most schools and those colleges working at sub-degree level the fundamental distinction between the objectives of politics teaching and of political education has to be established and widely understood. The development of the idea of political literacy to some extent involved an attempt to offer, or to invite, such a distinction. As the only really significant runner in the field at this time it must remain the safest bet for those who share a concern for political education. I believe that a clearer understanding of political literacy may go some way towards overcoming this particular obstacle to progress.

For some, of course, political education will always be interpreted as the teaching of politics. As long as the movement for political education exists they will add their public support to it while harbouring private ambitions for an increase in the extent of politics teaching and in the number of politics teachers. Leaving such views aside there is fairly widespread agreement about what is and is not proposed in the name of political education. Undoubtedly political education is intended for all — for all children in a school or college, and for all schools and colleges. This broad aim presupposes certain objectives; possibly even a certain social philosophy — one which assumes an important relationship between the education of all individuals and the condition of the political order. The objectives of political education are not individual-centred (at least not exclusively) and certainly not knowledge-centred, but rather are society-centred. It follows from this that for political educationalists knowledge, in the restricted sense of factual data, is simply not enough. However, beyond the dissatisfaction with knowledge alone there is much less agreement. Each set of proposals to supplement basic knowledge carries with it a particular set of objectives and often a strategy for implementation. These are the issues over which the most ardent campaigners for political education are bound to disagree. Whilst there most certainly are such disagreements, it would be quite wrong to cite this as evidence that there is conflict over the fundamental meaning of political education. Tapper and Salter, in a rather perfunctory analysis of the political education movement in Britain, remark on the 'internal self doubts' of the campaign and provide the pertinent warning that it looks as if '. . . it may end up as a discussion arena for interested parties rather than as a viable instrument for change'.[1] It is well worth reminding ourselves that the views which political educationalists hold in common, and which set us off from most political scientists and others who may doubt the value or practical possibility of political education, are far more significant than those matters over which we may disagree.

'Politics' (or 'Political Science' or 'Government') will not do as political education for obvious reasons. As a time-table subject, usually defined and delimited by examination syllabuses, it is almost everywhere offered as an optional subject to pupils and college students beyond the age of 14. Although theoretically available to all students to whom a choice of subjects is offered, it would be impossible in practice for all to elect to study politics. If politics became too popular quotas and disqualifying procedures would be imposed. Although it does not have to be that way politics, like most school subjects, is rationed to a few; especially that select few who continue their schooling beyond the age of 16.

An accepted outcome of politics teaching is that students are assessed and graded according to their ability to recall facts. Frequently this grading is part of a wider selection process for higher education or employment opportunities. Whilst some students have such opportunities increased or reinforced as a result of politics teaching, the majority do not: in comparison with the successful minority the majority are labelled as failures. In stark contrast political education is not intended to classify students and to separate out the 'competent' from the 'incompetent'.

There are other problems. Politics is generally seen as a particular body of knowledge which is more or less distinctive and which can be distinguished from other subjects. The teaching of politics is concerned with the transmission of this set of knowledge to students. The success of the teaching process is measured by the amount of knowledge received and recalled by students. Now even if political education could be reduced to such behavioural, fact-transmission/recall objectives without ceasing to be political education, there would be little correspondence between 'politics' knowledge and 'political education' knowledge.

Political education is not a subject in this sense at all. It has, as I have said, objectives which go beyond the mere transmission of knowledge. Certainly there is a knowledge base, some of which will be recognized as politics. Much more will come from other subject areas — from sociology, economics, history, geography, literature and media studies. A large proportion of the subject matter will be derived from outside the traditional boundaries of school knowledge by drawing on, for example, students' everyday knowledge, experiences and interests, and on information from the mass media, pressure groups and other informal sources. In drawing on this range of subjects and other sources the purpose would not be to try to create and legitimate another subject. Although it may be possible to refine and enhance politics teaching in respect of one or two of these deficiencies, a wholesale change along the lines indicated is not merely unlikely but, in any case, is in my view unnecessary and undesirable. There are other more urgent reforms needed for the teaching of politics in Britain.

In England the political education movement in general and political literacy in particular was to some extent a product of dissatisfaction with politics teaching. In the 1960s politics teaching in schools was mostly confined to British Constitution lessons. Those who are not familiar with the syllabuses and textbooks which were current at the time may have some difficulty in appreciating what it was about this subject that resulted in 'Brit. Con.' becoming an expression of contempt. Unlike many other examination

syllabuses the specification of British Constitution gave little
guidance on what the examiners expected. In 1969 the University of
London Advanced Level[2] Syllabus regulations included such topics
as:

> The nature, sources and characteristics of the British Constitution . . . The
> Royal prerogative. Constitutional conventions . . . Public opinion.
>
> Parliament; its position, functions, personnel and powers . . . Parliamentary
> privilege and procedure . . . The Privy Council and the Cabinet. Committees of
> the Cabinet. Ministerial responsibility. The position of the Prime Minister. The
> principal government departments. The civil service. The outlines of public ad-
> ministration. Various forms of control over administration, including Treasury
> control, control by Parliament and the Cabinet, and ministerial and parliamen-
> tary control of public corporations . . .

There seemed to be an unstated assumption that there was general
agreement about the meaning and the scope of these headings: that
there was, for example, an agreed specification of what constitutes
'public opinion' or the 'position' of Parliament. So teachers were
forced to turn to past examination papers for real guidance on the
requirements of examiners. Questions such as: 'Discuss the com-
position and functions of the House of Lords since 1945' (1969
Paper 1 Question 7), reveal an obsession with petty parliamentary
and other 'constitutional' facts and an apparent desire to avoid
anything which may be open to alternative interpretations. This
was for most teachers, and for the subject itself, quite demeaning.
Most institutions of higher education and employers would not
recognize British Constitution as being equivalent to other subjects.
Many headteachers held the same view, with the result that where it
was offered there was little or no time-table provision and students
either took it as an extra subject or as the only remaining alternative after they had been turned away from those subjects which
were their prime choices. In short, it was regarded as a soft option;
and not without considerable justification. In the first issue of the
Newsletter of the Politics Association[3] (Spring 1970), the chief examiner for the London 'A' level published an article entitled 'The
Philosophy of an Examiner'. In the following six issues there were
thirteen articles or letters which either challenged the original piece
or were defensive replies by its author. The debate rumbled on
throughout the first volumes of *Teaching Politics*, the journal
which succeeded the original *Newsletter*.

Two points were patently obvious. First, there was a lot of discontent among teachers. There was much evidence for this in other writings and especially at teachers' conferences and in-service training courses. It was also clear that this particular examiner (and others who entered the debate) were at cross-purposes with the teachers. For both sides the issue was about standards. In defence of the standards of British Constitution the examiner insisted:

> I tend to be pedantic and pull to pieces sloppy English, obscure expression, untidiness . . . I am very hard on such offenders . . . Leave them in no doubt that such carelessness is academically criminal . . .[4] We must raise the standard of British Constitution by making the papers much more sophisticated. We must ask questions that force the candidate to think hard about the answers; he will have to organize his knowledge, keep his factual material separate from his ideas, work out his attitude and construct an argument.[5]

At the same time, teachers were calling for syllabus reform with such comments as:

> . . . the nature of politics must be studied — the nature of power, bureaucracy, and the allocation of values . . . The student must learn the methods of political enquiry . . . As the basis of political argument is ideology this must be included in a syllabus . . . the major political ideals . . . and political concepts like the state, sovereignty, representation . . . .[6]

They wanted a *change* in the subject-matter whereas the examiners merely wanted to ask more demanding questions about the *existing* subject-matter. Eventually the teachers prevailed and most British Constitution 'A' level syllabuses have had a face-lift; a change of title, more detailed and more extensive syllabuses, often with a number of alternative papers to choose from. But what, at that time, could be regarded as a step forward for the teaching of politics in schools, was, when considered from the point of view of political education, a serious set-back.

Bernard Crick, now Professor of Politics at Birkbeck College, University of London, had led the attack on British Constitution in 1969. In an essay advocating teaching about politics in schools he rejected British Constitution as hardly relevant, potentially boring and scarcely Politics.[7] This apparently struck a resonant chord in staff-rooms up and down the country. The cause was taken up and eventually 'British Constitution' was transformed into 'Politics and Government': it became a 'proper' subject with a manifest line of descent from undergraduate politics courses. Syllabuses and option paper headings mirrored undergraduate specialisms. The same books were recommended both for 'A' level and for first year university courses. Student numbers and departmental allowances increased. Career prospects improved. It was no longer sufficient to be able to distinguish a Private bill from a Private Members bill; one had to know the difference between 'demand conversions' and 'output feedback'. The subject matter has certainly changed, but merely by substituting one set of facts for another. Whereas the content may well be more relevant and less boring, it is not necessarily 'Politics'. The irony of the situation is that the examiners were equally victorious inasmuch as they had retained their basic perception of Politics while making the examination papers 'more sophisticated'.

Teachers of politics and government in England are now inclined to be equally sophisticated. They teach their subject specialism almost exclusively to the over-16 age group in sixth form colleges and colleges of further education. Teaching about social and political affairs in the lower school or in non-vocational courses is 'infra dig.' and is commonly left to social studies or liberal studies teachers. The swift elevation of politics teachers to the heady heights enjoyed by economics and sociology teachers seems to have, for the time being, at least, produced a disdain for the non-academic areas of the curriculum. Consequently the advance of political education has probably suffered from the neglect by politics specialists in schools and colleges.

Crick's theme was clear — at least in retrospect. He was advocating politics and criticizing 'constitution'; calling for political education rather than 'Politics and Government'. Any worthwhile education, he wrote, must include some explanation of the naturalness of politics. But the point of departure, the basic premise, is all important. By starting with 'the constitution' it is almost certain that we will head off in the wrong direction entirely and even engender a distaste for the real stuff of politics. Crick suggested British Constitution might be understood as an evasion of politics born out of a nervousness of teaching about what some regard as a slightly improper or a deviant activity. He drew a striking analogy with sex education. Here there is a nervousness about the role of the school and doubts about whether it is desirable or possible to make a distinction between offering prudent advice and laying down moral laws. The usual compromise is to duck the issue altogether and teach in a functional anatomical way as if reproductive organs and activities have an existence apart from real thinking, caring people. And so it is with political education: the hidden curriculum of misrepresenting politics as a relatively stable and agreed set of offices and institutions, and of procedures and conventions is that public disagreement over policies and procedures is portrayed as being a little distasteful.

The analogy with sex education is striking not least because it catches our interest even before the argument is presented. But, like all analogies, it has its limitations. The structural anatomical account of sex is recognized as one among many plausible accounts of a particular activity, the determining characteristics of which are almost universally recognized and accepted. Crick's main point was that 'constitution' *is not really politics at all* and British Constitution teaching is of little value to political education. Political education should be, he asserted:

> something realistic, racy and down-to-earth which focuses on politics as a lively contest between differing ideals and interests — not as a conventional set of stuffed rules . . . it is rarely an advantage for a student to have taken 'British Constitution' at school, often the contrary. And this is not simply . . . because . . . his mind is astonishingly full of irrelevant and picturesque detail about parliamentary procedure and 'constitutional institutions', so that he has none of the inquisitive turbulence about the manifold relationships of ideas to institutions and to circumstances that is surely the essence of a political education.[8]

The shortcomings of British Constitution teaching stem, not from any unique characteristics of British institutions nor from any limitations of British teachers, but from those notions about what constitutes an academically respectable subject discipline upon which it is predicated. The very fact that these notions were the motive force in the transition from 'British Constitution' to 'Politics and Government' has meant that most of today's syllabuses are just as incompatible with political education as their forerunners were. Notions about the nature of an academically respectable subject are more or less universal. Crick's indictment of British Constitution would apply with equal force to any syllabus, in any country, which is based on the prevailing notions of what constitutes good political science. His alternative proposal, political literacy, is as widely applicable and should not be seen as a limited response to local conditions.

Tracing the origins of the term political literacy has become something of a pastime among those associated with its early exposition and if I am mistaken about its genesis, others will justly derive some satisfaction in knowing better.

When a suitable term was being sought by Crick and those engaged on developing political education in Britain[9] Ian Lister, Professor of Education at the University of York, drew our attention to the idea of 'politeracy'. 'Politeracy' had been discussed by Graeme Moodie, Professor of Politics at York, in an address given to the 3rd Annual Conference of the Politics Association in 1972.[10] During the 1960s various writers had employed the phrases 'political literacy' or 'political illiteracy' but without any considered explanation. Moodie was probably the first to give an account of what this might entail.[11] Moodie provided a number of clues to what he had in mind. He carefully distinguished it both from British Constitution, (which he castigated as 'a surrogate for political education and sometimes a surrogate for any kind of education at all') and from 'the new GCE Politics syllabuses'. The approach to teaching 'politeracy' should be orientated towards political problems instead of from assumptions about a subject discipline. The perspectives employed ought to be those of the ordinary citizen rather than those of the rulers, let alone those of the academic political scientists. Moreover, the objectives should involve sensitizing people to the existence and nature of political problems and the means of tackling them wherever they may be found — in schools, colleges, trade unions or businesses. To this end it must provide an understanding of concepts, the ability to argue from and about facts and some inoculation against the spurious and the demagogic use of both facts and concepts. Above all it should have some practical value or application.

Lister's suggestion was readily accepted and so the principal task of the Programme for Political Education was to try to set out in more detail what political literacy should involve. This was, in many respects, a dialectical exercise: Crick, Lister and others offered, in a series of working papers, theories and proposals which were developed, modified or even contradicted by the experiences of teachers in collaborating schools seeking to put the suggestions into practice. Even within the Programme for Political Education there was no one definitive version of political literacy. This was, in part, a consequence of the structure and organization of the project. But it was also a consequence of the general objectives of the exercise. The Programme was, and still is, a series of related projects and curriculum development initiatives. Thus the possibility of divergence and even disagreement was inevitable. Moreover, this diversity was intended: the project accepted that in political education, as in politics, there 'is a range of legitimate differences as to both the objectives and the methods of political education'. These were not merely tolerated but were encouraged and supported. The only provisos were that no approach should be so inflexible as to rule out other approaches, or should actually negate the objectives of political literacy.

The broad foundations to political literacy were laid down in those first working papers.[12] The first point which should be emphasized is the wide scope of the notion of politics which was employed. Examples of 'the political', it was asserted, can be found in the sayings and doings of politicians and political activists, in the teachings of political scientists, and in everyday life — the family, the locality, in educational institutions, clubs, societies and in almost any kind of formal group situation. So the politically literate person would be able to recognize and understand the political dimensions of any human situation. One principal characteristic of all political situations is a differential distribution of 'resources' such as power, status, skills, time, and space. As political disagreements generally arise over conflicts of interests or ideals concerning the distribution of such resources, a basic understanding of politics would involve an appreciation of the main political issues. An issue is defined as a disagreement over policy goals, values, methods and/or results. Such disagreements would arise when members of a group realise that they may be affected by a decision in a way that strikes them as unfair and not inevitable. The issue becomes political when it disrupts cooperative relations between the individuals or the groups concerned and when joint decisions have to be sought if cooperative relations are to be maintained or restored. Clearly this implies that the relationships concerned are not purely voluntary but that some degree of compulsion or commitment or some kinds of sanctions are involved. It also means that politics cannot be confined to the activities of the state but must extend to all areas of life. To propose that, for example, schools and schooling may be understood as political is not necessarily to suggest that *all* their social characteristics are political, nor even that some of their characteristics are *always* political; merely that, by their very nature, school communities sometimes manifest some phenomena which all reasonable people would accept as being essentially political in character.

Political literacy is specific to particular contexts and situations. The knowledge, skills and attitudes appropriate in the context of the state would not necessarily be the same as those in other contexts. Within any given context political literacy requires a basic understanding of the structure of power, how resources are distributed and how the affairs of the institution are normally conducted. Given that there ought to be a general awareness of the nature of political disputes, political literacy will necessitate notions of policy, of policy objectives and an ability to recognize how well policy objectives have been achieved. In the wider context a politically literate person would know what the main political disputes in contemporary politics are, what beliefs the main contestants have of them, and how they are likely to affect him. The knowledge component of political education ought to include an awareness of alternative sources of information. Not only should politically literate people acquire the kinds of knowledge needed which they did not possess but they must also know how to set about informing themselves. Such knowledge would not be confined to customary procedures and systems but would extend to considerations of possible alternative arrangements.

Of special importance is the knowledge of political concepts. A politically literate person would show some consistency and subtlety in the use of basic concepts — those concepts which are minimally necessary to construct simple analytical frameworks. In a personal paper, Crick argued for the following twelve concepts (Figure 1) which, he claimed, reflect the average person's view of political arrangments — relationships between himself and government.

FIGURE 1

Government

| Power | Force | Authority | Order |

Relationships

| Law | Justice | Representation | Pressure |

People

| Natural Rights | Individuality | Freedom | Welfare |

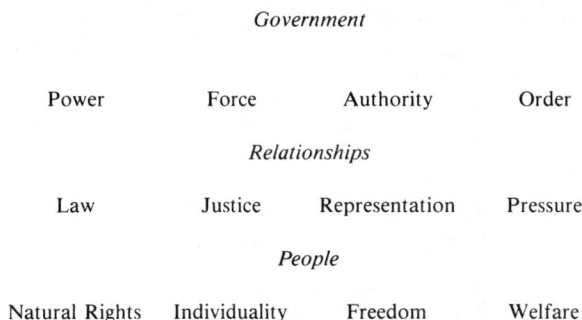

Crick's paper provided comprehensive explanations of the concepts and a rationale for their place in the political literacy scheme. Nevertheless, as a personal contribution it had only the same status as all other contributions from teachers and other individuals involved in the development work. Whilst it proved very useful in many contexts, being essentially a state-politics model it was less appropriate to issues and analyses of 'politics of everyday life'. Moreover, whereas the concepts suggested may well be commonly used in conversation and in media accounts of political issues, they are not all basic or primary in the sense of being fundamental to a simple analysis of political issues. A further paper by Dr Robert Stradling offered an alternative arrangement of concepts (Figure 2). However, political literacy does not require or depend on the adoption of either set of concepts, it merely proposes that some familiarity with political concepts is essential for a political education.

It is absolutely clear that this view of political education asserts that even a wide knowledge of political matters is, by itself, not adequate. Politically literate people would usually, although not necessarily, also be politically active. At least they would have the knowledge, understanding and skills which would be necessary to enable them to operate effectively within a particular context and,

FIGURE 2
A Developmental Approach to Political Thinking

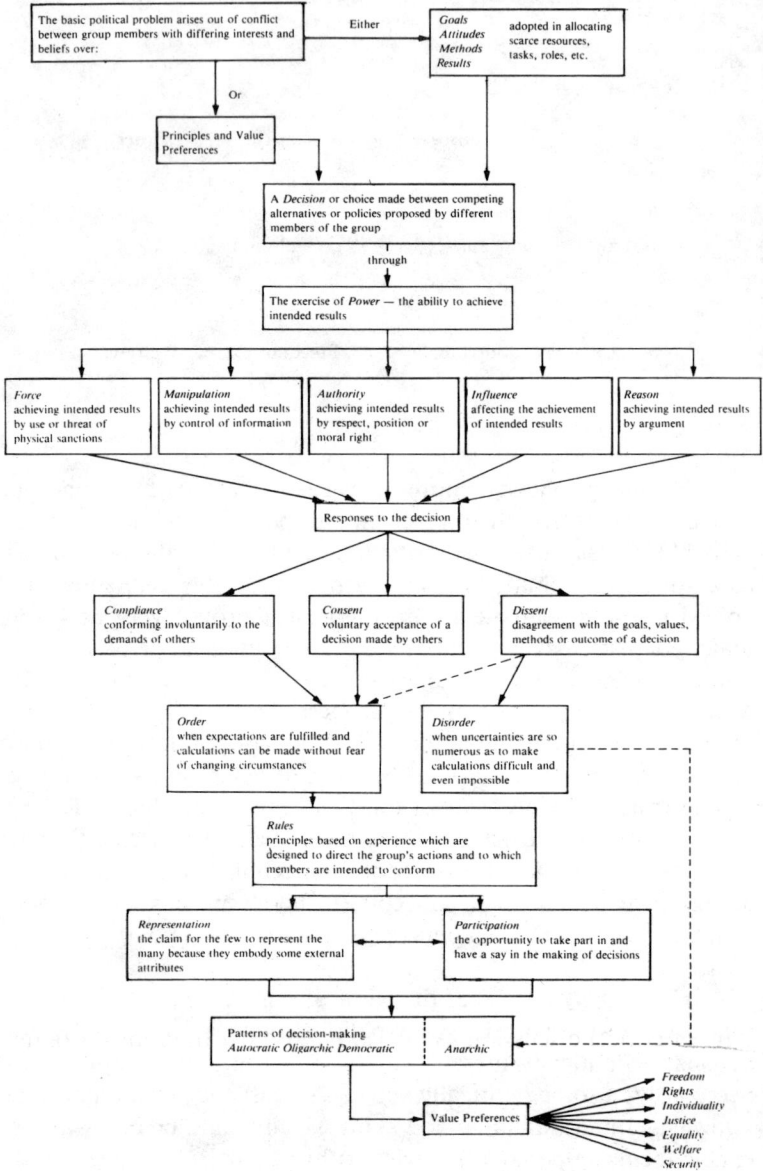

The basic political problem arises out of conflict between group members with differing interests and beliefs over:

Either

Goals
Attitudes
Methods
Results
adopted in allocating scarce resources, tasks, roles, etc.

Or

Principles and Value Preferences

A *Decision* or choice made between competing alternatives or policies proposed by different members of the group

through

The exercise of *Power* — the ability to achieve intended results

Force
achieving intended results by use or threat of physical sanctions

Manipulation
achieving intended results by control of information

Authority
achieving intended results by respect, position or moral right

Influence
affecting the achievement of intended results

Reason
achieving intended results by argument

Responses to the decision

Compliance
conforming involuntarily to the demands of others

Consent
voluntary acceptance of a decision made by others

Dissent
disagreement with the goals, values, methods or outcome of a decision

Order
when expectations are fulfilled and calculations can be made without fear of changing circumstances

Disorder
when uncertainties are so numerous as to make calculations difficult and even impossible

Rules
principles based on experience which are designed to direct the group's actions and to which members are intended to conform

Representation
the claim for the few to represent the many because they embody some external attributes

Participation
the opportunity to take part in and have a say in the making of decisions

Patterns of decision-making
Autocratic Oligarchic Democratic

Anarchic

Value Preferences

Freedom
Rights
Individuality
Justice
Equality
Welfare
Security

as such, the choice between whether to participate or not would be a real choice rather than a theoretical one. Political literacy involves the ability to use one's knowledge, not only in familiar contexts but also in other contexts beyond one's immediate environment. It involves the ability to devise strategies for influence and an awareness of the likely effect of one's actions, especially on others. Action would not be uninformed and unreflective. The politically literate person would be able to give reasoned justifications for his actions, for the ends sought and for any other consequences of his actions. Moreover, he would be able to criticize the relevance and worth of the arguments and evidence mustered by various interests concerned in an issue. Finally the skills of political literacy require some experience of participation and there is a recommendation that opportunities should be provided in schools and colleges for genuine experience by students of their internal decision-making procedures.

Political literacy does not purport to be value-free but rather includes and depends on a particular set of attitudes. Perhaps of foremost importance is the acceptance of the naturalness of political conflict; the politically literate person will see that the very nature of politics lies in there being a plurality of values and interests of which he must have some minimal understanding. Although being generally predisposed to participate this would not be merely enlightened self-interest but would involve respect for the sincerity of others' interests and a willingness to respond to them morally. The underlying attitudes are defined as procedural values for they are intended to provide a guide to one's political behaviour without prescribing one's substantive political beliefs. Five procedural values were offered — freedom, toleration, fairness, respect for truth and respect for reasoning — and, in a second personal paper, Crick outlined a definition of each of these values in the context of political literacy.

Whilst at first sight, these values may be regarded as a summary of the Western liberal-capitalist tradition this was explicitly denied. Indeed the values of Western liberalism should be as much the subject of critical discussion as the values of other traditions. Political literacy should involve an understanding of the plausibility of differing value systems and what, for example, is entailed by different interpretations of concepts like democracy and equality. The critical or sceptical stance of political literacy would not be confined to detached analyses of factual statements or of claims for the superiority of certain procedures and values but should extend even to critical appraisals of this (or any other) scheme for political education.

The specification of political literacy given in the project documents of the Programme for Political Education was really more of a framework for further development than a foundation. This is apparent from Figure 3 which detailed what was minimally involved. Thus it was an approximate guide with inevitable obscurities and ambiguities, and as such it was open to considerable refinement, modification and correction. Consequently, in the course of the development work, teachers and others made numerous contributions which elaborate and specify the concept in a wide range of teaching contexts. It would be quite impossible to summarize all such contributions or to determine which will, in the longer term, turn out to be the more significant. However, for me there are two which stand apart from the rest, these being the further work undertaken by Stradling for the further education sector and a paper by Peter Tomlinson on cognitive development and political literacy.

Stradling directed a project to develop detailed schemes for teaching political literacy to craft apprentices in further education.[13] Such objectives necessitated an account of political literacy which, whilst being more comprehensive and precise, was presented in a manner which was not intimidating but rather would serve as a useful guide to teaching objectives and syllabus construction. Stradling's account, summarized in Figure 4, is in effect a checklist of the basic characteristics of political literacy, presented in such a way as to render the scope of the concept and the possible inter-relationships much clearer than previous accounts. Although Stradling offered some reasoned suggestions of his own, no particular priority or sequence is laid down or implied and, to that extent, this specification is more versatile. The nature of the knowledge, the skills and especially the attitudes and values involved is made more explicit. This is largely because the elucidation of political issues, which was undertaken towards the end of the Programme for Political Education, has been employed here as one of the organizing principles. Thus, for example, there is a stress on group relationships which was not apparent in the first specifications.

FIGURE 3
Perception of Issues

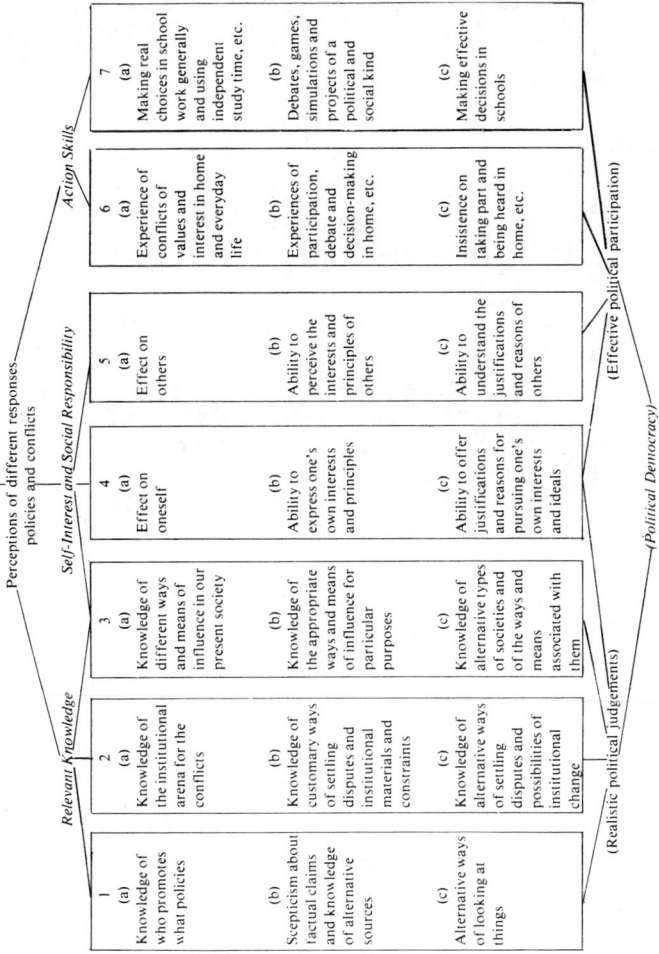

Perceptions of different responses, policies and conflicts

	Relevant Knowledge		Self-Interest and Social Responsibility		Action Skills	
1	**2**	**3**	**4**	**5**	**6**	**7**
(a) Knowledge of who promotes what policies	(a) Knowledge of the institutional arena for the conflicts	(a) Knowledge of different ways and means of influence in our present society	(a) Effect on oneself	(a) Effect on others	(a) Experience of conflicts of values and interest in home and everyday life	(a) Making real choices in school work generally and using independent study time, etc.
(b) Scepticism about factual claims and knowledge of alternative sources	(b) Knowledge of customary ways of settling disputes and institutional materials and constraints	(b) Knowledge of the appropriate ways and means of influence for particular purposes	(b) Ability to express one's own interests and principles	(b) Ability to perceive the interests and principles of others	(b) Experiences of participation, debate and decision-making in home, etc.	(b) Debates, games, simulations and projects of a political and social kind
(c) Alternative ways of looking at things	(c) Knowledge of alternative ways of settling disputes and possibilities of institutional change	(c) Knowledge of alternative types of societies and of the ways and means associated with them	(c) Ability to offer justifications and reasons for pursuing one's own interests and ideals	(c) Ability to understand the justifications and reasons of others	(c) Insistence on taking part and being heard in home, etc.	(c) Making effective decisions in schools

(Realistic political judgements)   (Political Democracy)   (Effective political participation)

FIGURE 4

Knowledge		Skills		Attitudes and Procedural Values

Skills

Propositional Knowledge

Within given political contexts (eg. the state, work place, union, college, school etc.) the politically literate individual should know something about:

1. the structure of power;
2. customary ways of taking decisions and settling disputes;
3. alternative ways and means of taking decisions and settling disputes;
4. where the resources (money, goods, time, space etc.) come from and how they are allocated;
5. alternative ways of allocating resources; and disputes;
6. the main political issues and disputes;
7. who promotes what policies, goals or values, and why.

Practical Knowledge and Understanding

1. Some understanding of the nature of political disputes and issues (whether they are about goals, values, methods or results) and their causes.
2. Some understanding of how these political disputes might affect oneself and the groups to which one belongs.
3. Some understanding of how these disputes affect other people and the groups to which they belong.
4. Knowledge of how to influence the decision-making process in given contexts, including knowledge of alternative means of influence and their relative appropriateness for particular purposes.
5. A developing understanding of basic political concepts (Conflict, Decision-Making, Power, Consent-Dissent, Order-Disorder, and Rules).
6. Knowledge of how to obtain information which one lacks.

Intellectual Skills

1. Ability to interpret and evaluate political information and evidence.
2. Ability to organise information through basic political concepts and generalisations.
3. Ability to apply reasoning skills to political problems and construct sound arguments based on evidence.
4. Ability to perceive the consequences of taking or not taking specific political actions in given contexts.

Action Skills

1. Ability to participate in group decision-making.
2. Ability to effectively influence and/or change political situations.

Communication Skills

1. Ability to express one's own interests, beliefs and viewpoints through an appropriate medium (oral or written).
2. Ability to participate in political discussion and debate.
3. Ability to perceive and understand (if not agree with) the interests, beliefs and views of others.
4. Ability to exercise empathy (i.e. to imagine what it might be like in someone else's shoes).

Attitudes and Procedural Values

1. Willingness to adopt a critical stance toward political information.
2. Willingness to give reasons why one holds a view or acts in a certain way and to expect similar reasons from others.
3. Respect for evidence in forming and holding political opinions.
4. Willingness to be open to the possibility of changing one's own attitudes and values in the light of evidence.
5. Value fairness as a criterion for judging and making decisions (i.e. regardless of whether the outcome will personally benefit or harm oneself).
6. Value the freedom to choose between political alternatives (goals, methods, values, parties or groups).
7. Toleration of a diversity of ideas, beliefs, values and interests.

Tomlinson's contribution was of a quite different order.[14] He set political literacy in the wider context of some psychological and philosophical perspectives on aspects of education. Beginning with the assertion that political education should be seen as an extension of moral education he speculated about a possible relationship between political literacy and the development of moral judgement. The similarity between John Wilson's account of moral education[15] and Crick's procedural values remarked on by Tomlinson is unsurprising as Wilson had presented a paper to one of the planning meetings for the Programme for Political Education. More significantly Tomlinson, in common with various philosophers, saw morals and politics as being essentially linked. This being the case it should be possible to identify relationships between the theories of Piaget, Kohlberg and others and cognitive development in political awareness. As an example Tomlinson cites Kohlberg's claim that there are three aspects involved in any moral judgement; the *mode* of judgement of obligation and value; the *element* or principle involved; the *issue* or institutional area concerned. These three aspects are elaborated as follows:[16]

ASPECTS OF MORAL JUDGEMENT

I The modes of judgement of obligation and value

    A Judgement of right
    B Judgement of having a right
    C Judgement of duty and obligation
    D Judgements of responsibility — conceptions of consequences of action or of the demands or opinions of others one should consider over and above strict duties or strict regard for the rights of others.
    E Judgement of praise or blame.
    F Judgements of punishability and reward
    G Justification and explanation
    H Judgements of nonmoral value or goodness

II The elements of obligation and value

    A Prudence — consequences desirable or undesirable to the self
    B Social welfare — consequences desirable to others
    C Love
    D Respect
    E Justice as liberty
    F Justice as equality
    G Justice as reciprocity and contract

III The issues or institutions

A Social norms
B Personal conscience
C Roles and issues of affection
D Roles and issues of authority and democracy, of division of labour between roles relative to social control (Polity)
E Civil liberties — rights to liberty and equality to persons as human beings, as citizens, or as members of groups
F Justice of actions apart from fixed rights — reciprocity, contract, trust, and equity in the actions or reactions of one person
G Punitive justice
H Life
I Property
J Truth
K Sex

Now if Tomlinson is right and if there is a necessary link between political and moral education, then by applying Kohlberg's or Piaget's work to political education the possibility is opened up of being much more precise about political literacy with respect to both the specification of those attributes which the politically literate person would possess as well as the objectives and the content of teaching programmes.

If the worthwhileness of an enterprise can be judged by the amount of criticism which is levelled at it then the proponents of political literacy can feel encouraged — but only a little. The published criticisms may be broadly classified into three types, only one of which is directly concerned with the concept of political literacy itself.

A small number of people appear to be simply opposed to political education in general and to any curriculum development exercise in this area whatever its recommendations might be. Although the hostility has been expressed only in brief letters or reviews the authors either take the view that political education is not needed or that it would be politically too risky. However, this neat division conceals considerable divergences of view. Some argue that it is not necessary to develop political education because it is already sufficiently well provided for, whereas others merely claim that it is not a worthwhile aim of education. Similarly there are on the one hand those who fear the prospect of generating discourteous or even rebellious activism, while on the other hand there are those who are alarmed at the possibility of creating servile and deferential apathy. Few of these critics trouble to consider the idea of political literacy and for that reason further discussion of their views is not merited in the present context.

Although other criticisms include some sympathy with the aims of political education, they express misgivings about either the specification of political literacy or the manner in which the curriculum development exercise was undertaken. Criticisms of project procedures, like those of political education in general, do not warrant detailed attention in the context of this account. However, a brief resumé will provide a useful preface to a review of the major criticisms of political literacy.

In an important article published early in the life of the Programme for Political Education, Pat and John White made a substantial number of criticisms offered as a constructive contribution to the project planning.[17] In their opinion the intentions of the project, as a theoretical and practical curriculum development exercise, had not been sufficiently well thought out in advance. They were especially doubtful that such development could proceed on the assumption of there being a general consensus on the aims of political education. The counter-claim that it was 'agreement' rather than 'consensus' which was being sought or assumed cannot adequately answer their criticism for it appears, rather naively, to overlook the obvious — that without some assumed agreement the project could not have proceeded at all.[18] More convincingly the Whites argued that to limit the exercise to secondary schools and further education colleges was illogical and possibly even counter-productive. In their view, political education should start in the primary schools and be available to all children as part of a common curriculum. Undoubtedly limited resources and, in particular, the procedures for obtaining support and funding had a significant effect on the organization of the project. And whereas this must be more or less so for all curriculum development projects, in the case of political education the need for caution, compromise and containment may well have transcended all other influences in the crucial formative stages.

The main criticisms of political literacy were directed at the concept of politics which it entails: for some the scope was too wide and for others it was too narrow. On both sides there were those who simply meant it was unacceptable and whose indictment of the extended/restricted scope of politics was really an indictment of any form of political education.

Kenneth Minogue, in a doctrinaire broadside on the aims of political education — 'Can One Teach Political Literacy?'[19] — made no more than two direct references to the concept. He asserts that:

> most people regard politics as a spectator sport, in which the main actors are office-holders or those actively bidding for office. This Report, however, is keen to foster the illusion . . . that politics is fundamentally participant — cheering and booing are actually taken as politics itself. Now while it is true that no one is necessarily excluded from politics, it is also true that most people will never really take part in politics.

Here he either implies an insistence on politics being confined to the state arena or, alternatively, he reveals a complete misreading of political literacy. The latter is certainly a possibility for he also wrote: 'The Report [of the Programme for Political Education] is by a variety of hands, but expresses a single coherent point of view.' Now if there is one point over which we are all agreed, authors and critics alike, it is the very antithesis of the foregoing observation.

The Whites were concerned that the conception of politics may be too limited. Commenting on the twelve basic concepts suggested by Crick they observed that not all political relationships are between 'ruler' and 'ruled'. Geoff Berridge also took up this point in a more generalized attack on Crick's influence on politics teaching and examination syllabuses.[20] Both articles rightly argue that for many people politics includes relationships between sovereign states as well as conflicts between or within many other groups and societies. However, they both inexplicably overlook the broad understanding of politics on which the basic specification of political literacy is founded — the assertion that politics is to do with all the causes, circumstances, outcomes — indeed all aspects — of conflicts over the allocation of resources (also broadly understood) in *any* social situation. Such a concept of politics which may be applied to a wide diversity of human relationships must be qualitatively different from one which is defined as being necessarily limited to the state arena. The basic grounds for disagreement therefore must be over whether this broad specification can be regarded as 'politics' — a debate which can be located within the long tradition of political discourse. Unfortunately they also overlook the fact that in a programme of political literacy this particular understanding of politics would be set alongside various alternative views and would be as much the subject of critical consideration as the substance of politics itself. However, if they were merely remarking that Crick's suggested set of concepts are more appropriate to a traditional view of politics which centres on the state this, as I have previously observed, had already been acknowledged and an alternative set — Stradling's issues-based scheme — had been included.

Sir Keith Joseph expressed reservations about the conception of politics for different reasons.[21] There appeared to him to be an assumption that governments are the main source of well-being in a society and this leads to the further assumption that political issues may be symptomatic of a shortfall between public needs and government performance. Joseph suggested that these assumptions ought to be reconsidered and alternative values introduced which stress the economic basis of most political problems:

> Issues before institutions . . . yes; but perhaps before issues come the ingredients of issues; cause and effect; relationships; political economy as a base for political literacy.

Issues, he argued, tend to be presented by the media, often vividly but superficially and sensationally, focussing on the symptoms rather than seeking to penetrate the inwardness of an issue. If political literacy is to avoid such superficiality it ought to go beyond mere symptoms. Clearly Joseph was not challenging the potential of political literacy, only the rather restricted emphasis which was apparent at that time. The scope has since been widened. Joseph identified the need for consideration of decision-making procedures and this omission was remedied accordingly. But there is obviously a limit. The Whites and Joseph had suggested economic concepts should be added. The same kind of reasoning which they employed would identify a range of concepts so vast as to invalidate any grounds for making a distinction between the objectives and content of political education and the rest of education. One has to stop somewhere, and to draw the line at basic political concepts is an obvious expedient.

One other criticism of the original political literacy papers was also effective in bringing about an amendment to the specification. The Whites drew attention to the emphasis on the individual. The aims of political literacy appeared to be the benefit of the individual and possibly the improvement of government. What about, they asked, the common good of society as distinct from the good of each individual? The omission was never intended and clear reference to groups as well as individuals has since been made in Stradling's work for 'Political Literacy in Further Education'.[22]

Political literacy has also been criticized for its lack of precision. Whilst I am content to accept this view, it has often been expressed in company with other comments which reveal an ignorance of some fairly definitive aspects of political literacy. Ted Tapper and Brian Salter, in their somewhat premature obituary to the political education movement, referred to political literacy as 'the catch-all phrase used to describe the individual characteristics which hopefully will be acquired through the formal teaching of politics.'[23] Whether or not the expression 'catch-all phrase' was intended to be derogatory matters little for it is a fairly astute summary of the project's philosophy, strategy and objectives. This stands in stark contrast alongside their assertion that political literacy 'will be acquired through the formal teaching of politics'. Minogue made the same blunder. Drawing an analogy with religious education, he remarked:

> exactly the same sort of misguided attempt to turn it into an academic subject, such as we find in the present Report [of the Programme for Political Education] is now turning [religious education] into comparative religion.

Incredibly, John Hipkin, in a review of the report wrote:

> . . . groups who tied in the teaching of politics with public examinations fared better than those who followed project policy and eschewed them . . . success seems to require that politics become a subject in its own right and take its place in an established curriculum of cognate subjects . . .[24]

The only possible explanation for such observations which purport to cite conclusions which are diametrically opposed to those actually appearing in the project report would imply a less than conscientious reading of the report. Certainly Geoff Whitty had a valid point when he identified ambiguities in the report of the Programme for Political Education and claimed that most of the work on political literacy 'has been at a very high level of abstraction'.[25] However, the only confusion on the question of political literacy requiring the formal teaching of politics as an academic subject tied to public examinations is in the minds of Minogue, Tapper and Hipkin.

Chris Brown was the first to draw attention to a characteristic of political literacy which probably ever will remain an intractable problem.[26] The problem may have been avoided if political education had indeed sought the status of an academic examination subject with a publicly accredited body of factual knowledge — had indeed been content to remain a sophisticated version of British Constitution. However, the stress on the importance of skills and attitudes and the characterization of political literacy as a 'disposition' rather than an encyclopaedic familiarity with political facts was likely to generate controversy –- and it did.

Brown claimed that the political literacy objectives amounted to no more than training children to be conforming and uncritical members of society. His argument rested on the evidence of three features of political literacy — a proposed sequence for treatment in the classroom, the intention that political literacy would lead to a 'proclivity to action', and the set of five procedural values. In an early project paper it had been tentatively suggested that teaching could start with 'knowing how our present system works', then proceed to the 'attitudes and skills necessary for an active citizenship' and only finally reach a 'consideration of possible changes of direction or of alternative values and systems'. Had this proposal remained in the final recommendations of the report a charge of seeking to train conformists might well have been justified. Not only was the suggestion deleted but an explicit retraction was included, a point which I shall later develop.

Participation is quite another matter. Brown claimed that 'participation implies acceptance'. That is one possible understanding of participation and the 'proclivity to action' associated with political literacy, but it is by no means the only interpretation. Minogue certainly did not consider that participation implied acceptance, rather he feared that it may lead to mass discontent and 'the production of demonstration fodder':

There is the occasional disclaimer: though the politically literate are allowed the bracketed alternative of 'positive refusal to participate', they would have a hard time beating the apathy rap. But the Report finds a great variety of ways of encouraging the sort of ill-considered reforming activism which has been the curse of Britain over the last quarter of a century. Political literacy appears as a struggle against strong tendencies towards passive 'quietism' in Britain today.

Both Brown and Minogue, together with Tapper, have made the mistake of muddling the aims of political literacy with their own worst fears about the consequences of political education.

Discussion of the procedural values of political literacy is often characterized by the same kind of conceptual shift from analyzing aims to expressing fears. Tapper and Salter made their shift of attention explicit:

Unlike most of the social scientists working in the field of political socialisation, [the advocates of political literacy] have been interested in actually changing what goes on in the classroom, and to have been seen as working for the shoring up of the present society would have been a disastrous image. In spite of this conscious attempt to present another image, certain doubts remain as to the true intentions of those who are advocating political education.

Whitty summed up their fears succinctly thus:

There is some evidence then, that certain aspects of the political education movement are, either in intent or likely outcome, not too far removed from explicit political indoctrination into an uncritical acceptance for the status quo.

I propose to consider the main thrust of this allegation later. At this point it is sufficient to note that part of Whitty's evidence were the procedural values of freedom, fairness, toleration, respect for truth and respect for reasoning. He quoted an opinion that political literacy is an 'indirect indoctrination into the values underlying our form of democracy'. He can draw no comfort from the support which Minogue gave to this view:

. . . there is very little else [political education] can be (apart from ideological indoctrination) except an assertation of what is here called 'the values of Western European liberalism'. . . . [The procedural values] are in many respects admirable. . . . But there is no doubt that this version of them is unmistakably a rather bald summary of what a liberally minded Briton has taken away from his reading of his history.

Unfortunately Minogue's claim became less convincing when, in the same context, he shifted his attention and expressed somewhat different fears to those of Brown, Tapper and Whitty:

> Given that we live in a dangerous world full of power-hungry exponents of ideological truth whose aim it is to do away with degenerate bourgeois shams like parliaments and a free press, the politically literate man begins to reek of Kerensky and the Weimar Republic.

One answer to these criticisms might point out that their various conclusions stem from an erroneous assumption that the five values of political literacy are substantive political values. I find it difficult to present that answer with any real conviction. Crick may wish to draw a distinction between substantive and procedural values and such a distinction may be possible in theoretical terms, but at the level of classroom practice it has so far proved difficult to distinguish them. For the time being I prefer the clearer statement of attitudes presented by Stradling (Figure 4). The expedient is that they are presented more as methodological or behavioural objectives for the analysis of political issues. However, this presentation does not adequately meet the charge of indoctrination into Western liberal values. My own interpretation of political literacy can carry no more authority than those of any others among its proponents. But as one who has had the opportunity to observe it in practice in school and college classrooms I may be in a better position than most of the critics to offer an account of its essential characteristics.

It will be no easy task to unravel those aspects of political literacy which have generated fears both of quietism and of hyperactivism. It may be best to start by quoting those objectives which are expressed in fairly explicitly political terms — paradoxically, those upon which the charge of 'education for domestication' have been principally based:

a. The purely and properly conserving level of knowing how our present system works, and knowing the beliefs that are thought to be part of it.

b. The liberal or participatory level of development of the knowledge, attitudes and skills necessary for an active citizenship.

c. Beyond both of these there lies the more contentious areas of considering possible changes of direction of government or of alternative systems.

As I mentioned earlier, the explicit suggestion that these should be prescribed stages for the classroom presentation of issues and the implicit notion that there is some kind of hierarchical or temporal relationship between these three objectives were denied in the Report of the Programme for Political Education.[27] Stripped of all references to grade or order and presented as a summary of political literacy, these three objectives are, in my view, best understood as three modes of awareness or types of understanding which, when taken together, are the essential ingredients of a political education. When expressed in this way there is a useful correspondence between these aspects of political literacy and the types of understanding discussed by philosophers of knowledge.

Gilbert Ryle made the important distinction between 'knowing *that*' and 'knowing *how*'.[28] Knowing 'that' is propositional knowledge; knowing that, for example, proposals to enable council tenants to purchase their houses is Conservative party policy or that proposals for further state ownership of sectors of the economy is Labour party policy. Ryle asserted knowing 'that' must involve more than the ability 'to parrot an answer' or more than mere strong belief. It needs, on the one hand, a correct understanding of the concepts involved and, on the other hand, that the proposition in question be a true statement about the world regardless of whether or not it is claimed to be true. But knowing 'that' must be more than true belief: it also requires good grounds to substantiate that belief.

Knowing 'how' is procedural knowledge; knowing how to look up the decision of local government bodies or knowing how to harness the services of a Trading Standards Officer. Knowing 'how' involves more than being able to recite the correct procedures; it requires success in the performance of such procedures. There is a crucial difference between that person who is merely lucky or just performs correctly by habit and one who knows 'how'. The latter would be able not only to repeat successful performance but also to improve upon it, adapt it to varying circumstances and have sufficient insight to counsel others on their performance.

Knowing about the institutions and procedures of any political arrangement is the propositional knowledge involved in knowing 'that'. The knowledge, attitudes and skills 'necessary' for participation need be no more than procedural knowledge. If political literacy was confined to propositional and procedural knowledge alone then the charge that it is indoctrination into the status quo would be well deserved. Richard Pring has identified a further type of awareness, essential to a complete social education, which illuminates the third objective of political literacy. Pring claimed that

> . . . extending the know-how is not enough. To reflect upon, to look critically at, to make explicit the hidden assumptions beneath the know-how . . . is the beginning of disciplined thinking, of systematic thinking, indeed of theory.[29]

It is possible to know 'that' and to know 'how', in the fullest sense intended by Ryle, without being able to theorize about one's knowledge or performance. In the specific context of political education this condition would indeed amount to a thorough socialization into the norms and values of the prevailing political order. But political literacy requires a further mode of awareness which, however inadequately expressed, is quite explicitly intended to meet accusations of indoctrination. Pring has well described this as the activity of 'wondering whether' about propositional knowledge and 'wondering how' about procedural knowledge; of, for example, doubting given assumptions, questioning evidence and considering alternative explanations — in short, a critical awareness.

For the purposes of political education, a more comprehensive account of this third type of understanding may be found in Paulo Freire's notion of '*conciêntizac̃ao*' (conscientisation):

> *Conciêntizac̃ao* is a permanent critical approach to reality in order to discover it and discover the myths that decive us and help to maintain the oppressing dehumanising structures.[30]

The essential link between the notion of conscientization and political understanding is evidenced by Karl Mannheim, who claimed:

> Political discussion is more than theoretical argument . . . it is the tearing off of disguises, the unmasking of those unconscious motives which bind the group existence to its cultural aspirations and its theoretical arguments.[31]

Just as conscientization is one of Freire's conditions for literacy so a critical awareness or consciousness, is a necessary condition of political literacy — the essential third leg without which the stool could not possibly stand up. Literacy for Freire requires more than the knowledge of and ability to decode linguistic symbols. It involves, like political literacy, that further mode of awareness whereby a person is able to reflect critically on and take effective action in the world.

At this juncture it should be stressed that the world does not begin outside the school gates. Students' critical faculties should be brought to bear not only on school affairs in general but on the very programmes of political education which seek to promote those faculties. Even where, unwittingly or otherwise, the values of any political system are being offered as models of perfection, a political education conducted according to the precepts of political literacy should inoculate students against an uncritical acceptance of those or any other values.

Bernard Crick, in public lectures, has cautioned audiences against mistaking the 'critical' objectives of political literacy for 'radical' objectives. Radical would normally be understood as an ideological position which seeks not only a reform of existing structures and values but probably also involves a preference for one particular set of alternative arrangements. A critical perspective, on the other hand, would merely assess existing arrangements and evaluate them alongside alternatives without any prior judgement or preferences. This is undoubtedly the case if we limit our considerations to the broad educational objectives of a political education programme. However, there is no doubt that political literacy is a radical proposal for it certainly seeks changes in the present curriculum in most schools and colleges and implies a preference for alternative arrangements which many consider to be extreme. So in the context of schooling at least, political literacy clearly involves an ideological position. Moreover, this is not confined to the politics of curriculum reform but extends to the pedagogy of political literacy.

I have been at pains to stress that political literacy is not a subject and that as much emphasis is given to procedural knowledge and critical awareness as to propositional knowledge. Furthermore the propositional knowledge involved could not be a fixed set of facts which could form a nationally agreed syllabus. The propositional knowledge would have to be selected and reselected both from, and to relate to, contemporary events and classroom needs. Knowledge derived from teachers, books and the mass media would not have any more status than the knowledge which students themselves bring into the classroom. Political literacy, unlike many other areas of the curriculum, does not presuppose or depend on a view of students as necessarily being deficient in worthwhile knowledge. It recognizes the individual and collective dignity and basic right of students to express political views on matters that directly concern them. It is clear that effective political education lessons are unlikely to be confined to authoritative expositions from the teacher. How effective lessons would be conducted is less clear.

Some investigation of the teaching of political literacy was undertaken by the Programme for Political Education from which a few fairly predictable generalized conclusions were drawn. There is little in the report that would provide sufficient practical guidance to any teacher setting about devising appropriate courses and resources who does not have easy access to some other form of support such as the experience of other teachers or local authority advisory staff. Undoubtedly the future development of political education in Britain now depends on the extent to which help and support is given by local and central agencies to those many teachers who are most anxious to devise teaching schemes which adapt the political literacy approach to their individual circumstances.

How to identify effective teaching is the most intractable problem of all. It is certain that measurements of outcomes will not do. The ability of students to recall facts is hardly relevant and could not be regarded as a reliable index of other achievements. Even if suitable measurements of behavioural and affective achievements could be found, negative findings from tests in schools would not preclude the possibility of competence in real situations later in life. Beyond this is the impossibility of linking 'success' or 'failure' in the political sphere to the experience of a particular course in political education. Whether or not any educational objective which cannot be adequately assessed can nevertheless be regarded as worthwhile is a much wider issue than that involving political education. It is likely that proponents of political education will side with Lawrence Stenhouse[32] and those others who stress the primacy of the process of education over the product. In which case the valuation of an 'effective' programme of political education would be more concerned to compare the expressed objectives with the actual content of lessons and the pedagogy employed. It would be absurd to claim that political literacy provides a complete guide for such a valuation: the gaps and the temporary infilling are quite apparent. Nevertheless I remain confident that Crick's guidelines embody principles which are applicable not only in the context of the British tradition of parochial constitutionalism but probably in all other contexts regardless of culture and tradition.

NOTES

1. Ted Tapper and Brian Salter, *Education and the Political Order*, London: Macmillan, 1978, p. 85.
2. 'A' level: a public examination for 18 year old students administered by the universities.
3. The Politics Association is a British professional association of teachers of politics.
4. F. W. G. Benemy, 'Some Thoughts on Teaching British Constitution', *Newsletter of the Politics Association*, No. 2, 1970, p. 34.
5. F. W. G. Benemy, 'British Constitution Out! Government and Politics In!', *Newsletter of the Politics Association*, No. 3, 1970, p. 47.
6. M. de la Cour, 'British Constitution — 'A' Level', *Newsletter of the Politics Association*, No. 6, 1971, p. 29.
7. Bernard Crick, 'The Introducing of Politics' in D. B. Heater (ed.), *The Teaching of Politics*, London: Methuen, 1969.
8. Ibid., 2.
9. A special conference was arranged by Professor Crick in 1973 to prepare proposals for research and development in political education which led to the Programme for Political Education. See also Robert Stradling's 'Political Education: Developments in Britain', chapter 3 of this volume.
10. Graeme C. Moodie, 'Some Problems of Political Education', *Teaching Politics* 2 (2), 1973, p. 10.
11. The earliest use of the expression 'political literacy' which I can trace is by Harold Entwistle in his M. Ed. thesis 'A Concept of Democracy and its Implications for Education' (University of Manchester, 1958, p. 180). However, Entwistle seems to use the term 'literacy' as a shorthand summary of his support for the comparison which Oakeshott made between political education and the process of learning a language.

12. The project discussion papers are reproduced in section 2 of Bernard Crick and Alex Porter (eds.), *Political Education and Political Literacy* (London: Longman, 1978) which should be consulted for a more detailed account of political literacy.

13. 'Political Literacy in Further Education' funded by the Anglo-German Foundation for Industrial Society. See also chapter 3 of this volume.

14. Peter Tomlinson, 'Political Education: Cognitive Development Perspectives from Moral Education', *Oxford Review of Education* 1, 1975, p. 241.

15. J. B. Wilson, 'The Study of Moral Development' in K. G. Collier, J. B. Wilson and P. D. Tomlinson (eds.), *Values and Moral Development in Higher Education*, London: Croom Helm, 1974.

16. A useful summary of Kohlberg's theories may be found in Thomas Lickona (ed.), *Moral Development and Behaviour*, New York: Holt Rinehart and Winston, 1976.

17. Pat and John White, 'A Programme for Political Education: A Critique', *Teaching Politics* 5, 1976, p. 257.

18. My comments on these criticisms of the project are taken from or based on Bernard Crick, 'A Reply to a Critique of the Programme', *Teaching Politics* 6, 1977, p. 115.

19. Kenneth Minogue, 'Can One Teach Political Literacy?', *Encounter*, June 1979, p. 25.

20. Geoff Berridge, 'Crick and the Curriculum', *Teaching Politics* 7, 1978, p. 1; and 'The Concept of Politics Re-Visted', *Teaching Politics* 9, 1980, p. 72.

21. Sir Keith Joseph, 'Education, Politics and Society', *Teaching Politics* 5, 1976, p. 1.

22. See note 13.

23. Tapper and Salter, op. cit., p. 72.

24. John Hipkin in *Journal of Curriculum Studies* 11, 1979, p. 186.

25. Geoff Whitty, 'Political Education in Schools', *Socialism and Education* 5, (5), 1978. A revised version of the article is published as 'Political Education: Some Reservations', *The Social Science Teacher* 8, 1979, p.112.

26. Chris Brown, 'Contexts for Political Education: Social Studies' in Tom Brennan and Jonathan F. Brown, *Teaching Politics: Problems and Perspectives*, London: BBC Publications, 1975, p. 69.

27. Crick and Porter, op. cit., p. 12.

28. Gilbert Ryle, *The Concept of Mind*, London: Hutchinson, 1949, chapter 2.

29. Richard Pring, *Knowledge and Schooling*, London: Open Books, 1976, p. 122.

30. Paulo Freire, 'A Few Notions about the Word Conscientization', *Hard Cheese* 1, 1971, p. 23.

31. Karl Mannheim, *Ideology and Utopia*, London: Routledge and Kegan Paul, 1936, p. 35.

32. L. Stenhouse, 'The Humanities Curriculum Project', *Journal of Curriculum Studies* 1, 1968.

8

Politicians and Political Education: A View from the British Labour Party

Austin Mitchell

We're all political educators now. Political education has almost assumed the status of pre-marital chastity: praised in inverse ratio to its practice. Politicians have become as enthusiastic about a wider appreciation of their art form as their fellow toilers at the people-face, artists, writers and musicians. In Britain the 'Genus Laboriense' wants a spread of enlightenment, involvement and independent thinking. This may not be unconnected with the prospect that a better informed electorate is more likely to vote Labour. Tories tend to see political education as a blend of civics and Boy Scout responsibility, inculcating those virtues of obedience and duty so much admired by Conservatives and so necessary under their governments. Democrats want provision of a life-skill and a preparation for effective democracy. Yet sadly, now that support for the once daring idea of political education is so much an orthodoxy that only backwoodsmen, like the present British Parliamentary Under-Secretary for Education, a well-known political Don Quixote, formally challenge it, and so commonplace that many assume it is universal already, I feel, as a long-standing enthusiast, a growing sense of doubt.

This springs not from doubts about a principle so obviously right that the argument is not worth restating. It concerns the product and the scale of the effort. Both seem inadequate in the face of problems likely to become increasingly pressing. Much of what is currently offered in the way of political education is as relevant as books on anorexia nervosa in a famine. The scale of the effort, given the strains likely to emerge in our democracy through the uncertain eighties, is pathetic; like coping with a forest fire by squirting the young shoots from the fountain pens of a posse of amateur fire-fighters. Even then we are finding difficulty in agreeing who is to hold the pens, how many squirts are necessary and of what mixture.

Democracy asks people to make periodic judgements on a complex series of issues simplified to a party choice. It expects involvement, intermittent or continuous. It posits a government responsible to the people and acting on their behalf. Yet the people themselves exhibit a great deal of ignorance about government and its arts. In my previous incarnation as a specialist in the television branch of the extruded plastics industry I readily used the tools of the trade: that kit of concepts and alphabetical definitions which are the shorthand of punditry. Transferring the same toolkit to politics I found it as relevant as spouting second-century Aramaic on the doorstep. Electors, preoccupied with different realities, express them in different language. When I found people saying they would vote for me if I could get devolution down to one percent, thinking EEC meant Eastern Electricity Council, or asking why I was standing for Parliament when they had a perfectly good MP in the deceased Anthony Crosland, I began to re-assess.

The process was hastened by a review of the poll material in electoral ignorance. Pundits have expressed dismay at the findings of the Hansard Society's study of the political information of school leavers and at such gems as the fact that a quarter of those surveyed thought that Conservatives stood for more nationalization. Yet elders are not really betters. One National Opinion Poll survey showed that at the time when Parliament was legislating for European elections only 55 percent of the electors had heard of the European Parliament and 49 percent of the Commission. Only a third of those who had heard of the institutions knew that there were plans for elections. Asked to identify various of the alphabet organizations that shape our lives, 61 percent had never heard of the National Enterprise Board, 42 percent of the Equal Opportunities Commission and 33 percent of the Office of Fair Trading, an average identification of 36 percent for six organizations.

Absence makes the heart even less fond: 33 percent knew what NATO is, 16 percent SALT and 44 percent recognized Britain's government in exile, the IMF.[1] In May 1975 seven out of ten had heard of the government's 'Social Contract' with the unions, yet only 27 percent had any definite idea of what it was about. Even television has not turned household names into household faces: asked to identify from photographs, 51 percent recognized Tony Benn, 21 percent Sir Keith Joseph and 13 percent Sir Geoffrey Howe. Foreigners fare better, 22 percent recognized Giscard D'Estaing, 28 percent Helmut Schmidt and 48 percent the current hate symbol, Ayotollah Khomeini, though he may be less well known than that slightly lower tollah, the Mahdi, who had much the same standing in nineteenth-century Britain's esteem.

MPs, who are all convinced that they are not only known to, but possibly even know every one of their constituents, are occasionally shocked to find that in constituency studies the proportion knowing their MP is rarely over half. Indeed the 1972 Granada TV survey of public attitudes to Parliament found that three quarters confessed to knowing nothing or not very much about the institution and only 22 percent got as near as six hundred and something when asked the number of MPs. Insofar as they understood Parliament at all, their constitutional assumptions, such as the belief that Parliament appointed the cabinet and decided the election date, were generations out of date. The real role of Parliament had not percolated through which isn't surprising because most journalists don't understand it either.

Examples could be multiplied indefinitely. The basic fact is that there is a widespread public ignorance about politics, politicians and parties and even more about institutions and procedures. Any MP can contribute numerous examples (unfortunately always anecdotal and never quantified) of failures by constituents to understand what's going on in Parliament, how the machinery of government works, how to enforce rights, which department, or authority, or council, to approach on what issues. The public have not been educated to cope with an increasingly complex and sophisticated machine. We are sadly short of international comparisons. Those available indicate that we may be a more ignorant community than comparable industrial societies. Compared with such countries Britain might well feature as low on a political information scale as it does on the league tables for education, growth or

GNP per head. These similar placings may not be accidental. The optimist will answer that things are getting better. They are. The electorate is becoming better informed in the sense that it is more likely to recognize issues, party policies and politicians. In an expanding universe of facts it has more facts at its disposal. More people are staying at school for longer. Television has brought politics, and so many other subjects, to far wider audiences than were ever available before. Gladstone would have had to mount twenty Midlothian campaigns to get the audience delivered by five minutes on the television programme *Nationwide*. And *Nationwide* delivers a cheque too. Yet it is questionable whether the information increase is proportionate to the increase in scale and complexity of either the machinery or the problems. In any case, the information is collected like trivia and ephemera in an attic; plucked here and there at random, rarely organized into any coherent pattern or fitted into a framework of ideology or attitudes to make sense of them. Trivia, gossip, opinion and facts are fired without discrimination every night into millions of minds. Most pass straight through without trace or residue. Some remain not as a distillation but as a confused jumble of ill assorted, unrelated information, organized, if at all, mainly for negative purposes.

A little knowledge is a dangerous thing. Most electors in our half-educated democracy have enough at their disposal to take up the negative, more vociferous positions, but not enough to provide a scaffolding for the positive. This weakness is heightened by media emphasis. By a Gresham's law of coverage, news, trivia and events drive out explanation. The media can instantly highlight Jim Callaghan's attitude to Tony Benn; Margaret Thatcher's attitude to her minions or what wives and other victims think about strikers. When it comes to explanation, they mutter. The press does not want to explain. Television, because of the nature of a medium which gets fewer words in a half-hour bulletin than in a few columns of *The Guardian*, can't. To explain is to take a point of view and this isn't allowed so TV finds it easier to follow the cues and leads of the press rather like the Chinese followed the Antipodean Gold Rushes. So the mind of the electorate is focused on the trivial and the superficial, never the basic or the vital.

How important are ignorance and incomprehension? Political purists proclaim their shock and horror at manifestations of popular ignorance, a label usually applied to anything which sets back their own prospects. Yet the system continues to function. Indeed strenuous efforts have been made to turn apparent defects into benefits. Electors emerged from the first voting surveys as creatures of habit, conditioned by their background with elections decided by the differential abstentions and the fluctuating allegiances of the 'floating voters'. Rather than seriously weighing up the issues these 'floaters' proved less informed and less involved, they drifted rather than decided. Purists were provoked by these pioneer poll findings and the low levels of interest and information they revealed. For most people they probably had the same impact as other sociological research: putting what they already knew in language they did not quite understand. What they did undermine was not so much the credibility of the electorate but of the parties' picture of the way it worked: a rational decision between two fully considered cases which conferred a mandate on the winning party to carry through its programme.

Those who preferred their political science factual accepted not only that the picture drawn by the surveys was realistic, but that the situation it revealed may even have had certain advantages. Electoral armies may have been immobile. Yet the first-past-the-post electoral system was a machinery finely attuned to detecting small shifts of opinion and amplifying them to large readings on the seismographic scale of seat changes. Less rooted allegiances, a higher proportion of 'floaters', would mean a more mercurial, less predictable system. Greater participation and stronger enthusiasm may even be dangerous. Massive turnouts and frenzied participation had in the past often been symptoms of a system under strain rather than desirable civic virtues. The rooted allegiances themselves could be justified as having a certain economic rationality. Anthony Downs and others saw in these allegiances a rational assessment of the elector's own economic self-interest.[2] It could even be argued that, given the unimportance of one single vote, and the complexity of the calculus, those who put themselves on this automatic pilot were perhaps behaving more rationally than anyone energetic enough to feed party permutations and his own predilections into a personal computer to work out how he should vote.

Ignorance and immobility, while not exactly canonized, thus became more acceptable. This assessment chimed in with the mood of the times in the decades of affluence. Economic growth was providing a steady improvement in the standard of living and full employment. These in turn guaranteed satisfaction with the system. The British felt a strong pride in their system of government which was probably based on nothing more than insularity and abstract jingoism. Yet the system was really accepted and stable while it delivered. As long as it did so neither mass participation nor a high degree of political literacy were indispensable.

Since then the age of affluence has merged into the age of uncertainty in a transition so imperceptible that to set a date would be impossible. The underlying levels of apathy and ignorance remain much the same. Yet their repercussions in the new situation will increasingly emerge as very different. The easy acceptance of the system itself has been undermined. With the end of full employment and growth the system has ceased to deliver. Characteristics which in a growth situation may be benign then become liabilities.

The reasons for the economic failure are straightforward. All advanced countries face pressing economic difficulties generated by the increases in the price of oil and massive transfer of purchasing power from the advanced world to OPEC. The result has been a harder, more competitive world trading situation compounding greater difficulties of internal economic management. In Britain this situation has been much worse. Our own internal difficulties, the long failure to invest and grow at the same rate as competing economies, have left the British economy increasingly uncompetitive and subject to an accelerating process of deindustrialization. Prolonged comparative decline becomes absolute. The argument on when that point is reached is long and complex but it is certainly clear that Britain faces the world's difficulties in more acute degree. These trends emerged in the seventies. We survived them then with no overwhelming difficulty except that Britain became a much less pleasant place to be. They will be considerably strengthened in the eighties.

The political consequences, uniformly depressing, will get worse. A pattern of instability has already emerged. Governments have come in, grappled with the difficulties, failed either to solve them or to deliver and then been thrown out by a dissatisfied electorate. With five governments in the sixties and seventies Britain has had far less stability than the lesser breeds without the Westminster model in France, Germany, Japan or the USA. She has become far more mercurial. Steadily shortening honeymoons for each successive government are followed by a collapse in popularity in the polls, heavy by-election losses, and decimation in local government. Government ploughs on palsied by the fact that it is hated by almost two-thirds of the nation, most of whom cannot wait to get rid of it. A steady recovery eventually follows but neither long nor strong enough to produce election victory. The opposition then comes in and the cycle is repeated. Rooted allegiances remain the norm, yet there is an increasing proportion of the electorate which is now autonomous and available to be mobilized for change. So swings get bigger.

Failure to deliver means increasing alienation. This has been measured by a series of surveys, perhaps most graphically by an Opinion Research Centre Survey for *The Times* showing that over half of the electorate in 1980 considered that the present system no longer works properly.[3] If America has a silent majority we now have a grumbling majority. There is an increasing lack of faith in the system and indications here are that this has gone up more rapidly than in overseas systems which are delivering. There is also an increasing alienation from the two main political parties on which the system rests. This is combined with a growing feeling that the parties can do little to improve the lot of the people either as individuals or collectively. Four-fifths of the nation supported one or the other party at the start of the fifties: now only two-thirds. The decline is certain to resume as the Liberals, the SDP and the Nationalists, climb back under a Tory government. It is the outward and visible sign of a growing doubt about the relevance of the two main parties.

The people are also losing faith in the electoral system. Like several other surveys *The Times* study showed nearly three quarters of the population thought proportional representation a good idea. This is less a testimony to the virtues of a representation system whose proponents manage to endow it with all the attractive power of a crank religious sect, than to the reaction against the existing electoral system. If it worked well when shifts were slight and needed consolidating it works very differently when they are substantial. A limiter is then more appropriate. Also first-past-the-post works uneasily and unpredictably when the two-party system to which it is best suited is losing its hold. The result is so unpredictable and incalculable that negative protest and irresponsible voting are all encouraged. A large number of votes for the third party, running in 1974 to six million, are effectively wasted so there is little incentive to informed, considered voting and frustrated voters can hardly have any subsequent feeling of responsibility for, or involvement in, what happens.

The problem is compounded by the fact that the public cannot understand either what government is doing as it 'manages' the economy or why it is doing it. Instead the people react to the effects on their individual lives. This failure hardly matters when the system is delivering. When it is stuttering and the consequences are economic decline and loss of jobs, the problem becomes acute. In the twenties when economic policy was conventional wisdom writ large it might have been easy to explain that the government was forcing down wages and creating unemployment to make ends meet or balance its books: only the consequences of these apparently self-evident necessities were objected to. Keynes revolutionized the techniques of management but not the process of explanation. This weakness, bearable when Keynesian management worked, becomes crucial when the policies themselves become more extreme and when counter-cyclical spending involves borrowing requirements on a scale which easily terrify the unwitting. Unfortunately it is also at this moment that the politics become less effective: even if they prevent worse, they do not produce the old benefits. Indeed Keynesian policies are still impossible to justify at all to that sizeable section of society who feel that full employment saps morale and incentive, welfare spoils, work-spreading encourages laziness and government spending is a moral failure not a management technique. Indeed the masochistic 'things must get worse before they can get better' syndrome can cause retrograde policies to be greeted with relish even by those who do not feel such primeval resentments; the weight of taxation necessary to grapple with economic difficulties as acute as Britain's creates its own resentments. Governments attempt the explanation. They rarely get beyond the personalized homilies about household finances which Mrs Thatcher likes, or such graphic distortion as Mr Wilson's 1967 promise that the devaluation of the pound would not affect the value of 'the pound in your pocket'.

Failures of communication make it doubly difficult to govern a democracy in crisis. We are increasingly a participatory democracy though a very imperfect one and even this does not mean a better informed, more involved society. The participation is partial, predominantly restricted to the middle class and mainly mobilized for negative purposes. Many groups and institutions have the power to block, few can act positively to nurture and support. Trade unions have the strength to stop incomes policies but not to deliver their members or discipline them in support. The Confederation of British Industry can monitor pay but not enforce it or anything else. So participatory democracy really means that negative blocking groups from anti-motorway to anti-abortion springing up, usually too late, to fight vigorous rearguard actions against changes, often against improvements. Pro-groups are few and supportive ones tend to vanish in clouds of goodwill. People can be organized against, but rarely for. The brake is easy to apply, often automatically; the accelerator is disconnected. Public opinion works similarly. It just wants government to get on with its job of governing and to deliver. It reacts negatively, both against the consequences of failure and the techniques of correction.

This climate of attitudes becomes alarming in the light of the decline in prospect. If decline is accepted, it exacerbates all the divisions and antagonisms of a divided, cold-hearted, society. Though kind to animals, the British do not extend the same sympathy to people in distress or unemployment. A 1977 EEC survey of Common Market countries showed the British as the least sympathetic to the poor and unemployed, the most inclined to blame such misfortune on individual faults and weakness rather than social problems and the most likely to feel that government is doing and spending too much to alleviate their effects.[4] In such an atmosphere decline produces the politics of blame. Group fights group for shares of a shrinking cake. Workers seek through industrial action what growth is failing to provide. Government looks round for victims to blame for its own lack of success. The unemployed are relegated to a steadily growing ghetto which most people would rather not know about. The whole scenario puts Britain in the situation of the Common Market's Offshore Social Security Scrounger.

Decline promises stagnant misery and a rigid inflexible society rather than the adaptable, mobile, dynamic one which alone can adjust to the future. An active attempt to fight the difficulties promises a livelier version of the same depressing picture. The problems cannot be tackled without collective effort and sacrifice. Increasing unemployment imposes a burden on taxation. Positive efforts to solve it require reductions in overtime, spreading work, earlier retirement. Reviving competitiveness means either increased inflation through insulation and devaluation or a reduction in real incomes through incomes policies, or both. Procedures for squeezing out a surplus for investment have never produced dancing in the streets even in totalitarian systems let alone consumer democracies. Battered industries need aid; new ones need capital; Britain needs investment: none are painless. So every policy to grapple with the difficulties, or even spread the misery, demands collective effort, sacrifice, explanation and understanding.

Churchillian rhetoric rallies people to an enemy at the door. It could hardly rally an ill-informed community to attack problems it does not understand in ways it disapproves of, backed by institutions which cannot enforce them. This is not to say that the Dunkirk spirit does not transfer to economics. There is a willingness to accept an incomes policy which has always been more popular in the polls than with the organized interests. Yet the acceptance is conditional. Policy has to be fair and it operates in a country where there is a highly developed bush telegraph of pub, club and gossip to relay and amplify news of anomalies and unfairness and media which make their living out of portraying the other man's grass — in full colour. So we are a deadlocked democracy. The public hardly understands what is being done or why. Acquiescence and co-operation based on consent and understanding are not forthcoming. The groups which might mobilize support have blocking power but no positive power to bind.

Democracy promotes the deadlock. Its structure promotes escapism. Governments cannot maintain unity in their own forces: there are always opponents waiting in the wings with their own siren songs. Alternative strategists tell the Labour party that its sacrifices are futile. Opponents of incomes policy turn disruption into a creed. Tory monetarists squirmed through the Heath boom. Tory Keynesians wait impatiently for Mrs Thatcher's unconsummated marriage with Milton Friedman to end in divorce. Any economic policy contains the seeds of its own nemesis but the struggle is mainly a backstairs one largely kept from the public because the participants fear (rightly) that the argument would not be understood. The debate between parties is more open than the internal debate but no more responsible. The opposition is always there to jump on every corn, rub salt in every wound, and point out that if it were in power things would be different. Such is the nature of two-party politics: the opposition believes it can do better just because it feels itself to be better. To justify this built-in belief it needs the scaffolding of a body of belief. In opposition from 1974-79 the Conservatives found it in monetarism. This enabled them to attack Labour's interventionism, to capitalize on the grievances produced by high taxation and to argue that success would come from simply throwing Labour's policies into reverse.

The opposition convinced itself. An electorate without the information or education to question such simplistic assumptions accepted Tory confidence because it was not happy with Labour, not because it believed in or even understood an alternative which was essentially half-baked. Yet it could not see through it. The same imperatives push Labour in opposition. Incomes policies may be right: Tory ones are wrong. The basic problem of competitiveness is never broached, so a party which should have growth as the central symbol on its banner was able to enter office in 1964 with no policy towards the problem of sterling and in 1974 with no answer to de-industrialization and the growth of imports. It preferred to gloss over difficult problems and an electorate which did not understand allowed it to do so. This espousal of the politics of escapism by major parties is nothing compared to the eager mating instincts of the minor, whether Liberal, Nationalist or SDP.

Escapism and deadlock bode ill for a society facing increasing economic difficulties. The picture should not be overpainted. We are not in the realm of Sunday supplement scenarios of collapse and ungovernability such as those of the *Ice Age* portrayed by Margaret Drabble in her novelistic deep freezing of 1974-75. There will be remissions produced, for example, by the steady rise in tax revenues from North Sea oil towards the mid-eighties. An oil power in an energy-starved world can hardly collapse into destitution: not until the wells run dry. Yet even so the picture is currently and will remain one of a system unable to deliver; imposing apparently futile sacrifices and justifying ills greater than post-war experience has prepared us for. To break out of the trough of despondency governments would have to marshal, organize and guide the efforts of our people in a way not attempted since the much easier rallying process of war and post-war recovery.

Political education must be set in perspective against this. Normally regarded as a desirable, if optional extra, a further buffing in the polishing of the rounded individual, political education will have to become something far more if it is to be relevant to the age of uncertainty. It then becomes a major necessity, part of the process of adjusting our democracy to new pressures by making it more flexible and responsive and allowing it to mobilize and communicate with its citizens instead of resting on uninformed apathy. Political education is one way to produce a better informed, more involved electorate, one which understands what its government is doing and why. It is, however, only one approach. The problems will hardly be solved by education in the schools. This must be approached as part of a much wider effort to allow our democracy to adjust to the strains ahead.

In education the need is to approach politics as an art, not a science. Political science assumes a dry, desiccated approach, transforming what has to be a life-skill, part of the repertoire necessary for survival in today's world, into a dry academic subject which quantifies the unquantifiable, categorizes the chaotic. Politics has to be felt, not embalmed. Simply defined, it is the way in which people get on (or do not) in groups, an approach to life and problems. In modern society politics is a way of accommodating interests and allocating resources, a process of mediating demands and reaching decisions which needs to be experienced but is difficult to process into pedagogy. Structures can be described. Politics have to be felt. Because politics has been approached as an academic subject it has failed to excite interest. Two educational requirements have pushed it in the academic direction. The craving for impartiality has become a distortion as absurd as an atheist approach to God. It is understandable that the schools should be as cautious as they are in sex education. The problems are similar: not so much that the pupils will promptly go out and apply their new knowledge by picketing the school or experimenting with the physical dimension of interpersonal relationships, but fear of parental reactions. Such hostility has to be opposed. Though noisy, it is small in scale. To give way to it would dilute and distort the subject to the point of irrelevance. In any case the point at which bias, which is acceptable, becomes indoctrination, which is not, is clear. What is being taught is a process, not an ideology. Partisanship is part of that process, indoctrination is not. Individual views and partisanships must be brought into play and cannot be concealed by a pretence that a distilled essence is available which can be doled out impartially. Recognizing and dealing with partisanship is itself part of the process of being educated.

Academic pressures are heightened by a craving for respectability. In the educational world this is conferred by examination status. Yet exams put politics in the preserving jar. They become homogenized to fit into the dull and dutiful rigidities of examination schedules. The finished product ends up as a diluted version of university political studies of 'Power in Political Parties (Discuss)' or 'The Functioning of the Electoral System (Add up)'. The living, beery, sweaty reality, the passion, the choreographics of the committee machine and the shifting alliances of party government are either excluded or embalmed. Instead the emphasis is on a blend of sociology (the measurable) and the institutional (the describable) which is more susceptible to marking. Politics is not really a suitable subject for examination. To treat it as such is to petrify and rigidify in a way which undermines the case for teaching politics in the first place. Politics is a life-skill, not a basic bread and butter core-curriculum subject like chemistry or biology. It is a refinement, a feeling, an instinct, rather than a quantifiable commodity. It is not an appropriate intellectual discipline in the same way as, say science, history or even political theory. It has no central core and the educational approach to it falls between every possible stool, embracing a smattering of sociology, a dollop of political theory, a smidgeon of institutional theory and constitutional law, all mixed in with yesterday's newspaper clippings.

Looking at politics as a process, studying how decisions are taken and priorities allocated is the best approach. Yet in modern Britain this is as much a matter of fiction writing as factual analysis. The basic raw material is lacking because the reality is obscured not only from the public but from the members of Parliament who nominally run the machine on their behalf. MPs compensate for their own ignorance with dollops of gossip, doled out by ministers. Their views are formed on a continuous diet of who said what to whom, who triumphed, who was humbled. The nation then gets the same diet thinned with artificial dilutants and colouring matter. The last concerted attempt to peer through the chink in the curtain was Anthony Howard's stint as Whitehall correspondent of *The Sunday Times*. His tenure was weeks not months. The remaining pundits now dole out a tepid stew flavoured with leeks but containing few chunks of real meat. The only books to give even a remotely credible picture of events have been diaries, today's gossip deep-frozen, and a few journalistic reconstructions. The academics have filled in the wide gaps in their own knowledge with the polyfiller of pedantry. Freedom of information is indispensable before politics can become an academic or educational discipline. Without it, teaching politics is rather like teaching a language with nouns in plenty but verbs treated as strictly confidential.

Neither the academic emphasis nor the examination gearing are welcome. Political education as she is currently spoke might add to that well-informed minority who can spot trends and discuss with detachment. It makes little contribution to our basic problem: an uninformed electorate unable to understand what is being done to it and why and prey to alienation and unreasoning negativism. The requirement should be the universal provision of a basic curriculum geared not to examinations but to providing a life-skill and an understanding of the processes. Facts have a half-life of weeks but a feeling for the métier can endure. It can provide a greater understanding of the pressures under which politicians work and the realities which shape their end, rough-hew them how they will. To demolish the Churchillian image of political leadership, and show the realities of compromise and mediation would be in itself a considerable achievement. It would be to reveal the true nature of politics and politicians rather than to underline that unrealistic image which politicians may like for themselves given their propensity to don Churchillian rhetoric (or in Mrs Thatcher's case, trousers) but which only guarantees disappointment and alienation. They can never live up to it. They should not try.

The core curriculum must be geared to different levels of ability and understanding. It should provide certain necessary features. Politics is now a necessary life-skill. Knowledge of the institutional world of big labour and big business, big government, institutional welfare and the complex systems of control and organization is a means of survival. Students have to be prepared for change and adjustment, and a world of pressures quite unkown to their parents. The next generation cannot be turned out of school with no knowledge of welfare rights and how to exercise them, levers of power and how to pull them, participation and how to use it, of pressures and how to mobilize them.

The second requirement is a practical emphasis: problems and how to solve them, an approach which can be reinforced by mobilizing the knowledge and experience of those directly involved. Politics is one subject fortunate enough to have a vast, and underemployed, Labour (and Conservative) force available. The same is true of administration, unions, business and local government. In my experience these resources are not tapped. Of half a dozen secondary schools in Grimsby, only one has ever called on their member of three years' standing to tackle the subject 'MPs are a good thing (Discuss)!' This may be a symptom of good sense and taste on their part. I prefer to see it as an indication of lack of interest. The chief executive, three mayors, the Labour and Conservative leaders on the District and County Councils, and the managers of the Department of Health and Social Security and the Job Centre, all of whom will play a not inconsiderable part in the lives of apprentice Grimbarians, have been similarly underused. Unless my Conservative opponent has cornered the market first, contact of Grimsby youth with the realities of the political and administrative jungle will come as a rude awakening. The only educational interest came from a German publisher who used my initial election campaign as an example of how British politics work in an English text for German schools. *English G. Band 6A* was both interesting and well presented. Perhaps German school children now have a better working knowledge of Grimsby politics than anyone educated in the borough.

School politics cannot be rigidly defined as the comic-strip, kids' version of the political science taught at universities. Economic management is now the way in which government makes its biggest impact on its people. The area is a blend of politics and economics. It is crucial that this blend be part of the educational process. Hard and fast curriculum boundaries cannot preclude an effort to show what governments are trying to do, what are the limits of manoeuvre and what techniques and processes of economic management lie to hand. To produce a new generation of Keynesians is too much to hope for. It is not too much to expect a generation whose appreciation of the subject is better than the piggy bank economics, the personalization and the search for a Victim of the Month which now passes for economic literacy among both Tory backbenchers and the business community. In Britain we personalize the problems: economic problems are blamed not on competitiveness or the currency, but on laziness; the 'why work?' syndrome and extended tea-breaks and other symptoms thrown up by our galloping national inferiority-complex. We would do better to treat economics as a branch of politics.

Such is my politician's prescription: the Crick approach given the kiss of life and made universal, but shorn of the academic trimmings and the search for respectability. It is, however, only a partial approach to the looming problems described earlier. It will be as incomplete and as inadequate as any other effort to change society through the schools unless it is combined with two other efforts on a far broader front, to allow our system to adjust to the age of uncertainty.

Education does not stop as the school door closes. It is a lifelong experience. The vast reservoirs of ignorance and prejudice are mainly concentrated, in Britain at least, in the middle and older generations. To lower the level or dilute the mixture can only be done by bringing politics out of the ghetto and making them an appropriate part of the massive process of adult education which our society needs in this, and many other, spheres. The main strength of the political system has been the binding force of conditioned allegiances. As these gradually break down and attenuate, the only compensating alternative will be an informed, involved, electorate, weighing up decisions and then accepting responsibility for them rather than delegating the dirty work to politicians and then cursing them for failing in a job which is too big. Public finance for political parties must be a part of this process. In an age of dwindling membership and involvement, both parties, but more particularly Labour, will be locked into a spiral of decline unless public money is available on an appropriate scale to turn them into what they should be anyway: machines for popular education. Yet the main weight of the effort will be an educational approach which recognizes that political economy is a more relevant subject than flower arrangement. Every available resource from whatever framework of adult education the Tories leave standing through service groups, unions and workplace groups to the media (rescued from their present jester status as entertainers) must be mobilized in this process. Deny it as we might, life is serious and punk is escapism, not a way of coping with reality.

Political education in the schools and on a much wider basis can only do so much. It needs to be combined with a series of institutional reforms designed to allow the system to respond to the emerging pressures, to soften its rigidities and to accelerate and strengthen the developing educational processes. These reforms lie outside the scope of the present essay so it might be better to list the necessary reforms rather than expound them at length. My own list would include:

— Proportional representation. To give every vote a value and an investment in the result and to provide for greater stability.

— Televising of Parliament. As an indispensable part in the education process. What use is a national forum no one listens to?

— State aid for political parties. To turn decrepit election machines into the machines for political education which a modern party must be.

— Devolved regional governments. To diffuse power more widely, bring government closer to the people and break down the centralized power structure which gives British government such an impersonal remoteness.

— Open government. Secrecy can hardly be acceptable when the system is no longer delivering.

— Greater participation at work, in unions, in institutions such as schools and colleges, on the basis that this is a right but with the knowledge that *plus participer c'est plus pardonner*.

— Stronger, better disciplined and more democratic interest groups. Groups need to involve and educate their members but they must also be able to deliver and bind them.

— More vigorous media. The press may be irredeemable (though a greatly strengthened Press Council can try), but a genuine multi-channel television could cease taking its cues from the press, abandon the balance requirement and open itself up to the parties and groups to put their views and carry on the debate.

These reforms are a necessary part of the adjustment process. Without them the impact of the educational improvements is considerably blunted. Indeed part of it could be set at nought: unregenerate media can undermine efforts at political education; a stultifying electoral system can totally frustrate the educated vote. Coming hand-in-hand with a programme of political education, the structural reforms do offer some chance of breaking out of the trough of ignorance, prejudice, alienation and indifference. They will help us to survive the stresses and strains of a decade very different from what has gone before. As a nation we have failed to in-

vest in our industries, to grow into the virtuous cycle, to educate
our workforce or to inform our people. The forces of retribution
work on nations as well as individuals. Unless we understand the
problems and co-operate to solve them the strains will be severe.
An educated electorate is no guarantee that we can cope. An ignorant, prejudiced, sullen and ill-informed one makes it more certain that we cannot.

NOTES

1. *NOW!*, 1 February 1980.
2. A. Downs, *Economic Theory of Democracy*, New York: Harper and Row,
1965.
3. *British Public Opinion,* Spring 1980, p. 33. Interestingly less than a third
wanted to leave well-, or semi-well, alone.
4. *The Perception of Poverty in Europe*, Brussels: EEC, 1977.

III

NEGLECTED AREAS

9

The Political Education of Adults

Harold Entwistle

Both political theorists and educationists have traditionally taken
the view that political education is primarily a matter for adults.
Children have been assumed to have neither the relevant experience
nor the appetite for learning about what is taken to be concerned
essentially with a segment of life of significance only for the enfran-
chised adult. Within the past decade, however, there has been
strong advocacy that teaching about politics should be firmly
rooted in the school curriculum.[1] In part, this has been a response
to a reduction of the voting age to eighteen. It has also been influenced by psychologists who have insisted that early learning is
significant for cognitive development. Bruner, for example, has insisted that his advocacy of a 'spiral curriculum' is rooted in 'the
hypothesis that any subject can be taught effectively in some intellectually honest form at any stage of development'.[2] If this is the
case, it ought to be as true for the teaching of politics as for any
other discipline.

Nothing which is said in this paper about the indispensability of
political education for adults is intended to question this recent

trend towards political education for children. In fact, neither ought to stand alone. The unity of a lifelong educational experience which the spiral curriculum entails, depends upon the learning of concepts, principles and skills on the ground floor of one's schooling as well as upon the continuous sophistication of these as one climbs the educational spiral staircase throughout one's entire life. Adult political education should benefit from political knowledge acquired in childhood.

II

A number of conceptual distinctions are necessary to developing an argument about the need for and possibility of adult political education.

First, there is the question of what properly constitutes adult education. Historically in industrial societies, adult education has usually been 'remedial' or 'compensatory' in origin and intention. It has been concerned with the education of either those adults who had no formal schooling at all, or those whose schooling was elementary: those having had neither the benefits of secondary schooling nor a college education. According to Farmer, in the United States, 'time and time again, adult educators have sought to make education available to the disadvantaged and the oppressed through folk schools, adult education for immigrants, manpower efforts, and literacy programs.'[3] In Britain, Tawney wrote of the primary mission of the Workers' Educational Association (WEA) being to 'the educationally underprivileged minority, who cease their full time education at or about fifteen . . .'.[4] There is ample documentation of educational initiative by and on behalf of the working class, especially within those institutions which have constituted the labour movement: trade unions, co-operative and friendly societies, radical and socialist political parties and the evening and Sunday schools created by political movements like Chartism.[5] There seems little doubt that these various examples of the education of adults would have to be written into any history which attempted to describe and account for political and economic reform on behalf of the socially disadvantaged through two centuries of industrialism. Whatever the persistence of poverty and ignorance in the third quarter of the twentieth century, the condition of the working classes in Britain today bears little resemblance to that of the working classes observed by Engels in 1844. And such amelioration of its political and economic predicaments which has been achieved has been, in part, the work of a politically educated working class.

However, this educational history of the working class raises three questions which must be central to any consideration of the possibilities of adult political education in the future. The first of these is the question of how deeply adult education has cut into the working population as a whole: were those who benefited from adult schooling an unrepresentative minority? Secondly, notwithstanding its undoubted effectiveness as political education, to what extent has this inculcation of political maturity been a by-product of the general education of adults rather than deliberate teaching about politics? Put another way, to what extent is a good general education a form of political education? This is related to a third cluster of questions which have to be asked about adult political education. Ought it to be theoretical or practical, concerned primarily with understanding or with action; and, if the latter, must it be neutral, essentially a sociology of politics concerned with the existing political machinery and institutions available to the democractic citizen; or can it be ideologically biassed, critical in equipping the learner to associate with others in order to replace the existing political hegemony: in short, could there be, for example, education for socialism, or would teaching and learning in such an ideological context have to be dismissed as mere indoctrination?

With reference to the first of these questions, some students of the working class and of adult education doubt whether adult classes have touched any but a small minority amongst the working class. Historians of adult education in the United States have found it a marginal activity: 'adult educators have typically found their offerings of educational assistance more suited to and more frequently utilized by the upwardly mobile than the hardcore disadvantaged'.[6] In Britain, this notion that adult education has been mainly attractive to status-dissenting members of the working class — even to an untypical labour aristocracy — has recently been canvassed in a revisionist account of the clientele of Tawney's first extra-mural classes.[7] Hoggart has claimed that the working-class

adult student is the member of an 'earnest minority' or 'saving remnant' having interests and commitments which set him apart from
the majority of working-class people.[8] And, in the present day, the
assumption is that this remnant available for recruitment to adult
classes has been further eroded by the 'creaming off' of intellectually able working-class children for recruitment to higher education. It has become a commonplace that University Tutorial and
WEA classes recruit mainly from the professional middle classes.
In adult education circles there is continuous debate on whether
and how the movement can be restored to the working class. In the
United States, adult educationists ask the question, 'How do you
provide adult education when there is little or no motivation, no
drive for upward mobility?'[9]

In order to address this question, however, especially on the
assumption that the point of political education is to stimulate
political action aimed at social change, it is necessary to ask
whether adult political education *is* required by everybody. Even to
raise this question will, no doubt, be dismissed as élitist. Adult
educationists usually share the equalitarian educational philosophy
of liberal educationists generally; the belief dies hard that everyone
ought to have access to the best schooling available and the hope
persists that somewhere there is to be found a curriculum and
teaching strategies sufficiently attractive to woo even the most
reluctant of adult learners. However, it is not only conservative
educationists who accept, with the socialist Christopher Jencks,
that those with an appetite for things of the mind are, indeed (and
irrespective of social class), a minority. If those historians are correct who find that the working-class clientele in adult classes was
only ever a minority, perhaps one ought to examine the demands
and possibilities for adult political education in terms of Gramsci's
notion of the organic intellectual. Committed to radical political
activity aimed at overthrow of the existing social hegemony, and
dedicated to the political education of Italian workers towards that
end, Gramsci emphasized the need for leadership from an élite
amongst the working class. These intellectuals, organic to the
working class itself, have the responsibility for articulating the
predicaments of the subaltern classes (workers and peasants)
because appropriate, creative, counter-hegemonic solutions to their
dilemmas cannot be the product of mass thought:

Critical self-consciousness means, historically and politically, the creation of an élite of intellectuals. A human mass does not 'distinguish' itself, does not become independent in its own right without, in the widest sense, organising itself; and there is no organisation without intellectuals, that is without organisers and leaders, in other words, without the theoretical aspect of the theory-practice nexus being distinguished concretely by the existence of a group of people 'specialised' in conceptual and philosophical elaboration of ideas . . . innovations cannot come from the mass, at least at the beginning, except through the mediation of an élite for whom the conception implicit in human activity has already become to a certain degree a coherent and systematic ever-present awareness and a precise and decisive will.[10]

Here Gramsci was calling explicitly for the establishment of an 'élite', a word which he repeatedly used in this context. But this also has intimations of Hoggart's notion of the 'saving remnant' and its almost religious implication that the 'earnest minority' does, indeed, lead the mass out of bondage into a promised land. For, despite being in a minority within the working class, the adult student was also often active in the trade union, the co-operative or friendly society and the political party or group, frequently in the role of leader. Hoggart does not use the term 'organic intellectual', but some such organic relationship to the majority of the working class is implicit in his conclusion about the social role of the 'saving remnant': 'it seems difficult to overstress the importance to a society of people such as this, who are prepared to address themselves to study, usually after a day's work and often in unpropitious conditions, inspired by a sense, however disguised it may sometimes seem, of the power and virtue of knowledge.'[11] Whilst Gramsci did not speak of a saving remnant, the kind of social leavening evoked by the phrase was implicit in the role of the organic intellectual. Indeed, he saw the educational and cultural institutions of the British labour movement as models for the 'cultural associations' which he took to be necessary for the political education of the Italian working class. He instanced the Fabian Society, at the time of its affiliation to the International, which had 'succeeded in putting into this work of cultural and spiritual liberation, a great part of the English intellectual and university world'.[12] Gramsci assumed that, initially, organic working-class intellectuals would need to be educated by traditional intellectuals from other social classes.

However, the notion dies hard that even if intellectuals are crucial to the direction of working-class political activity, both equity (the opportunity for everyone to learn to lead) and prudence require universal access to political education. The history of the labour movement, no less than histories of the ruling class, may point to an 'iron law of oligarchy', but external vigilance is necessary if the arrogance, corruption and decay to which élites are prone is to be avoided. If there must be education for political leadership, this implies that there must be political education for those who are destined or choose to be followers; for 'ordinary' citizens to whom politics is not a major interest or preoccupation, who may choose to be politically active only occasionally when their own interests, or interests with which they are altruistically sympathetic, are threatened; or who wish simply to keep an eye on the political universe in order to judge wisely when opinion is canvassed periodically at election times. Again, our liberal educational wisdom is that this ought to include everyone in a democracy and (if, in Kant's words 'ought implies can') that, consequently, everyone should be capable of sufficient political education to enable him to vote intelligently and responsibly. Although Gramsci believed that not everyone was capable of being 'an intellectual' no one was so devoid of intelligence as to be beyond the range of rational argument.[13]

Notwithstanding this kind of optimism about the intellectual potential of all men, adult educationists (as we have already noted) point to the persistence of a core of the disadvantaged who seem entirely resistant to any educational initiative. Sociologists have pointed to the existence of groups who seem to make a virtue of 'cognitive poverty'. In this respect, Klein's description of some patterns of English working-class culture seem in line with Lewis's characterization of the 'culture of poverty' found amongst marginal populations, especially in Latin America, but also a familiar feature of slum and ghetto populations in the world's major cities.[14] According to Lewis, in addition to being a condition of chronic economic poverty, the culture of poverty is noteworthy for the cognitive poverty of its 'members', instilling a fatalism with reference to any possibility of ever achieving a different way of life. People develop this fatalism early and, when adult, they do not seek access to power through membership of political parties or labour unions, nor do they make use of even those welfare agencies which exist for amelioration of poverty.

III

If these marginal groups are a favoured target for adult political education, what pedagogical possibilities exist which give reason for optimisim in face of historical evidence that adult education reaches only untypical minorities at the other cultural extreme of the subaltern classes? Recently, adult educationists, especially in North America, have turned to Freire's pedagogy as a model. Fraser see Freire as standing in the mainstream of adult education in the sense that his 'pedagogy of the oppressed' is in line with historical American initiatives on behalf of the disadvantaged.[15] And, with reference to a question we posed earlier, Freire's pedagogical initiatives are frankly ideologically biassed. Their context is that of political oppression and economic exploitation and his own commitment to liberation of the oppressed.

Freire conceives political education as a by-product of education for literacy. And, although he does not make the point explicitly, it follows from his ideological stance that political education related to teaching and learning about existing 'mainstream' political institutions would merely be an example of what he calls 'extensionism', only further alienating the oppressed. On this view, what the oppressed need is not knowledge of how to engage with traditional political institutions, for this would only signal their acceptance of the existing social hegemony. What they need is knowledge and skill appropriate to the creation of novel, liberating political institutions, which uniquely address their own peculiar predicaments.

Critics of Freire have raised questions to do with both the philosophical underpinnings of his pedagogy and the practical effectiveness of his methods pending systematic study and evaluation of their efficacy in different practical contexts.[16] In particular, doubt has been cast on the possibility of their transferability outside the Third World context and into advanced industrial societies like the United States. Boston, a self-styled 'loving critic', concludes that 'it cannot be stressed too strongly that even an indirect translation of Freire is simply folly.'[17] But in an early essay, Freire

himself saw his work as addressed peculiarly to the problems of
Brazil, a nation lacking a history of popular democratic institutions.[18] Although he does not name them, he implies that there are
nations whose culture does provide a fertile soil for the growth of
popular democracy. For these, perhaps a different approach to the
political education of the disadvantaged is appropriate. But, in
principle, Freire does emphasize three necessary conditions for
adult education which are familiar in the theory and practice of
education elsewhere and which are important for any continuing
initiatives in the field of adult political education.

First, there is the fundamental importance of language in
political education. Secondly, a related emphasis, there is the
necessity for dialogue in the educational situation. Thirdly, there is
the stress upon daily empirical experience as the point of departure
for the awakening of political consciousness; that is, upon the importance of micro-politics rather than macro-political activity as
the theatre for individual political participation.

Familiarly, Freire's pedagogy of the oppressed involves the approach to conscientization ('*consciêntizacão*') and, hence, liberation of the person, through a campaign to promote adult literacy.
Historically, literacy has been conceived as the essentially liberating
intellectual skill. For although voting procedures put a premium
upon illiteracy, the assumption has been that the quality of
democratic citizenship depends upon there being a highly literate
population. John Stuart Mill put the point cogently over a century
ago: 'of the working classes of Western Europe at least it may be
pronounced certain that the patriarchal system of government is
one to which they will not again be subject. That question has been
several times decided. It was decided when they were taught to read
and allowed access to newspapers and political tracts.' Although
some modern radical educationists have made precisely the opposite point about mass literacy — that it facilitates social control
by producing 'good' citizens, in the sense that being literate simply
makes us compliant, passive, obedient citizens and consumers —
the ideology of Third World liberation and development still takes
for granted the liberating and creative potential of literacy.[19] But
both the economics of schooling and the sense of urgency which are
constraints upon educational provision in the Third World have
seemed to point to the need to attack adult illiteracy as a priority,

rather than persisting with traditional ways of producing a literate population through the costly, leisurely and not always effective processes of schooling young children. In Tanzania, President Nyerere has put this point as follows: 'First we must educate adults. Our children will not have an impact on our own development for five, ten or even twenty years.'[20] For Freire, the conclusion that adults should be the target for literacy programmes also meant rejecting the unrealistic vocabularies of traditional reading primers, 'disconnected from life, centred on words emptied of the reality they are meant to represent, lacking in concrete activity . . .'.[21] Instead, the approach to literacy would be based upon identification of a culturally realistic vocabularly aimed at 'the problem of teaching adults how to read in relation to the awakening of their consciousness'.[22] This involved the search for 'generative words' combining 'phonetic richness' with 'pragmatic tone', that is words implying 'a greater engagement of a word in a given social, cultural and political reality'.[23] Hence, Freire's pedagogy of the oppressed was an attempt to cultivate cultural (including political) awareness through 'the word'. It is interesting that the unique and highly successful nineteenth-century example of adult education in the Danish Folk High school was built upon Bishop Grundvig's notion of the educational potency of the 'the living word'.

Especially in Britain, there is a tradition of approaching the study of politics linguistically. Seminal texts have been titled *The Grammar of Politics* and *The Vocabulary of Politics*. Oakeshott's influential inaugural lecture, 'Political Education', likened political education to learning a language.[24] A suggestive, if limited, piece of research into the standards of political education in Britain, derived its conclusions that there was little evidence of political education amongst a group of intelligent sixth formers by reference to their inability to define accurately a list of words in a political vocabulary test.[25] And it is in line with this emphasis upon language in politics that the revival of interest in political education in Britain is associated with a stress upon political education as the acquisition of political literacy. This requires 'a knowledge of those concepts minimally necessary to construct simple conceptual and analytical frameworks', concepts drawn 'from everyday life — yet employed more systematically and precisely than usual'. Crick suggests that the appropriate vocabulary would include the words power, force, authority, order, law, justice, representation, pressure, rights, individuality, freedom, and welfare.[26]

However, just as the sophistication of literacy in a general sense is assumed to deepen and widen possibilities for active engagement with the realities of daily life, so the object of political literacy is the possibility of a more active, informed and responsible engagement with the realities of the body politic:

> The ultimate test of political literacy lies in creating a proclivity to action, not in achieving more theoretical analysis. The politically literate person would be capable of active participation. The politically literate person must be able to devise strategies for influence and for achieving change.[27]

Hence, one conclusion to be drawn from the Anglo-Saxon political tradition, as well as from Freire, is that adult political education should be concerned first with helping people to learn the language of politics.

A second and related message from Freire is that learning should be a dialogue, not a monologue, implying a reciprocal relationship between educators and educatees. It is not a question of authorities simply teaching the 'correct' vocabulary of politics, but of teachers and learners together generating the relevant vocabulary for understanding and meeting their own peculiar predicaments and dilemmas. Freire speaks not of teachers and learners but of the 'educator-educatee' and the 'educatee-educator'. One does not need to share Freire's mistrust of teachers as authorities in order to conclude that the educational process should be conducted as a conversation. Adapting Marx's Third Thesis on Feuerbach, Gramsci also implied the importance of the teacher as educator-educatee and the learner as educator-educatee. He took Marx's notion that 'the educator must be educated' to imply, not simply that the teacher must be an educated person, but also that he ought willingly to adopt the stance of a student in relation to his own pupils: 'the relationship between teacher and pupil is active and reciprocal so that every teacher is also a pupil and every pupil a teacher.'[28]

Again, Freire's emphasis upon the educational imperative towards dialogue only recaptures what has usually been the preferred method of adult education. Adult classes typically employ the discussion method. Tawney reminds us of the insistence of Albert

Mansbridge (founder of the WEA) that the proper vehicle for adult education 'was to be found not in lectures . . . to large and miscellaneous audiences, but in a group or class sufficiently small for intimate relations to develop between its members and between them and the tutor . . .'.[29] It is evident that not the least effective part of Tawney's own classes was their informal postscript over tea and biscuits, or under the lamp at the street corner, sometimes extending into the early hours of the morning. Tawney paid tribute to the educational value of discussion in adult classes for those who taught them: 'If I were asked where I received the best part of my own education, I should reply, not at school or college, but in the days when, as a young, inexperienced and conceited teacher of tutorial classes, I underwent, week by week, a series of friendly, but effective, deflations at the hands of the students composing them.'[30]

E.P. Thompson has claimed that dialogue in adult classes also has an academic 'pay-off'. He has concluded that in his own field of social history, the dialectic between teacher and adult student (what he calls 'the abrasion of different worlds of experience in which ideas are brought to the test of life') has led to the scholarly exploration of areas long neglected in university schools of history.[31] With reference to this point about the seminal possibilities of dialogue between teacher and adult student, it is noteworthy that some adult educationists have insisted upon the importance of participatory research. This, 'based on the assumption that man is a social animal, offers a process that is more consistent with adult educational principles, more directly linked to action, and more scientific because it produces a more complex and thereby more accurate picture of reality.'[32] Participatory research is based on the assumption that research can itself be an educative process for both researchers and their subjects. Its advocates dismiss traditional research conducted along positivist lines as 'élitist' and claim that it is possible to develop research as 'a basic tool in the transformation process of a society. It does not need to be limited to those with higher education, trained in methods and techniques, in organization of thought or formulation of problems and discursive logic. Ordinary villagers, administrators and teachers can be participants, in, not only objects of, research.'[33]

Thus, a second conclusion to be drawn from the tradition of adult education, as well as from Freire, is that a fruitful teaching method for adults is one which incorporates dialogue. This has also been the conclusion of generations of adult educationists.

A third implication for adult political education in Freire is his stress upon the seminal potential of the learner's own empirical experience: 'he helps the learner to evaluate systems in terms of their effects on themselves and their communities rather than primarily from the role perspective of institutions or persons who have oppressed them.'[34] Traditional, macro-focussed courses on political institutions tend to be addressed to a political universe which is remote from the daily political experience of individuals, a world with which most will actively engage only periodically at election times and which they can observe on a continuing basis only vicariously through the news. With reference to the 'oppressed' of the Third World, macro-political institutions represent an extension (something handed out by others) making for the alienation of what Freire called massification, 'a state in which people do not make their own decisions although they may think they do'.[35] This recalls criticism of traditional, civics-oriented programmes of education for citizenship which teach that the act of voting in parliamentary elections is the fundamental democratic privilege and skill.[36] On the problem of attempting to establish a traditional, national, democratic state in Brazil, Freire observes:

> Not only did we lack experience in self-government when we imported the democratic state; more importantly, we were not yet able to offer the people either the circumstances or the climate for their first experiments in democracy. Upon a feudal economic structure and a social structure within which men were defeated, crushed and silenced, we superimposed a social and political form which required dialogue, participation, political and social responsibility, as well as a degree of social and political solidarity which we had not yet attained.[37]

Given this cultural climate, unfriendly to the conventional institutions of the democratic state, Freire concluded that the relevant empirical experience could only be with politics at the micro-level:

> I was convinced that the Brazilian people could learn social and political responsibility only by *experiencing* that responsibility, through intervention in the destiny of their children's schools, in the destinies of their trade unions and

places of employment through associations, clubs, and councils, and in the life of their neighbourhoods, churches, and rural communities by actively participating in associations, clubs, and charitable societies.[38]

This amounts to advocacy of what I have called 'associational democracy', a conception of democracy no less applicable to advanced industrial society than to Third World nations emerging from colonialism.[39] This conception is based on the assumption that it is those micro-institutions (economic, cultural, educational, religious, philanthropic, recreational) encountered by people in their daily lives which offer to them the reality of participating in the management of affairs which touch them closely in relation to their work, their play and their domestic affairs, as well in their dispositions to be altruistic or charitable in relation to their fellow men. Local drama societies, football clubs, churches, political parties and groups, labour union branches, mothers' unions and townswomen's guilds, chambers of commerce, learned societies, co-operative societies, philanthropic associations, consumer groups — all have their politics. Their members have to make and administer policy. Nor is associational democracy merely the politics of the parish pump. Voluntary associations are the channels through which, for most of us, engagement with politics at the macro-level is possible. In non-totalitarian, pluralistic societies, large areas of national life (with reference to religion, education, philanthropy, recreation and the arts, as well economic affairs) are managed 'voluntarily' through associations. Voluntary associations exist within a national community whose character they may wish to shape. National governments recognize this when constructing consultative mechanisms for tapping the experience, expertise and informed opinion which accumulates in voluntary associations. Again, in stressing the political potency of associations, Freire is only underlining what is a well established and recognized dimension of the democratic political tradition. Their potential for the exercise of democratic citizenship has been well attested by political theorists.[40]

Thus, a third conclusion to be drawn from our political tradition, as well as from Freire, is that adult political education should begin with the study of institutions having a high potential for promoting active involvement by citizens within the body politic.

IV

We noted earlier that on both sides of the Atlantic, adult educational initiatives have traditionally been on behalf of the socially and educationally disadvantaged and it is in that context that it seemed relevant to focus this discussion on the implications of Freire's pedagogy of the oppressed. But this assumption that political education for adults is peculiarly relevant to the disadvantaged returns us to one of the questions we raised at the outset: can a pedagogy which is ideologically biassed be properly characterized as 'education'?

It is difficult to avoid the conclusion that teaching politics to the disadvantaged or the oppressed cannot be an ideologically neutral activity. Liberation of the oppressed — especially when these constitute an overwhelming majority of the population — inevitably requires radical solutions whether revolutionary or reformist in character. Liberation of entire social classes, even nations, from repressive regimes requires radical political and economic reforms and it is difficult to see how any educationist confronted with this kind of social phenomenon, and a clientele of the disadvantaged, could insist on the importance of taking a neutral, disinterested stance towards the institutional status quo. Freire does not identify himself or his pedagogy as 'socialist', but his rhetoric is reminiscent of a tradition of socialist political philosophy in the West. Goulet sees Freire as '*ideologically* committed to equality, to the abolition of privilege, and to élitist forms of leadership wherein special qualifications may be exercised, but are not perpetuated';[41] Freire's work has been especially influential in Tanzania whose educational ideology is explicitly socialist and where, especially, 'the increased emphasis on adult education is directly related to the new socialist direction to which Tanzania is committed'.[42] Much the same linkage between radical political philosophy and adult educational initiatives could be established from a reading of the educational histories of industrial nations in the West. In Britain, as in the example of Chartist schools, adult educational institutions were frequently founded upon the assumption that the political, economic or social status quo was an intolerable imposition upon the working class. And those traditional intellectuals, like Tawney, who brought the universities into the field of adult education were usually socialists of one complexion or another. It is true that these did not always see their mission as one of promoting radical social change through adult education. Indeed, in an article first published in 1914, Tawney disavowed any extrinsic or utilitarian objective for the tutorial class: 'To these miners and weavers and engineers who pursue knowledge with the passion born of difficulties, knowledge can never be a means, but only an end; for what have they to gain from it save knowledge itself?'[43] But forty years later he celebrated the success of the WEA in phrases which do accept the relevance of adult education for social change. Knowledge is now seen as 'a stimulus to constructive thought and an *inspiration to action*'; education was 'a social dynamic'; 'study and reflection, without which practice will not yield its lessons, is essential to the mastery of politics'; and, finally, workers who had left school at about fifteen need 'a humane education both for their personal happiness and *to help them to mold the society in which they live*' (emphases added).[44]

The ambivalence about whether adult classes are to provide knowledge for its own sake or for extrinsic ends like social change, probably arises from the fact that the early adult classes were in literature and history, not in political theory. Hence the illusion that they were not instruments of deliberate political teaching biassed towards advocacy of social change. But, as the later Tawney concluded, an overspill into political action was inevitable. In a different national context, Gramsci also concluded that familiarizing workers with the mainstream, humanist, cultural tradition — what he called 'the entire thought of the past' — could only have radical political consequences. How, if you are oppressed, could you learn history, for example, without being stirred from out of a fatalistic acceptance of the constraints of a life of ignorance and poverty? 'If it is true that universal history is a chain made up of efforts man has exerted to free himself from privilege, prejudice and idolatory, then it is hard to understand why the proletariat, which seeks to add another link to that chain, should not know how and why and by whom it was preceded, or what advantage it might derive from this knowledge.'[45] Of course, others — the privileged — might draw different conclusions from a reading of history, ascribing their social superiority to superior moral or intellectual qualities;

or, simply wishing to preserve their privileges, draw lessons from history on how best to perpetuate oppression.

Gramsci's educational prescriptions were quite explicitly conceived as an education for socialism. And in some Third World countries where particular varieties of socialism are the dominant ideology, it seems possible, without contradiction and without intimations of oppression, to advocate 'adult education for socialism'. Tanzania is an example of this, a nation whose leadership is committed to its development in terms of '*ujamaa*', a concept of socialism derived from the principles of social organization and community indigenous to African tribal life. In this context, what is called political education involves the transmission of ideas and skills which favour the development of 'socialist man'. From the viewpoint of the political conventional wisdom in the West this looks unpromising, an illiberal commitment to one controversial view of man and social organization.

However, two points are relevant here. First, although liberal-democratic educational theory has it that schools should teach individuals to discriminate critically amongst different points of view, it remains the conventional wisdom that capitalism is the only ideological option in the advanced industrial world. And educational theorists from Dewey and Russell down to modern neo-Marxists have criticized schools in capitalist societies for their 'hidden curriculum' which effectively socializes the young into skills, attitudes and values which are functional only for the survival of corporate capitalism. In particular, these critics have pointed to the emphasis upon competition between learners and the encouragement of what has been called 'possessive individualism', a concept of the individual which is unfavourable to notions like 'community', 'co-operation', and 'equality'. At least in his early writings, Dewey was frankly socialist in his assumptions.

A second relevant point concerns how socialism is defined and the extent to which such definition has reference to values which are consistent with educational norms. The moral promises of socialism (even if these become corrupted in practice) are essentially liberating of the individual. Again taking Tanzania as the example, there is insistence upon 'democracy in decision making'; 'an emphasis on people's participation in their own development plans'.[46] The following definition of Tanzanian socialism, and of what it implies educationally, is clearly quite consistent with liberal educational principles:

> Democratic socialism cannot function from above. Instructions cannot be passed down from the leaders to the people. The people must understand their own power and their own capability for change. . . . If the people are going to make the most of decision-making and fully participate in planning in a meaningful way, then people's consciousness about the nature of their world, their power for change and their skills for producing change must become increasingly articulate and sophisticated. . . . There is a large difference in emphasis placed upon Adult Education in socialist Tanzania because of the nature of socialism. . . . Socialism is an ideology that can only prosper if and when all Tanzanians themselves adopt it as their own — it demands enlightened masses. 'You can impose capitalism, you can impose totalitarianism, but no one can impose socialism' (Ministry of National Education, 1972). Only when man sees and intelligently accepts socialist values will they become committed socialists.[47]

According to this description, the 'new socialist man' shares all the characteristics of the autonomous, rational individual of liberal educational theory. Moreover, the requirement of the final sentence exactly satisfies Peters' notion that an educational process is only morally legitimate when employing procedures which enlist the learner's own witting and voluntary assent to the personal improvement which the concept of education entails. It is also interesting that Crick, who has been a tireless advocate of political education, should conclude his inaugural lecture, 'Education and the Polity', with an 'Ideological Postscript' confessing that his views on the relationship of politics to education have been coloured by the fact that he is 'a moderate Socialist'. For him the unfinished business of education relates to realization of the principles of the French Revolution — 'Liberty, Equality and Fraternity'. This last, especially, is at the root of socialism and it is also, when formulated as the Brotherhood of Man, at the basis of the Christian religious tradition. (It is also noteworthy in this context that Crick's argument calls for a significant transfer of educational resources to the education of adults.) No doubt it is the correspondence between socialist values and those of liberal educational ideology which has led socialist educationists, like Gramsci, to conclude that a commitment to socialism cannot fail to grow out of an individual's exposure to the mainstream of Western humanistic culture which, Crick insists, has tended to be 'an improving, reformist, ameliorative, not simply a contemplative culture'.[48] Tawney confessed that he was never tempted to resort overtly to propaganda: 'A doubtless very improper conceit persuaded me that the world, when enlightened, would agree with me. I thought, therefore, that the longest way round was the shortest way home, and that my job was to promote enlightenment.'[49]

However, in pluralist societies where ideological neutrality has to be the explicit policy of publicly provided schools, a curriculum which exclusively canvasses the virtues of a single political ideology is out of the question. Hence, education for socialism, whether it consists of teaching about socialism or of an examination of the traditional humanist culture aimed at finding there moral and intellectual support for socialism, must be conducted in an institutional context which is voluntary. Given the compulsory nature of schooling in childhood and early adolescence, this suggests two things: that ideologically biassed political education should be reserved for adults and that it should be private, undertaken in institutions which are not supported by public finance (i.e., in political parties, trade unions, factory councils, co-operatives).

Marx himself took the voluntary participation of adult students in controversial topics to be axiomatic. He assumed that 'truths' which are partisan, dependent upon 'party prejudices', should not be taught in schools: it should be left to adults to form their own opinions on these matters 'about which instruction should be given in the lecture hall, not in the schools'.[50] Lenin reached a similar conclusion about the inappropriateness of using the schools for political indoctrination. Speculating on his reasons for drawing this conclusion, Lilge suggests that he believed 'the schools had more fundamental things to teach that could not be accomplished anywhere else'. 'Nor', Lilge concluded, 'can the difficulties of teaching Marxist ideology to minors have escaped him.'[51] From a different perspective, Bereiter has even concluded that the school must confine itself to instruction, education being such a value-laden enterprise that it is only appropriate for adults: 'Education, therefore, insofar as it deals with these characteristics of a person (i.e., beliefs, values, personal traits, etc.), should be provided only in the form of options for people who are old enough to choose how they want to change themselves.'[52] And we assume that in a democratic society, the direction of a person's political commitment is something that he must choose for himself. Marx was assuming that coming to grips with 'partisan truths' was something which the adult must choose to do for himself. The assumption is that the fact of being an adult is prophylactic against indoctrination. The voluntary adult student is assumed to have acquired from his schooling the basic intellectual tools, and from his experience as a worker and in domestic life a realistic perception of the social universe such that he is not easily persuaded to embrace unquestioningly any political ideology. The adult's protection against indoctrination also lies within the pedagogical process itself. It is partly for this reason that the insistence upon dialogue is important. Tawney concluded that the way to achieve impartiality was not to attempt

> to chase all the partialities out; for being human, we can none of us be other than partial. It is to draw as many as possible of the partialities in, on two conditions. The first is that, if the spirit moves their votaries to propagate a creed, they shall do so by the frank exchange of an open argument, not by subterranean intrigues. The second is that they shall accord to the opinions of their neighbours, however nauseating or absurd, the same respectful hearing which they claim for their own.[53]

V

This essay has concentrated upon a tradition of adult education addressed to the educationally and socially underprivileged. I have tried to show that its modern counterpart, directed towards the oppressed of the Third World, draws essentially upon a similar motivation and pedagogy. In modern industrial societies, with greatly increased opportunities for secondary and higher education, the clientele for this traditional form of adult education seems a declining minority. However, the conclusion that those who lack political literacy are a minority, significantly diminished by the expansion of schooling, is probably too sanguine. It has been estimated that in the United States 60 percent of the adult population 'cannot read well enough, or think abstractly enough, to understand drivers' manuals, income tax forms, and many other obligations of modern citizenship.'[54] It seems that a majority of Americans is in need of political education, and one has no reason to believe that there would be fewer political illiterates elsewhere in the West. But given the voluntary nature of adult education, the problem is how to convince the politically illiterate of their need for further education in order to bring them into appropriate educational situations.

One approach to this problem would be to intensify efforts to make the teaching of politics a compulsory component of the school curriculum. Of course, this would have to be ideologically neutral (so far as avoidance of ideological bias is ever completely successful) emphasizing the vocabulary of politics which is widely shared in democratic societies by people of different ideological persuasions. A second approach would be to bring political education into those voluntary associations to which people belong in pursuit of their interests or in defence of their standard of life. Historically, a good deal of adult education has been provided in this way, incidentally to the major purpose for which associations exist, in trade unions, friendly societies and consumer co-operatives. For Gramsci, the appropriate place for adult political education was within the industrial context itself, especially in factory councils. As adults, committed to a particular occupation, workers needed education with reference both to the technical aspects of their work and to its political and cultural implications. On this view, political activity is not a chronological outcome of political education. The two are concurrent, as workers engage with theoretical knowledge whilst involved in productive work and grapple with the political and social predicaments generated by economic activity. But Gramsci repeatedly had resort to the aphorism, 'Pessimism of the intellect, optimism of the will'. One persists with an educational endeavour whilst recognizing that it may touch only few of those for whom it is intended. Perhaps the most significant contribution of political education located in economic and industrial associations would inevitably be in the nurture of organic intellectuals, 'the leaven in the lump', dedicated to improvement of the political culture.

This suggests a final comment on adult political education as it relates to the political culture and the response to politics of those who perceive themselves to be politically sophisticated, no less than that of the politically illiterate. On the threshold of the eighties there is widespread pessimism about the possibilities of politics, a loss of confidence in the political process. This produces different conclusions about what we can expect from politics and, hence, about the tasks of political education. One writer concludes that we must learn to diminish our political expectations: 'Sometime in the Eighties, the electorate may have to admit that political influence is at the margins.'[55] Implicitly, political education would reduce our expectations of political activity. By contrast, another regrets the retreat into monetarist economic solutions to our current dilemmas: 'Such preachings distract attention from the political approaches, however difficult or unwelcome they may be, which remain available to the problems of production, collective bargaining, energy conservation and development, and the ordering of the world's financial and monetary affairs.' On this view the task of political education is not to sober our expectations but to raise them: 'What is both more urgent and more realistic, it seems to me, is to hope for some revival of belief in political action.'[56] It is this latter kind of conviction which, historically, has motivated the provision of adult education. The burgeoning interest in political education in schools, which we noted at the outset, derives from this assumption that the young need to be convinced of the potency of political action. It would be odd if adult political education, in whatever institutional context it might be located, were less optimistic.

NOTES

1. See D. Heater, 'A Burgeoning of Interest: Political Education in Britain', *International Journal of Political Education* 1, 1977-78.

2. J.S. Bruner, *The Process of Education*, Cambridge, Mass.: Harvard University Press, 1963, p. 12.

3. J.A. Farmer, 'Adult Education for Transiting' in S.M. Grabowski (ed.), *Paulo Freire: A Revolutionary Dilemma for the Adult Educator*, Syracuse, New York: Syracuse University and ERIC Clearinghouse on Adult Education, 1972, pp. 2-3.

4. R.H. Tawney, *The Radical Tradition*, The Minerva Press, 1964, p. 92.

5. See, for example, R. Barker, *Education and Politics: 1900-1951*, Oxford: Clarendon Press, 1972; M.T. Hodgen, *Workers' Education in England and the United States*, New York: Kegan Paul, Trench Trubner and Co., 1925; H. Silver, *English Education and the Radicals: 1870-1950*, Routledge and Kegan Paul, 1975; B. Simon, *Studies in the History of English Education*, 3 vols., London: Lawrence and Wishart, 1960 and 1974.

6. Farmer, op. cit., p. 3.

7. L.R. West, 'The Tawney Legend Re-examined', *Studies in Adult Education* 4 (1), October 1972.

8. R. Hoggart, *The Uses of Literacy*, Harmondsworth: Penguin Books, 1958, pp. 266-69.

9. Farmer, loc. cit.

10. A. Gramsci, *Selections from the Prison Notebooks* (Q. Hoare and G. Nowell Smith, eds.), London: Lawrence and Wishart, 1971, pp. 334-35.

11. Hoggart, loc. cit.

12. A. Gramsci, *La Formazione dell'Uomo: Scritti di Pedagogia* (G. Urbani, ed.), Rome: Editore Riumiti, 96, 1967 (translated).

13. Gramsci, *Prison Notebooks*, p. 339.

14. See J. Klein, *Samples from English Cultures*, 2 vols., London: Routledge and Kegan Paul, 1965; O. Lewis, *Anthropological Essays*, New York: Random House, 1970.

15. Farmer, op. cit., pp. 2-3.

16. See essays by Stanley, Boston and Griffith in Grabowski, op. cit.

17. B.O. Boston, 'Paulo Freire: Notes of a Loving Critic', in Grabowski, op. cit., p. 91; see also D. Goulet, 'Introduction' to P. Freire, *Education for Critical Consciousness*, New York: Seabury Press, 1974, pp. ix-x.

18. P. Freire, 'Education as the Practice of Freedom' (1965), in Freire, *Education*.

19. For a discussion and evaluation of competing claims about the value of literacy to the working class, see H. Entwistle, *Class, Culture and Education*, London: Methuen, 1978, pp. 95-108.

20. Quoted by B.L. Hall, *Adult Education and the Development of Socialism in Tanzania*, Kampala: East African Literature Bureau, 1975, p. 2.

21. Freire, *Education*, p. 37.

22. Ibid., p. 43.

23. Ibid., pp. 49-51; see also ibid., pp. 49-55 and Appendix for description of the research and constructive work involved in compiling and structuring this generative vocabulary; for the description of an attempt to apply Freire's methods to Swahili in Tanzania see M. Gulleth and L.D. Olambo, *Experiments With the Freire Method of Teaching Literacy*, Dar-es-Salaam: Institute of Adult Education, University of Dar-es-Salaam, 1973.

24. See M. Oakeshott, *Rationalism in Politics*, London: Methuen, 1962.

25. General Studies Association, 'A Negative Document: The Political Vocabulary Test', *Bulletin*, no. 12, Winter 1968.

26. B. Crick, 'Basic Concepts for Political Education', *Teaching Politics*, September 1975.

27. B. Crick and I. Lister, 'Political Literacy' (T. Brennan and J.F. Brown, eds.), *Teaching Politics*, BBC Publications, 1975, p. 53.

28. Gramsci, *Prison Notebooks*, p. 350.

29. Tawney, op. cit., p. 85.

30. Ibid., p. 82.

31. E.P. Thompson, *Education and Experience*, Leeds: Leeds University Press, 1968.

32. B.L. Hall, 'Participatory Research: An Approach for Change', *Convergence* VIII (2), 1975.

33. M.L. Swantz, 'Research as an Educational Tool for Development', *Convergence* VIII (2), 1975.

34. Farmer, op. cit., p. 4.

35. P. Freire, 'Extension or Communication' (1968), in Freire, *Education*, p. 114, n. 9.

36. See H. Entwistle, *Political Education in a Democracy*, London: Routledge and Kegan Paul, 1971, ch. 3.

37. Freire, *Education*, p. 28.

38. Ibid., p. 36.

39. Entwistle, *Political Education*, ch. 6.

40. Ibid., pp. 76-78.

41. Goulet, op. cit., p. 41.

42. Hall, *Adult Education*, p. 132.

43. Tawney, op. cit., pp. 80-81.

44. Ibid., pp. 84-92; see also J.E. Thomas and G. Harries-Jenkins, 'Adult Education and Social Change', *Studies in Adult Education* 7 (1) 1975; this essay is a discussion of the relationship of adult education to social change by reference to the different conceptions of 'reform' and 'maintenance'.

45. A. Gramsci, *Selections from Political Writings* (Q. Hoare, ed.), New York: Lawrence and Wishart, 1977, p. 13.

46. Hall, *Adult Education*, pp. 13, 49, 132, 135.

47. Ibid., p. 62.

48. B. Crick, *In Defence of Politics*, Harmondsworth: Penguin Books, 1964.

49. Tawney, op. cit., p. 90.

50. Marx's statement to the General Council of the International, 1869, quoted by M.J. Shore, *Soviet Education*, The Philosophical Library, 1947, pp. 84-85.

51. F. Lilge, 'Lenin and the Politics of Education' in J. Karabel and A. H. Halsey (eds.), *Ideology in Education*, New York: Oxford University Press, 1977.

52. C. Bereiter, *Must We Educate?* Englewood Cliffs, NJ: Prentice-Hall, 1973, p. 89.

53. Tawney, op. cit., p. 90.

54. S. Shriver, 'The Politics of Education', *Adult Leadership*, 19 (5), 1970.

55. J. Cole, 'The Fault, Dear Britain', *Observer*, 30 December 1979.

56. P. Jenkins, 'Political Remedies in our Own Hands', *Guardian*, 28 October 1979.

10

Applying the Perspectives of History and of Psychology to Three Models of International Education

Judith Torney-Purta

For generations the school systems of nation states have used the opportunity available to them to mold students to the needs and demands of the domestic political system. This is probably a more conscious process in the United States than it is in the United Kingdom where, as Heater has recently noted (1978) only within the last decade has political education emerged from a state of stagnation. Although in most Western democratic societies educators have carefully avoided instruction which might be thought of as indoctrination, fostering of patriotic feeling for the country and of positive attitudes toward the government have nevertheless been important aims of education, especially in the United States.

In the process of achieving these goals, factual material about historical events has been mixed with symbolic rituals whose intent is to establish individuals' loyalty to the nation. In both the United States and the United Kingdom in the last decade or two attention

Author's note. Sections on the history of international education, UNESCO's program, and global perspectives are drawn from chapter 2 of *International Human Rights and International Education* by Thomas Buergenthal and Judith Torney, published by the US Government Printing Office in 1976.

has also been paid to training for the skills required for participation in the national government. To support these generalizations is not to argue that there are no important differences between civic education in the US and the UK, nor is it to argue that this education has been conducted in an absence of controversy about methods or objectives. It is to argue that within the area of social education the overriding aim has been to bind individuals to the nation state and not to units which are larger (world government, international organizations or human kind) or smaller (ethnic or local community groups).

This is understandable. Almost all conceptions of national security rely on the loyalty of citizens to the nation and its government and minimize their ties to other groups which are territorially broader or narrower than the nation. Thus 'one-worldism' is dismissed as naive or misguided at the same time that ethnic group loyalty is seen as divisive. The underlying assumption is that individuals possess a quantum of loyalty which can be invested either in the form of positive identification with one's own nation or in positive identification with a world community. Those who make this assumption decline to support international education in the belief that it will weaken national loyalty. This assumption has never been subject to empirical test. In fact, many psychologists would argue that an individual's potential for loyalty and identity can be enhanced in an almost limitless fashion by participation in different groups rather than being 'used up' by relationship to one.

The current status of international education can be understood more fully if the perspectives of two disciplines are applied, the first that of history and the second that of psychology. Both suggest ways in which it may be possible to capitalize on social and political circumstances and to incorporate an understanding of the basic elements of optimal program design. These two perspectives are also helpful in distinguishing between three models of international education which will be discussed — international human rights education; schooling for global citizenship; and development education.

HISTORY OF INTERNATIONAL EDUCATION
FROM THE 1900s TO THE 1960s

Within the history of education directed toward national aims,
some attention has been given to international education, world
studies, and education for peace. Many of these efforts have been
lost as footnotes to the history of education, however. For example, the period from the close of the nineteenth century to the
beginning of World War I has been referred to by an educational
historian (Scanlon, 1960) as 'the greatest effort in the history of
civilization to build a realistic basis for world peace'. During this
period Francis Kemeny, a Hungarian, made the proposition that
there was an international component in all cultures which was the
result of cultural borrowing; nationalism and internationalism
could only be viewed as complementary, in his opinion. He suggested the formation of an organization to set up international conferences for teachers, develop international agreements on the
structure of education, formulate international statements on the
rights of man, revise textbooks to eliminate hatred, and make a
concentrated effort to eradicate racial prejudice (Kemeny quoted in
Scanlon, 1960).

Other organizations established with similar aims during this
period included the Carnegie Endowment for International Peace.
Mr Carnegie in his letter to the trustees in 1910 was optimistic, envi-
sioning a time when war would be 'discarded as disgraceful to
civilized men'; Carnegie cautioned the trustees that when that happened they should devote the endowment's resources to 'the next
most degrading evil or evils' (Carnegie, 1974: 5). The American
School Peace League, whose aim was 'to promote through the
schools and the educational public of America the interests of international justice and fraternity', was also founded during this
period. In the early 1900s schools in the US, England, France and
the Netherlands celebrated 18 May as Peace Day in commemora-
tion of the Hague Peace Conference. Fannie Fern Andrews, an
American, attempted to involve both the ministries of education
and non-governmental organizations abroad in expanding the
School Peace League throughout Europe. In 1911, with the ap-
proval of President Taft, she took on a post in the United States
Office of Education to set up an international conference to plan

for an international bureau which would include a research clear-inghouse and publications program. In 1912, invitations were issued by the Netherlands to sixteen European countries, the United States, and Japan to attend such a conference at the Hague. Only France and Switzerland accepted, and the conference was postponed. In 1914, the invitations were again issued, but the beginning of World War I intervened and the conference was never held.

In the United States in 1912, the National Education Association passed a resolution praising the work of the School Peace League; the report of the NEA Commission on the Reorganization of Secondary Education, issued in 1916, recommended the develop-ment of international world-mindedness, stressing the concept of interrelationships among nations. The effect of these pro-nouncements of educational organizations seems to have been limited. A review of the curriculum in use during this period in-dicated that social studies in the United States had little interna-tional content and consisted of materials about heroes, stories about Indians, and information about holidays stressing national loyalty and patriotism.

Following World War I, during the deliberations over the League of Nations Covenent, the International Council of Women and the Conference of Women Suffragists (including Fannie Fern An-drews) met with representatives of the Allied governments to pre-sent a plan for an International Office of Education. They argued that the popular acceptance of the League depended upon teaching young people about its aims and organization and also that univer-sal schooling was the only way by which the aims of human freedom expressed by the League might be realized. They therefore proposed that the Covenant of the League of Nations provide for the establishment of a permanent bureau of education.

Many nations, jealous of their sovereignty, feared that the League would impose a particular form of education on them, and this bureau was never established. However, the League's Commit-tee on Intellectual Cooperation sponsored international education conferences and by its mission to China in 1931 established the principle that international organizations have a responsibility to aid developing countries. One of the lesser known activities of the committee was the Sub-Committee of Experts for the Instruction of Children and Youth in the Existence and Aims of the League of Nations, which met in Geneva in 1926-7. The document produced by the sub-committee contained recommendations on ways to make the League known to young people and to develop 'the spirit of international cooperation among young children, young people, and their teachers' (cited in Prescott, 1930).

Prescott, an American educator, was impressed by the 'leverage' on national educational authorities which this recommendation provided for the introduction of international material. Some of his conclusions foretell those in the international education literature of today. After a study tour made of six European countries in 1926, he wrote that 'the spirit of the school' is more important in international education than specific curriculum. He also cited the conservative force of tradition which

> resists the introduction . . . of material . . . that would set children to thinking about present international relationships, that would inform them about the various solutions that have been suggested or tried . . . that would demonstrate the extreme interdependence of nations at the present time and the multiple causes of international friction . . . (Prescott, 1930: 114)

Other well-known educators such as Maria Montessori during the 1930s in Europe were discussing a long-range concern for the role of education in promoting world peace. She viewed the child unspoiled by education as a 'teacher of peace' from whom adults could derive many useful lessons. She proposed the study of the structure of society and the existence of mankind as a single nation as the basis of a 'science of peace'. Similar interest among educators in the United States was evidenced by publications such as the 1937 yearbook of the National Society for the Study of Education, which was entitled *International Understanding Through the Public School Curriculum*. In the period before 1940 in most countries of the world beliefs in international education were held primarily by individuals who happened to have traveled abroad or who shared a particular vision of world order. It was not a concern of the average school principal, teacher or school board member. And World War II intensified the stress on national loyalty and discounted the vision of many of the advocates of world peace through education.

UNESCO AND THE ASSOCIATED SCHOOLS

From the point of view of the international community the establishment of UNESCO in 1945 is the most important event which took place in education during the post-World War II period. Its Constitution represented the culmination of several years of work by the Allied ministers of education meeting in exile during the war. For a time it appeared that education might be excluded from this organization's mission for the same reasons of concern for domestic jurisdiction advanced at the time of the League of Nations. However, this concern did not prevail, and an entire sector of UNESCO is devoted to education. Moreover, the UNESCO Constitution is permeated with the conviction that education is an indispensable element in the construction of a lasting peace. Its preamble proclaims:

> that since wars begin in the minds of men, it is in the minds of men that the defences of peace must be constructed . . .

and continues,

> that the wide diffusion of culture, and the education of humanity for justice and liberty and peace are indispensable to the dignity of man and constitute a sacred duty which all the nations must fulfill in a spirit of mutual assistance and concern . . .

The Universal Declaration of Human Rights, adopted unanimously by the UN General Assembly in 1948 is another landmark recognition of the importance of international education and the role of human rights in it. In Article 26 the Declaration states that education,

> shall promote understanding, tolerance and friendship among all nations, racial or religious groups, and shall further the activities of the United Nations for the maintenance of peace.

UNESCO is unique among the organizations in the UN system in its mandated concern for building the psychological and educational foundations for peace and unique among educational organizations in the requirement that human rights be given prominent consideration in its program.

Early in UNESCO's history (from 1947 to 1952) conferences of teachers explored how education could best contribute to international understanding. These conferences seemed to have their principal impact upon the participants; in 1952, therefore, it was decided that a more systematic approach was needed. In 1953, a network of secondary schools closely associated with UNESCO was established in fifteen countries (not including the United States); these UNESCO-Associated Schools conducted projects of their own choosing on three themes: the rights of women; the characteristics of other countries, peoples, and cultures; and the principles of human rights and their relationship to the work of the United Nations.

These early Associated Schools frequently utilized an historical approach to the United Nations including its peace-keeping functions. This involved dealing with the idea that different governments have the right to hold different points of view and with the role of the United Nations as a public forum for the peaceful resolution of international disputes. The problem-centred approach, focusing on the struggle against disease, the conservation of resources, and the UN's efforts in solving world problems was also used in many of the projects of the Associated Schools.

The UNESCO summary of the Associated Schools' programs issued in 1971 concluded that:

> the majority of projects have been successful in achieving their general objectives of increasing knowledge of world affairs, giving pupils a sounder comprehension of other people and cultures, and developing attitudes favourable to international understanding. (UNESCO, 1971: 15)

Those who examined these projects also concluded that the impact of the programs depends to a large extent on

> the preconditions of education for international understanding. An especially important factor is the atmosphere of the school. . . . The principles of human rights should be reflected in the organization and conduct of school life, in classroom methods, and in relations among teachers and students and among teachers themselves. (UNESCO, 1971: 23)

The ultimate aim of the Associated Schools Project is not only to improve the international understanding of students in participating schools but also to insure that this aim is reflected in the curriculum and syllabi promulgated by ministries of education and other influential groups. This has turned out to be somewhat more difficult than establishing the programs in individual schools.

A 1975 report indicated 1,000 participating institutions in 63 member states including countries with widely differing cultural traditions, stages of development and social/economic systems. The largest proportion of these institutions are secondary schools, but primary schools and teacher-training institutions (and a few institutions of higher education) also participate.

In many countries of the world, especially those in Eastern Europe and the developing world, the UNESCO Associated Schools Project is the major impetus to the inclusion of international education themes and topics in the curriculum. Although a network of schools exists in the United States, it functions alongside and in connection with a variety of other global and international education programs. Much the same situation characterizes the UK. In both nations independently during the last few years, movements to reinvigorate the Associated Schools Project have taken place.

At the present time an evaluation of the Associated Schools Project is being undertaken by two scholars who have not themselves been involved in implementing it. And the Associated Schools continue to play an important role in UNESCO's international education plans because they provide important links for international cooperation among a variety of nations whose other opportunities for multilateral connections in education are relatively limited.

EDUCATION FOR INTERNATIONAL UNDERSTANDING AND HUMAN RIGHTS

The major conceptual contribution which UNESCO has made to education for international understanding has been broader than the Associated Schools. In 1974 the General Conference of UNESCO passed a 'Recommendation on Education for International Understanding, Cooperation and Peace and Education relating to Human Rights and Fundamental Freedoms'. Representatives of the large majority of the member states of UNESCO participated in drafting this Recommendation thus giving it a consensual status as an international document. An article from its Guiding Principles will give the flavor of this document:

> In order to enable every person to contribute actively to the fulfillment of the aims referred to and promote international solidarity and cooperation, which are necessary in solving world problems affecting the individuals' and communities' life and exercise of fundamental rights and freedoms, the following objectives should be regarded as major guiding principles of educational policy:
>
> (a) an international dimension and a global perspective in education at all levels and in all its forms;
> (b) understanding and respect for all peoples, their cultures, civilizations, values and ways of life, including domestic ethnic cultures and cultures of other nations;
> (c) awareness of the increasing global interdependence between peoples and nations;
> (d) abilities to communicate with others;
> (e) awareness not only of the rights but also of the duties incumbent upon individuals, social groups and nations towards each other;
> (f) understanding of the necessity for international solidarity and cooperation;
> (g) readiness on the part of the individual to participate in solving the problems of his community, his country and the world at large. (para. 4)

Since 1974, this recommendation has served as the organizing plan for the programs of UNESCO in this area. It has also represented a conceptual breakthrough because it has linked educational for international understanding with human rights education, a connection which previously was implicit but not explicit in UNESCO's program. It recognizes that when programs such as disarmanent education, international understanding education, and peace education are conducted under the auspices of UNESCO, they must include education regarding the existence of an international consensus on basic human rights and international procedures designed to protect these rights. It is important to note that this recommendation was passed by the General Conference of UNESCO two full years before President Carter's election (after which human rights was given an enhanced position on the American foreign policy agenda) and also before the signing of the Helsinki Accords (which established human rights as a topic for discussion in the East-West debate). UNESCO now requires member states to report periodically on actions they have taken to implement the Recommendation on Education for International Understanding and Human Rights.

In 1977, a UNESCO congress on Teaching Human Rights was held in Vienna. Following that congress, a group of representatives drafted a Seven-Year Plan for Teaching Human Rights which proposes the involvement of a number of structures of UNESCO (its programs in social science as well as education) and calls upon educators in member states to undertake new initiatives. UNESCO has commissioned a Guidebook for Teachers (Graves et al., in press) which will aid them in incorporating programs of international understanding in their classrooms. This book will provide specific suggestions in areas such as teaching about other cultures, international conflict, and human rights and will be written by scholars from nations in different world areas.

In the United States, teaching about human rights has been the focus of the US National Commission for UNESCO's international education efforts. Information about the international protection of human rights is the subject of many volumes of international law. However, the average fourth grade teacher can hardly be expected to walk into a law library, take out a case book on international human rights, read a half a page of text and a half a page of footnotes, and construct an appropriate lesson for his or her class. So, the first step taken by the US National Commission for UNESCO was the publication of a book, *International Human Rights and International Education*, which introduced the 1974 Recommendation to educators (Buergenthal and Torney, 1976). More important, it gave them basic information about international organizations and procedures protecting human rights which could be used to develop materials and programs. That publication was followed by a conference in 1978 at which representatives of Finland, the Federal Republic of Germany, Canada and the United States met to form more detailed plans concerning international human rights education. Individuals who specialized in international law, teacher training, curriculum development, and educational research developed four general objectives for human rights education:

1. To make students aware of the universal yearning for human rights as part of a sense of human community.
2. To transmit to students basic knowledge concerning international instruments to protect human rights and associated institutions.
3. To give students experience in thinking critically about these issues and their application in illustrative cases.
4. To encourage concern or empathy for those who have experienced violations of their rights. (Torney, 1978: 2)

Although these objectives were agreed upon by representatives of four nations, it is clear that each country's school system must make particular adaptation of the material for their own educational structures.

At the present time in the United States, the average student hears about the concept of rights only in the national context. The study of the US Constitution is begun in the elementary school when students are asked to give examples of their enjoyment of freedom of religion (going to the church of their choice) and the freedom of the press (reading the newspaper of their choice). In many states a passing grade on a test covering the US Constitution and Bill of Rights is required for admission to secondary school, but a secondary school graduate would not be atypical if he or she had never read about the Universal Declaration of Human Rights in any textbook. Because schools teach so much about domestic guarantees of rights and so little about international processes and procedures, it is understandable that many Americans believe that the concepts of rights was invented in their country. In a parallel area, a survey conducted by the National Assessment for Educational Progress showed that a substantial percentage of thirteen-year olds believe that the United States is the only country in the world which has certain political institutions, such as a written constitution.

A small interview study recently conducted in the United States with children aged nine through thirteen explored both the issue of nation-centredness in the perception of rights and the issue of basic consensus on principles of human rights (Torney and Brice, 1979). About one third of approximately forty students said they had never heard of the term human rights. When these students were given examples of rights and asked if there were any persons or organizations that tried to help people enjoy such rights, none mentioned the United Nations or other international organizations. The most common response was that the US President or government should tell other leaders how to give rights to the people in their country.

In spite of this restriction in their view of human rights protection to the national context, these young people were in almost unanimous agreement about the principles of human rights. They were asked questions taken directly from the Universal Declaration of Human Rights (without identifying their source or labeling them as human rights questions). For example, one question read, 'If it was decided in another country that it was all right to buy and sell people like slaves and there were no rules or laws against that, would that be right?' Another question was as follows: 'Suppose that a group of people in another country decided that in their country it was all right to put someone in prison for several years without going to court and having a trial. So they had no laws saying that people should have a trial before being put in jail. Would that be right?' A third question asked: 'What if someone in another country was arrested and the police thought that he was guilty, but the person would not admit it. Would it be right for the police to beat the person to get him to admit to the crime or to get evidence?' In response to these questions (and others like them dealing with basic human rights), ninety to one hundred percent of the children said that no law enacted by a country could justify actions which violated rights. This suggests that although they know very little about the international protection of human rights, there is nevertheless a deeply held belief in American children that human beings have certain rights by virtue of being human. Because there is a lack of information connected with this belief, human rights is an especially important content area for education.

A number of attempts are currently underway in the United States to produce material useful for international human rights education and to stimulate its use by teachers. Publications of the Center for Global Perspectives in Education, the Center for Teaching International Relations and the World Education Center have included teaching materials on this topic. Lists of materials available on apartheid also include useful sources. The state of New York is beginning an effort to integrate material on human rights into its curricula and to pilot an elective course on this subject in the secondary school. In developing these materials and programs, the link between human rights problems and international procedures and institutions needs to be constantly reinforced. (See chapter by Torney-Purta in Graves, et al., reviewing twenty-seven activities for teaching human rights.)

In summary, the human rights thrust stimulated by the 1974 UNESCO recommendation provides a model which can stand on its own independent from the Associated Schools. The recently strengthened human rights procedures of many international organizations and agencies, including UNESCO, where teachers, social and natural scientists, and artists may now file individual complaints against governments for the violation of their rights, provide a supportive context for educational programs. International human rights education is not a passing fad, but a concept deeply rooted in principles of justice and the practice of international cooperation.

SCHOOLING AND GLOBAL CITIZENSHIP

The history of interest in education designed to reflect the individual's membership in a global society may be traced back to 1966 when the US Office of Education funded a proposal of the Foreign Policy Association to prepare 'An Examination of Objectives, Needs and Priorities in International Education in the United States' Secondary and Elementary Schools', frequently referred to as the Becker/Anderson report (after its two authors). A series of papers from well-known scholars in several disciplines on the global character of the subject matter were commissioned and existing school programs were examined. The unstated definitions of international education with which schools appeared to operate were examined: first, international education as that which deals with 'strange lands and friendly peoples'; and secondly, international education as that which is taught in specific courses such as world history, international relations, or foreign area studies. Becker and Anderson found these definitions inadequate.

For example, though one of the more widely claimed purposes of international studies is the reduction of students' ethnocentric perception of the world, if international education is thought of merely as education about other lands and other peoples, a 'we-they' distinction has been built into the very heart of the enterprise. Also, the tendency to divide the world into 'things American' and 'things non-American', for purposes of study, obscures the degree to which study of American history, society and social institutions has important international dimensions which can serve either to detract from or augument the development of students' understanding of the world beyond their nation's boundaries (Becker and Anderson, 1969: 17).

In attempting to formulate a satisfactory preliminary definition, these authors enumerated three aspects of the international environment: societies (territorially based association including nation states); social institutions and associations that cross or span societal barriers (e.g., the United Nations, the World Bank, NATO, business firms, religious organizations, youth associations); and interactions both among groups and individuals across societal boundaries. They concluded, however, that even definitions stressing these elements did not sufficiently emphasize the global nature of present world reality. Accordingly, the definition finally adopted was as follows:

> International education consists of those social experiences and learning processes through which individuals acquire and change their orientations to international or world society and their conception of themselves as members of that society. . . . For the purposes of understanding human behavior, it has become useful to think of the human species as having reached a point on the scales of interdependence, common values, and shared problems where we can analytically view the planet's population as members of a single, albeit loosely integrated, society. It is fruitful to think of individuals as having orientations to international society and conceptions of themselves as members of that society. (Becker and Anderson, 1969: 30-31)

In contrast to previous definitions, which had stressed education about other nations, these authors constructed a typology of objectives clustered around two major themes. First, they delineated the 'objects of international understanding'. There were three particular objects through which the school curriculum might be helpful in giving students a fuller understanding of the essence of international education: 1) earth as a planet; 2) mankind as one species of life (including both the existence of commonalities and the source of human differences); and 3) the international system as one level of human social organization. The last item included,

> but was not confined to knowledge about the UN in terms of the function it performs as a center of decision-making, a site for diplomatic negotiations, an agent in the channeling of economic resources from the developed to the developing nations, a forum for national propaganda, a peace-keeping or policing institution.

The processes by which national societies interact and the major international social problems are dealt with (e.g., control of conflict or war, foreign policy decision-making, reduction of social and psychological cost of world-wide urbanization), were subsumed under the third object of international understanding. Having delineated these three objects which individuals or groups need to comprehend, the authors then considered the capacities which ought to be developed in individuals: being knowledgeable about phenomena; being able to make analytic judgements; and following these, being competent to arrive at normative judgements in the form of attitudes (in particular, 'humane evaluations'), possessing the ability to critically observe current history, being able to analyze policy and, finally, the motivation to act.

Previous work had given little attention to specifying the objects or dimensions of international understanding. Education for this complex human goal had more frequently been assumed to require only the development of empathy or positive attitudes toward other countries and negative attitudes toward war. The Becker/Anderson report was notable for giving a lessened emphasis to the role of nation states, to the part played by international leaders as major actors, and to the functions of the United Nations and its agencies. These were only elements in a much longer list of important 'objects' which should be understood by the individual who strives for international competence.

In establishing the educational legitimacy of terms such as 'the global perspective in education' the Becker/Anderson report has been a landmark. It has been widely quoted, and has expanded the group of those who pursue such objectives from an élite group of teachers who happen to have traveled extensively or studied other cultures to a concerned group of teachers, curriculum specialists, and administrators of various persuasions who have a vision of the global system and how education can prepare an individual student to live more effectively in it. It has provided the framework within which many organizations, ranging from the US Office of Education's Global Education Task Force to local school districts, have constructed recommendations and programs.

More recently, Anderson (1979) has expanded on the ideas set forth in the earlier report and has examined evidence from a wide range of disciplines on the emergence of a global society. He argues, presenting extensive documentation drawn from history, geography, economics, political science and sociology that globalization of the human condition may be thought of as taking place according to a geometric progression described by a J-curve. The evolution of global systems of transportation and communication have been among the essential elements of this globalization. Portions of his arguments derived from history, and from sociology/anthropology will serve as examples:

> The evolution of a single world wide political system is a product of three historical trends: (a) the globalization of the European state system that emerged in the Seventeenth Century, (b) the emergence of non-European states to positions of power in the system, and (c) the growing power of the Third World.

> Six major types of changes have occurred in the structure of the international system: (a) the growth of nonstate actors, (b) the decreasing coherence of nation states, (c) the growth of transgovernmental relations, (d) the expanding substantive scope of international politics, (e) the changing character of military conflict, and (f) the growing obsolescence of traditional doctrines of international relations. (Anderson, 1979: 240)

This process has had several effects.

> First, there is an expanding portion of humanity whose lives are directly affected for good or ill by world politics . . . second, the size of the world's political elite is growing . . . and third, opportunities for self-conscious and deliberate citizen involvement in world affairs are increasing. (p. 246)

A parallel argument is made from sociology/anthropology:

There currently exists a global culture.

The creation of a global culture is a result of two historical processess characteristic of the modern era and particularly of contemporary history. These are (a) increasing interrelatedness between societies and (b) increasing cultural congruence among societies . . .

Increasing interrelatedness combined with increasing cultural congruence serves to globalize human culture by creating dimensions of shared culture and domains of common culture constitute a global culture.

Anderson continues:

The emergence of a common global culture does not eradicate all of traditionally diverse regional, national, and local cultures. Rather the development of a global culture creates a structurally complex cultural system in which global culture co-exists in uneasy relationship to traditional, local and microcultures.

Global culture evidences regional, national and local variations, but these variations are variants on a common theme. (Anderson, 1979: 316-17)

Anderson concludes that 'progressive historical globalization of the human condition has brought into being a human society on a planetary scale.' Further, the demands upon citizens in an age which may be characterized in this way 'call for competencies which have not traditionally been emphasized by schools' (Anderson, 1979: 335). This need for new competencies is tied directly to citizenship education. Citizenship, in Anderson's view, need not be restricted to relationships between an individual and the government of a single nation but can relate the individual to diverse groups and systems at many levels. Citizenship is not limited to traditional activities such as voting and obeying laws, but includes a much wider range of actions and decisions. In order to be a competent citizen, by this definition, one needs to be competent first, in perceiving one's involvement in global society; second, in deciding between courses of action which influence and are influenced by global society (including the transnational and long-term consequences of decisions); third, in reaching judgements about world problems and alternative futures; and fourth, in exercising influence through personal, social and political activities. A very complete typology of these capacities and abilities is presented with the aim of defining 'citizenship for a global age'; and stimulating education programs which can equip students for these roles.

It is reasonable to assume that this report will have an influence upon American programs of international education which is at least as substantial as the Becker/Anderson report of ten years ago. The documentation in Anderson (1979) is massive and persuasive. (The report itself is a useful resource for those who wish data from which to develop curriculum.) The educational objectives detailed within the four categories of competencies are wide-ranging and imaginative, though some may prove difficult to justify to educators and to implement in materials and strategies within the American context. Even more substantial modifications may be necessary to adapt them to other contexts. This report will certainly make educators who are not currently involved more aware of global education. However, its potential impact should also be assessed in light of the known impact of the earlier work in this area.

A recent review of US activity in global education over the last decade (Collins, 1979) has concluded that although some progress has been made, there are still substantial problems. To cite a few,

> Global education does not now hold a position of high priority in the minds of the majority of educators. . . . Students also seem more concerned about themselves than about other areas of the world. Most educators attempting to deal with global studies are handicapped by their lack of formal training, their unfamiliarity with the teaching techniques and materials and their lack of personal cross-cultural experience. (Collins, 1979: 11)

Collins argues that materials are available; however, as long as global education has no strong advocates and must be implemented by individuals who are uneasy about their training, progress will be very slow. He continues: 'Global studies are still seen . . . as solely the concern of the social studies, particularly the area studies, world history and world geography' (p. 13). It should be noted that some of these courses are offered only as electives in which a small minority of students register. Furthermore, these courses often do not deal with key topics of current importance but stress the accumulation of facts and a compartmentalized approach to the areas of the world. When attempts are made to globalize the curriculum beyond these courses, it is often seen as a threat to the interests of those in other subject areas. Collins continues: 'Global education suffers more severely than most fields from . . . "felt instability" ' (p. 16). He notes that few of the organizations or individuals currently active in the field have been so for more than five years. Global education thus suffers from the image of being a new 'fad' which will pass. Those given responsibility in education units for global education frequently are also expected to advocate a diverse package of other topics ranging from career education to drug education. Finally, Collins concludes: 'Education has always suffered from a lack of objective evaluation. Global education, on the other hand, hasn't suffered . . . it appears to be largely unaware of the problem' (p. 15). Lack of evaluation makes it very difficult to convince those who make policy or implement curriculum that global education makes any difference. Although some may argue that Collins presents an over pessimistic view, it would be unrealistic to argue that global education has successfully transformed the awareness of American young people.

An evaluation of what is called The Cycle of Neglect of World Studies in the UK paints a similar picture:

> Teachers lack world awareness and knowledge, as well as confidence to teach these themes.
>
> Books on world themes are often expensive or of lower quality. School exams include few world themes.
>
> There is lack of educational research in this field. (Wright and Wright, 1974)

To advance education for citizenship in a global age, or education with a global perspective, or world studies beyond the current position is clearly a continuing challenge. The conceptualization of global society which Becker and Anderson have laid out will continue to stimulate programs as well as discussion among educators, but it is not likely in the foreseeable future to occupy as important a place as national political education on the agenda of the United States and United Kingdom.

DEVELOPMENT EDUCATION

The term development education is sometimes used inter-
changeably with global education or education for international
understanding. However, it also has a special character and a
slightly narrower focus than the concept of global education
presented in the preceding section. 'Development education' was
first used in the late 1960s and early 1970s by individuals who worked in international governmental and voluntary agencies which
raised funds for assistance to developing countries. At that time
there was an increasing awareness that the United Nations'
Development Decade was likely to have a much more modest impact on the transfer of resources from the rich countries of the
north to the less-developed countries of the south than had been
hoped. The term was used to describe the expansion in the information outreach of agencies whose only goals previously had been to
raise funds for development assistance. This attempt to focus
educational attention on promoting an understanding of world
poverty was a response to growing dissatisfaction with inducing
people to give funds in response to a crisis (a famine or flood) and a
desire instead to inform individuals about complex problems which
have only long-range solutions (Dunlop, 1980).

Force, who has recently reviewed a number of Constituency
Education Programs, for Church World Services (1979), notes that
an important aim of development education (especially that conducted for adults) has been moving people from information to
commitment. The interconnection of questions of justice at home
and abroad is stressed. There are two routes to understanding
world problems. Stimulating individuals' global awareness by con-
centrating on the overseas challenge means alerting people to events
by presenting them with symbols of reality and attempting to
engage their empathetic response. It may be possible to make people aware of conditions in other parts of the world which they have
not previously perceived as influencing their own lives, but the process often loses its power because it relies on symbols and indirect
experience. In contrast, he defends the process of 'conscientization'
as one which relies on local challenge; it may be stronger according
to Force, because it relies on sensory impressions and personal experience in an individual's own community. This model recognizes

individual differences — some people are more receptive to overseas challenge, others to local challenge. The eventual interconnection between these two paths is essential, however.

Programs of development education in voluntary organizations, especially those in the churches during the 1970s, made the assumption according to Force that

> massive efforts in information and education would produce 'new people' ready to change their life styles, their production patterns, the structures of their societies, the exploitative relations between rich and poor. (Force, 1979: 25)

In fact, he cites one report, which recommended that a quarter of available funds should be spent for education at home 'until attitudinal changes shall have occurred'. (This is similar to Carnegie's concern for the use of endowment funds for peace, but only until 'war had been abolished'.)

The difficulty of attitudinal change, combined with problems in involving individuals in action for justice, led Force to speak strongly in favor of a pluralistic approach to development education adapted to particular circumstances. Encouraging charity and compassion for others whose underdevelopment is the result of 'backwardness' is presumably acceptable only if other approaches are not feasible. Fostering the structural understanding of underdevelopment as the result of unequal economic relations (due to colonialism) is more likely to produce concern for justice, but often does not go far enough in changing individuals' behavior. The third stand, which defines underdevelopment as a result of dependent development requires a pedagogical approach based on 'liberating experiences, involvement in action that expresses solidarity with the poor worldwide, search for alternatives in social organization, production, and life style' (Force, 1979: 27). This third approach defines problems as having their origin in the First World, not the Third World and seeks a radical reorganization of power structures. This model, which would have extraordinary difficulties in being incorporated into most school systems, has even had considerable problems within voluntary organizations. Although not unduly optimistic, Force concludes that: 'We should aim to spend as much time educating ourselves and our constituency about the causes of world poverty and injustice and in the ways

they might be removed as we do to raise money to alleviate them
. . .' (Force, 1979: 99). This implies an improved understanding of
the 'structures of power, domination, and dependence'. It means

> campaigning to change the attitudes of those in power; more involvement by
> people in the First World with underprivileged groups in their own countries
> (e.g., migrant workers); more participation by people from the Third World in
> voluntary agencies based in the First World. (Force, 1979: 100)

Force presents these issues as an agenda for future discussion and
action based on his examination of program content, but they also
correspond in some interesting ways with the results of some empirical research conducted independently which surveyed approximately 160 individuals in churches who were active in world
hunger and social action concerns and compared them with a sample of 160 individuals who were active in churches without a social
action focus. Also tested were 115 members of Bread for the World
(a voluntary organization). This study demonstrated some differences among groups in perceptions of the causes and potential
solutions for problems of world poverty; more strikingly, the study
revealed that the major source of positive feeling about voluntary
activity on the part of involved individuals was their belief that they
themselves are learning more about the problem and they are having a positive impact on the attitudes of other people. Reinforcement for continued activity was not dependent on the feeling of
having made much difference in solving the problems of hunger
itself, but rather included positive feelings resulting from close-to-
home educational activity (Torney, 1980).

Development education has not been limited to voluntary
organizations nor to the United States. It has always included a
stress upon understanding causes of world problems and on active
approaches to ameliorating injustice within one's own society, but
it has not in all cases gone as far as advocating changes in power
structures, such as those which Force proposes. A project carried
out by IFRED for FAO and UNESCO in 1973-74 surveyed in-
school development education in six European nations (France,
Federal Republic of Germany, Hungary, Sweden, Switzerland and
the United Kingdom). The purpose of the study was

to determine the present role of the school at the post-primary level in sensitizing children to problems of development and in forming new attitudes toward these questions. (UNESCO, 1974: 2)

The study examined the education of students of approximately ten to fifteen years of age who were in the first cycle of secondary education. The report refers to two approaches. In the first children are given information about Third World countries to further their understanding of relationships between industrialized and developing countries. In the second approach it is proposed that the scope of development education be broadened to link it 'to issues closely related to children's lives, their immediate environment and concrete experiences' (p. 5). A variety of issues were suggested: the situation of migrant workers, ecological studies, other community problems, and educational reform.

Although these issues seem very diverse and in some ways separated from the core concern of aiding developing societies, they are quite consistent with the general approach outlined by Force using involvement in local issues to stimulate global awareness. There is a further justification contained in the UNESCO report for development education which begins with local issues. If one assumes that

dependency and domination both between developed and highly industrialized countries and between different social strata within these countries are responsible for maldevelopment, students must come to understand the conflicts and antagonisms which exist in all societies. (UNESCO, 1974: 59)

Within the formal education system, development education is probably stronger in the United Kingdom than it is in the United States, in large part because of the catalytic effect of the Development Education Fund of the Ministry of Overseas Development upon curriculum innovation (Dunlop, 1980). A current definition has been offered by the ODM:

We use the term development education to describe those processes of thought and action which increase understanding of worldwide social, economic, and political conditions, particularly those which relate to, and are responsible for underdevelopment. Its purpose is to encourage widespread involvement in action for improvement. (Cited in Dunlop, 1980: 3)

Teachers' guides to presentations of development education published by the Center for World Development Education indicate the content in this area. A booklet entitled *The Changing World and Religious Education* suggests ways in which teachers might incorporate these aims into the curriculum in courses in religious education (offered in many schools in the United Kingdom). Having discussed the meaning of development, it continues to discuss its connection with values of social justice, empathy, and sharing. Another booklet, *The Changing World and Geography*, takes a more comprehensive approach. One aim of the booklet is to help geography teachers decide whether textbooks available in the United Kingdom adequately cover the 'development dimension'. By means of a checklist of desirable cognitive and affective outcomes, books commonly available for school use can be rated. Among the questions asked are whether the book:

1. deals with spatial variations in the levels of human welfare, measured on a variety of scales? Does it consider the validity of measures of human welfare, e.g., GNP?
2. shows any awareness of the cultural achievements of developing countries and the cultural debts that industrialized countries owe to them?
3. discusses the physical environment in terms of constraints upon, and opportunities for, development?
4. deals with the history of the developing countries concerned, with reference to their colonial background?
5. deals with the world distribution of resources and production?
6. deals with the content and direction of international trade, its changing patterns and the ways in which it affects the internal structure of developing countries?
7. presents a range of agricultural situations in developing countries and discusses questions of land ownership and land reform?
9. discusses the nature of aid relationships?
10. looks at alternative strategies for development?
11. examines the economic, social and cultural effects of tourism?
12. includes any discussion of the role of large multinational corporations? (Cited in Dunlop, 1980: 4-5)

It is assumed that by drawing teachers' attention to these criteria in selecting books, one will also stimulate them to seek out materials which deal more adequately with development issues.

In summary, development education as an approach to international education shares some of the same foci with human rights education and education for global citizenship, but it also has particular themes which receive extra stress, especially the link between close-to-home activity and international development.

The three models presented — international human rights education, global education, and development education — do not, of course, exhaust the possible approaches. These models may also be differentially appropriate for individuals of different ages and in different situations or cultures. And, in practice, each of them borrows to some extent from all the others.

THE PSYCHOLOGICAL PERSPECTIVE AND INTERNATIONAL EDUCATION

Up to this point the focus has been on the content and justifications given for each of the models. None has been totally successful either on a national or an international basis. Each continues to search for improvements to make them more salient and more effective. The perspective of psychology is useful in supplementing this analysis of history and content. In particular, there are two psychological concepts which can be applied to each model — questions about sequence (or timing) and questions about motivation.

Questions of Sequence and Timing Applied to the Three Models

A recent review of the educational research literature with regard to differing principles by which curriculum may be sequenced introduces one of these important issues from a pedagogical point of view (Posner and Strike, 1976). The question of sequence has been ignored in much of the international education literature. In fact, different sequences of content may result in unequal learning of content. Even if different sequences are equally effective, they may have hidden results in the form of differing conceptions by the student of how a subject is structured or of links between elements. Posner and Strike illustrate two kinds of sequences: those which are derived from the subject matter and those which are based on the learner. One method of sequencing is based upon empirical relationships among events, people and things. This includes spatial relationships (teaching the names of countries according to geographical location), time (teaching historical events in chronological order), and physical attributes including complexity (teaching about the structure of primitive society before teaching about complex industrial society). Other principles of sequence which they identify are based on the fundamental concepts of a discipline, e.g., class relations (teaching discrimination before examining racial or sex discrimination).

In addition to sequences derived from subject matter, there are, according to Posner and Strike, a number of sequences which rely more on conceptions of the learner and the learning process. First is the sequence based on empirical prerequisites, e.g., when the learning of one skill — such as alphabetizing words — is necessary before one can teach another — using the dictionary. Second is a sequence based on familiarity — e.g., teaching about local issues before teaching about other nations. The third principle is difficulty — teaching the spelling of short words before longer ones. Fourth are sequences based on interest — teaching things which are of intrinsic interest first. Fifth, there is a sequence based on the principles of development. These authors limit their use of 'development' to changes in the learner that result from maturation, which is a somewhat narrow view. Finally, they consider internalization as a learner sequencing principle (e.g., teaching students to recognize behaviors in others before recognizing these behaviors in themselves). The last set of sequencing principles is based on utilization (e.g., teaching things in the order in which one will have to use them).

There have been a few empirical studies in sequencing. Crabtree (1976) examined concepts derived from a social studies curriculum in regional geography using second graders. Three criteria were employed to test whether a sequence existed: first, whether each learner achieved concepts in a fixed order (invariance); second, whether each new concept represented the reorganization of concepts from earlier stages (hierarchic organization); and third, whether a concept once achieved could not be dissolved (irreversibility). By examining patterns of correct and incorrect responses on a test she demonstrated that, in fact, mastery of each higher order capacity was dependent on mastery of capabilities antecedent to it (as predicted by the conceptual sequence).

> Thus, mastery of the concept of areal association, the central analytic concept in the regional method of geographic analysis, was dependent on children's prior learning of discrimination and classification skills involving the critical observation of geographic data, and their ordering into appropriate, functionally defined regional categories. Once mastered, the concept of areal association, in turn, facilitated children's learning of the analytic processes which permit the search for patterns of accordance and, subsequently, patterns of spatial interaction between functionally related geographic features within and between regions. (Crabtree, 1976: 29)

A related approach to timing and sequence is represented by the cognitive developmental model as proposed by Kohlberg to describe progressive changes in moral development. This model has been of tremendous interest to educators.

The theory posits that an individual's judgements of morality move through an invariant sequence of stages progressing from hedonistic (oriented to reward and punishment) to conventional (rule oriented) to morally principled. According to this theory, exposing an individual to a state of moral reasoning slightly above his or her current one induces conflict which, when resolved by a kind of mental reorganization, results in a progression to a higher stage of moral reasoning.

Programs using this rationale introduce moral dilemmas in the classroom, where active discussion is encouraged between small groups of students who are at different levels of moral reasoning. Evaluation has indicated that participation in such discussion facilitates attainment of the next higher stage of moral reasoning in many students, although there is often no concomitant change in behavior in situations where it might be possible to cheat without obvious detection (Blatt and Kohlberg, 1975). These programs have most typically used the teacher as a discussion leader rather than as a model or source of information. Very recently Kohlberg himself has expressed some discontent with reliance on these methods to the exclusion of others and has concluded that attempts to convince children of the 'immorality' of cheating, aggressing, or stealing may not necessarily be indoctrination (as he previously viewed them) (Kohlberg, 1978).

Although moral education programs have had some successes, many educators in their haste to implement specific curricula appear to have lost sight of two of the most basic premises of Kohlberg's theory (and of the theory of Piaget's to which it is allied). These are notions of timing and sequence. Are educational efforts more likely to be effective if they are presented at one stage (phase or age) of an individual's cognitive growth than at another? Are educational efforts more effective if they are presented in the sequence which is 'natural' in the child's development? Brainerd (1978) argues that the answer to these questions is 'yes' and has outlined and summarized the implications of Piaget's theory in curriculum sequencing as it might be appropriate in a variety of fields:

> We should not try to teach children material that is clearly beyond their present stage of cognitive development.... We should try where possible to teach children new concepts in the same order that these concepts emerge during spontaneous cognitive development. (Brainerd, 1978: 273-75)

In fact, the three criteria which Crabtree used in defining sequence in her curriculum study are precisely those which stage theorists like Piaget and Kohlberg use — invariance of order, hierarchy, irreversibility. It could be argued that these notions about sequence are much more basic to the structure of cognitive developmental theory and useful for its application in international education than are the specifics of moral development content.

What assumptions regarding timing and sequence are made in the three models presented earlier — human rights education, global education, and development education? With respect to education about international human rights, I have argued elsewhere that middle childhood and early adolescence are optimal periods for these programs because certain cognitive abilities and the capacity to take the perspective of someone else are likely to have developed, but the young person does not yet have strong pressure to conform to adolescent groups by negatively judging ideas or individuals which seem different from group norms (Torney, 1980). The issue of optimal sequence in human rights education is derived from the premise, supported by Posner and Strike, that the sequence in which elements are presented may determine children's assumptions about the structure of the real world. It seems likely in this area that there is a strong primacy effect. The concept which is acquired first serves as the basis on which other knowledge is cumulated. It might, therefore, be argued that to present domestic definitions of human rights first and then to place little (if any) stress on international rights protection gives the child a concept which lacks an important dimension. If this is true, the optimal sequence would be to teach about the universal search for basic human rights in all nations (by study of the Universal Declaration of Human Rights) and then to teach about domestic guarantees (US Constitution) in this context. One might also consider a sequence which taught about human rights instruments first and then considered various world problems in that context — hunger problems as a denial of economic and social rights, imprisonment for political beliefs as a violation of civil and political rights, racial inequalities as an instance of discrimination. Empirical research comparing different sequences for their effectiveness is badly needed because there may be better ways than progressing from national to international.

The second model, citizenship education for global perspectives, has a very complex set of objectives which are somewhat more difficult to analyze for optimal timing or sequence. Some of the same timing principles delineated for human rights education, such as the importance of middle childhood and adolescence, probably also apply in this model. In terms of sequence, awareness almost certainly must come before more complex decision-making and action. However, it is probably also true that the individual who becomes active also expands his or her awareness. Education in global perspectives has suffered from many of the same untested assumptions about sequence that human rights education has faced. The global context is often considered in the last chapter of the social studies book; if time (or space) is short, this point of view is ignored completely. Anderson's most recent exposition (1979) suggests that one may need to begin simultaneously close to home and with a global context mind, since it is artificial to distinguish between domestic and foreign.

Most discussions of development education suggest that one can begin either with global concerns or local concerns; the preference appears to be for involving people locally, however, on the grounds that there are similarities between the power structures within local communities and those in the world as a whole, and individuals are more likely to learn from direct experience. As long as the educational process pays attention to both, it has a reasonable probability of successfully enhancing awareness of development issues.

The major conclusion to be drawn, however, is that concern for the psychological and pedagogical issues of sequence and timing has not been adequately considered in the design of international education programs. Presumptions about relations within the subject matter — moving from close to far have been used more frequently than those which involve conceptions of the learner. Sequences which have not been tried may be more appropriate than those which have been. But that possibility can only be explored exploring the effectiveness of alternatives through empirical research.

Concepts of Motivation Applied
to the Three Models

So much of the attention of social studies educators seems to have been focused on the details of the cognitive and moral developmental model that the issue of motivation, especially as it is dealt with in the social learning approach has been given little attention. For many years, psychologists felt that it was appropriate to stress contrasts between Bandura's social learning theory and cognitive-developmental theories. The more popularity the latter got among educators, the less attention was paid to the former. There are clear differences between these positions, but publications such as *Social Learning Theory* (Bandura, 1977) have made evident that recent versions of this theory take account of cognitive factors.

This is still not a developmental theory, however; that is, it does not describe specific structures which change sequentially and universally and which are characteristic of one chronological age period more than another; nor does it describe the kind of cumulative environmental-organismic interchange promoting development which is characteristic of theories like those of Piaget or Kohlberg. In other words, stage sequences are not part of social learning theory, although cognitive mediators play an important role in its most recent exposition. Since eclecticism is probably the most useful position to take in applying psychological theories to education, the contribution which social learning theory can make to this area along with other approaches is important, however.

Bandura identifies four distinct and important processes governing observational learning. Under attentional processes, he characterizes the model provided for the child according to its distinctiveness and complexity. He also points to the characteristics of the observer but gives little attention to age, for example. Social learning theory has traditionally maintained that the processes of acquisition through observational learning are the same for both children and adults.

A second major category of the component processes governing observational learning deals with retention processes. Whether an individual retains over time the behavior that he/she has observed varies according to such factors as the symbolic coding of that behavior, the cognitive organization of the individual, and opportunities for rehearsal of that behavior. The emphasis on cognitive and symbolic processes is new within the last five years. The theory no longer maintains that the only important characteristic of the observer is his/her reinforcement history.

A third component process governing observational learning is what Bandura calls motor reproduction processes. This stresses the aspect of the process which results in action not merely attitude or judgement. It is perhaps in this phase that one can best see the way in which social learning theory can fill in the gaps left by cognitive developmental theory.

The fourth category, motivational processes, and its distinction between external reinforcement, vicarious reinforcement, and self-reinforcement, is of special interest. Self-reward is the aspect of motivation which is of the greatest importance to educators in general and particularly to those involved in international education. Harter (1978) who has investigated the developmental course of some concepts which are closely related to social learning theory argues that during childhood two systems are internalized — one a self-reward system and another a system of mastery goals. These two systems together allow children to evaluate behavior and to self-reinforce that which lives up to their internalized standards. The intrinsically motivated individual in this formulation is one who can operate on a relative 'thin schedule' of reinforcement — that is, reinforcement may occasionally be necessary to confirm one's sense of competence, but it is not constantly necessary.

There are, of course, individual differences in the strength of this intrinsic motivation. And, according to Harter, some children perform more easily with intrinsic motivation in different areas (e.g., school, sports, interpersonal relationships). There is a developmental course to intrinsic reinforcement, which Harter describes at some length. A consideration of these relatively recent advances in the area of motivational psychology has a number of implications for the three models.

All of the three models stress various kinds of activity (in support of human rights, in citizens' influence activities, in participation relating to development problems). These activities, although they may be established originally through a process of external reinforcement or vicarious reinforcement, must eventually come to depend on individuals' processes of intrinsic self-reward if they are going to be maintained. If one were only concerned with children's learning of active approaches to solving problems in schools where teachers are ready to provide positive or negative reinforcement, one would probably not engage in international education at all. Processes of self-reward are of tremendous importance.

This raises other questions. What kinds of models of behavior should children be provided with? What sort of standards for self-reward should individuals be encouraged to develop? How can one capitalize on intrinsic motivation and self-reward when dealing with global issues without making them seem overly simple and without giving individuals an unwarranted sense of efficacy? On the other hand, how can one keep from presenting issues in ways which stress the hopelessness of action? What is the optimum level of challenge? How can one move individuals from attitudes favoring action to the action itself?

The international education models share similar difficulties in addressing the issue of motivation. It may be the case that when local activities can be integrated into global concerns, intrinsic motivation can be enhanced and systems of self-reward can be established.

The results of the survey of world hunger activists reported earlier also contain some clues about motivation. These individuals obtained reinforcement from the process of participating and the feeling that they were educating and informing others (even if they felt that the concrete steps towards eliminating the problem of world hunger were not striking). They also relied at least to some extent on occasional support and reinforcement from others who thought the work on hunger to be important. This argues that when one is working in an area where it is difficult to see results (either because of the size of the problem or its distance from the individual) self-reinforcement is best supplemented with some external social reinforcement.

The three models, in other words, have a similar problem to face in the area of motivation. Inadequate attention has been paid to it in the past.

CONCLUSIONS

Three models widely used in international education have been presented in their historical context and examined in light of the assumptions they make about sequencing and about motivation. To understand the future of programs in these three areas, however, requires more than projecting their development from the past ten years and more than spelling out the implications of sequence or motivation research for improving their internal structure. We may, as Anderson argues, have passed the take-off point of the J-curve for many elements of the globalization of society. However, we cannot predict that the implication of international, global, or development education individually or together will describe a similar trajectory. Examining educational innovation nearly always means applauding limited achievements rather than pointing to far-reaching successes. Optimism, as that expressed by Carnegie in predicting that war would become obsolete or by the individual who expected to change attitudes toward underdevelopment within a matter of less than a decade, is seldom justified. In the United States, for example, even 'the new social studies programs' which mobilized tremendous resources in the 1960s, a decade later are experiencing only limited usage in schools. Educational change and attitudinal change are always slow processes.

Complete pessimism is not justified either, however. International education has long had a group of individuals who are deeply committed to it as more than a subject area. There is an unusual sense of dedication in many of its proponents — those committed to enhancing regard for human rights by educating individuals about ways to press their governments to respect them; people deeply committed to make citizens aware of their relationship to global society and willing to participate in it; and individuals committed to a multifaceted approach to the problems of developing societies and to the reform of power structures. This list does not even include another group of substantial size — those who have a special interest in a particular world area (Asia, Africa) and who believe that international studies are best understood by projecting them through awareness of those areas and cultures. All of these groups continue in the hope that their approach will suddenly catch fire — that there will be a conceptual breakthrough rather than slow incremental change, that suddenly those in high positions in the political or educational system will see the power of these ideas or that international cooperation will suddenly intensify as a result of unpredictable events or extraordinary personal leadership. Each of these areas can point to the beginnings of success. Those interested in international human rights point to strengthened international procedures and rapid growth in the visibility of nongovernmental organizations and regional organizations which focus on human rights as important steps. Those who believe in the link between citizenship and global society point to increasing awareness of interdependence which has been thrust upon Western nations by the action of OPEC. The establishment of the Global Education Task Force of the US Office of Education and the special consideration given to the role of international education in the newly organized Department of Education represent what may be an organizational breakthrough. The establishment of the President's Commission on Foreign Language and International Studies, with its recommendations dealing with a variety of levels of education, it is also a hopeful sign. If provided with adequate funding, what are called 'lighthouse' programs within states as well as intensified attention to the training and certification of teachers suggested in the commission's report will give further legitimation to international education. Those who focus on development education point to the increasing awareness of the complexity of these issues by policy makers, as well as by the average citizen. In the long run, they argue that when the balance shifts so that the average individual is knowledgeable about these problems, governments in the First World will no longer be able to engage in policies which promote maldevelopment.

Although progress is being made, the complexity of problems of international human rights, global interdependence, and development will not easily be solved either on a macro-level or a micro-level — if macro is used to refer to the problem itself (e.g., human rights violations, or hunger) and micro is used to refer to individuals' understanding of these problems. The micro-problem of education is accentuated in both the United States and the United Kingdom by commitment to a belief in pluralism and choice in educational enterprises. International human rights education has as its most basic premise that free access to information from divergent sources and the opportunity to make up one's own mind and act upon one's freely chosen decision is the essence of education. Global education for citizenship places faith in the individual's decision to choose an action once he or she has been made aware of global society. Those in development education specifically call for a plurality of approaches on the grounds that some individuals may never move beyond 'giving money to feed the starving child'. Pluralism in education is a strength, but it also requires a differentiated view of success. Different approaches may demonstrate their effectiveness in different ways and appropriate evaluation strategies are especially important.

Another problem also exists at the micro-level. Programs will continue to operate on unexamined assumptions which may be erroneous, for example, that international education detracts from national loyalty or that education which focuses on activity within the classroom will automatically construct for itself a self-reinforcing system outside the classroom. These issues are present in many nations and in all three of the models. They argue for making a concerted attempt to examine assumptions and translate them into empirical questions. They also argue for examining history — the ideas which have generated programs which have lasted and flourished. But everyday work of the school cannot wait until all assumptions have been examined and all history analyzed. It cannot even wait until sufficient quality material exists in quantity, until requirements for the pre- and in-service training of teachers exist in a majority of areas, or until those who choose textbooks pay as much attention to sections on international as to sections on national political education.

The future of international education can be assessed at present in a relatively positive fashion, and considerable hope can be held out for the future. It is not possible in today's world to ignore the global context in which citizens act, to fail to see evidence of the long-range economic implications of maldevelopment, or to be completely deaf to the demands of people all over the world for respect of their human rights. It remains a challenge for educators to fully respond to the oft-stated belief that responsibility for the level of international awareness and international action in the next generation lies in their hands.

REFERENCES

Anderson, L. F., *Schooling and Citizenship in a Global Age*, Bloomington, Indiana: Social Studies Development Center, 1979.

Bandura, A., *Social Learning Theory*, Englewood Cliffs, NJ: Prentice-Hall, 1977.

Becker, J. and L. F. Anderson, *Objectives, Needs, and Priorities in International Education in the United States Elementary and Secondary Schools*, report to the US Office of Education on Project 6-2908, Bethesda, Md: ERIC Document Reproduction Service, 1969, p. 11.

Blatt, M. M. and L. Kohlberg, 'The Effects of Classroom Moral Discussion upon Children's Level of Moral Judgment', *Journal of Moral Education* 4, 1975, pp. 129-161.

Brainerd, C. J., *Piaget's Theory of Intelligence*, Englewood Cliffs, NJ: Prentice-Hall, 1978.

Buergenthal, T. and J. V. Torney, *International Human Rights and International Education* (US National Commission for UNESCO), Washington, DC: US Government Printing Office, 1976.

Carnegie, A., 'Letter to the Trustees', reprinted in *Basic Documents of the Carnegie Endowment for International Peace*, New York: Carnegie Endowment, 1974, p. 5.

Collins, T. H., *Global Education and the States*, Report to the Council of Chief State School Officers, Washington, DC, 1979.

Crabtree, C., 'Sequence and Transfer in Children's Learning of the Analytical Processes of Geographic Inquiry', *Journal of Experimental Education* 45, 1976, pp. 19-30.

Dunlop, O. J., 'Development Education: Origins, Aims, Obstacles and Opportunities', paper prepared for Council of Europe Seminar, 1980.

Force, D., 'Constituency Education: Pilot Program', a report to Church World Service, 1979.

Graves, N., O. Dunlop, and J. Torney-Purta (eds.), *Teaching for International Understanding, Peace, and Human Rights*, Paris: UNESCO, in press.

Harter, S., 'Effectance Motivation Reconsidered: Toward a Developmental Model', *Human Development* 21, 1978, pp. 34-75.

Heater, D., 'A Burgeoning of Interest: Political Education in Britain', *International Journal of Political Education* 1, 1978, pp. 325-346.

Kohlberg, L., 'Revisions in the Theory and Practice of Moral Development', in W. Damon (ed.), *Moral Development. New Directions for Child Development*, San Francisco: Jossey-Bass, 1978.

Posner, G. J. and K. A. Strike, 'A Categorization Scheme for Principles of Sequencing Content', *Journal of Educational Research* 46, 1976, pp. 665-690.

Prescott, D., *Education and International Relations*, Cambridge, Mass.: Harvard University Press, 1930.

Scanlon, D. G., *International Education: A Documentary History*, New York: Columbia University Press, 1960.

Torney, J. V., 'Summary Report: Symposium on International Human Rights Education', UNESCO Document SS-78/Conf. 401, 1978.

—— 'Middle Childhood at a Critical Period for Education about International Human Rights', in C. Falkenstein and C. Anderson (eds.), *Daring to Dream: Law and the Humanities in the Elementary School*, Chicago, Ill.: American Bar Association, 1980.

—— 'Attitudes, Beliefs, and Involvement in the Issue of World Hunger', report to the Ecumenical Task Force on Christian Education for World Peace, 1980 (with the assistance of J. Beckman, C. Mumby, and C. Cory).

—— and P. Brice, 'Children's Attitudes to Human Rights and Social Cognition', paper presented at the American Psychological Association, New York City, 1979.

UNESCO, *International Understanding at School*, Paris: UNESCO, 1971.

Wright, D. and J., *The Changing World in The Classroom*, London: IFRED, 1974.

Conclusion

Derek Heater

This book has had a limited, though it is hoped, useful purpose: to note the recently developing interest in political education in the Atlantic world. During approximately the last two decades a clearly detectable interest in and commitment to the issue of political education has blossomed in most of the centres of this geographical area. The decision of the editors to confine contributions to authors from this region was dictated partly by practical considerations such as personal knowledge of whom we could approach. There was also the consideration of coherence. Our contributors are all writing within the western, liberal democratic tradition. A whole range of assumptions are consequently taken for granted. These include the desirability of popular knowledge about and participation in matters political; a nervousness concerning the dangers of indoctrination; the freedom of schools at least not slavishly to support the political status quo.

The omission of any treatment of political education in communist and Afro-Asian-Latin American countries means that there has been little explicit discussion in this book of curricula shaped overtly by ideological considerations, the use of schools for conscious nation-building or the promotion of extra-mural educational activities to challenge the established system. The societies of North America and Western Europe are not, of course, totally innocent of such variations on the generous theme of political education. The USA is still nation-building, not to mention the Federal Republic of Germany; while the relative weight and danger of the socializing or radicalizing tendencies of educating young people politically have been hotly debated in the western countries that have witnessed such a bourgeoning of interest in the matter in recent years.

Two topics underplayed here, if not totally omitted, require comment, particularly as they interestingly reflect the ways in which the movement for enhanced provision for political education has developed in most countries. The first concerns the assumption, implicit or explicit in most of the contributions here, that political education is primarily the responsibility of the schools. True, we commissioned Harold Entwistle's contribution; perhaps it was a mistake not to have commissioned a similar piece on such organizations as youth clubs, though it is difficult to know how widespread and effective their work is in this field. The second topic underplayed is global education, world studies, education for international understanding or whatever label is preferred. In some courses a global perspective clearly is assumed to be a natural and essential part, perhaps in a concentric formulation of the subject from local through national to international. On the other hand, very many courses are clearly focused on the preparation of young people to understand and participate in their local and national civic communities. In some countries, indeed, pressure to introduce a global perspective into syllabuses and curricula has taken the form of movements parallel to those advocating political education, though indeed these lines of advance often appear likely to meet somewhat before infinity. However, since the matter is widely recognized as being so important, rather than omit it entirely we have the noble attempt of Judith Torney-Purta to compress the discussion of the major issues into a single chapter. Paradoxically books on education for international understanding that have so far been published have been written largely within a national frame of reference. A book similar to the present one but devoted entirely to this topic would be illuminating.

One commonplace frequently cited as a feature of our international era is the homogenization of culture and experience through the processes of rapid communication and the ubiquitousness of the products of multi-national companies. In short, we live in the transistor and Coca-Cola age. One of the purposes of this book has been to show the balance between common experience and national distinctiveness in the development of political education in the countries of the Atlantic world in recent years. Twenty years ago there was little active debate on the matter. However, during the past two decades we have all experienced in one way or another a sharpening of interest — due to academic development in the field of political socialization, the lowering of the age of majority and the politicization of student bodies. In comparing experiences it is particularly instructive to place side-by-side the contributions of Bob Stradling, Mary Jane Turner and Willem Langeveld.

What, then, in the light of the contributions to this volume can we judge to have been achieved and what still needs to be given particular attention? In narrowly academic terms the achievements of the past two decades have been heartening. The social need for more and better political education has been thrown out as a challenge; and at the lowest level of achievement it has at least been shown that the challenge cannot be ignored. The matter has become a live educational and political issue (the political dimension having been particularly evident in Germany, as is vividly shown by Dieter Schmidt-Sinns' contribution). Pressure to introduce more effective programmes of political education into schools has become a direct challenge of principle to the nervousness of governments and school administrators. Academics, through the founding of journals, the holding of conferences and the conduct of research and development projects have debated the pedagogical issues at a far higher level of sophistication than ever before. Context, content and method have all been discussed with the benefits of modern philosophical, psychological and sociological insights.

However, although all this intellectual activity has been most necessary, it can only be considered as a starting-point. One of the most sobering sentences in the present book is Mary Jane Turner's question, 'If we presume (and we are convinced that the evidence strongly substantiates it) that civic education has not changed markedly in the 200 years that the United States has been a nation, what factors can be identified that have contributed to this situation?' (p. 56). If truly effective progress is to be made, then the

enthusiasm and skills of classroom teachers must be more efficiently cultivated than hitherto.

Where, then, should efforts now be concentrated in order to
build upon achievements of recent years? I would wish to place
three items on my agenda.

First, objectives. Hundreds of blooms have flowered and
thousands of lists have contended. I wonder whether perhaps we
have not been over-ambitious? If we read 'political education' as
being synonymous with teaching Pol. Sci., the identification of
cognitive objectives is hardly likely to be all that contentious. But
political education is generally recognized as being both more and
less than that: less, because a too academic syllabus will make little
impression on pupils of average ability and interest; more, because
most advocates of political education place great weight on attitudinal and behavioural outcomes of their pedagogical efforts.
Alex Porter reminds us of the multi-dimensional nature of the concept of political literacy and Bob Weissberg of the complexities of
the socialization process. But what is it really desirable and prac-
ticable that young, politically educated people should be able to
do? Two matters here need more thorough investigation. In the
first place, what kind of 'good citizens' are we trying to produce?
(Politicians, like Austin Mitchell, are, of course, particularly exercised by this question.) Those who support the system? The answer
assumed by most writers is that the western democratic system is
worth preserving though detailed criticism of its operation is to be
encouraged. The objection to such a position is that it opens its ex-
ponents to the accusation of wishy-washy liberalism, especially if
the writers give the impression that they take it as axiomatic that no
other position is tenable. It may be, of course, that this liberal
stance is neither wishy-washy nor as objectionable as alternatives.
This point could be more thoroughly discussed. This is the educational version of the classic dilemma of the democrat — can he
tolerate propaganda and movements designed to destroy
democracy? One must ask the parallel educational question, 'Has a
school the moral and social right to undermine the social/political
system of which it is part?' Fred Newmann discusses this issue most
thoughtfully. But are we realistic to expect the majority of our
young people to take the prospect of participation (except in the

minimal sense of voting in elections) at all seriously? Feelings of efficacy among the majority of people are notoriously low. Perhaps this point of view smacks of defeatism. However, what I am really suggesting is that teachers should assess with cool realism what participative situations the majority of citizens are likely to find themselves in and concentrate on training in the skills particularly relevant to these.

The second item on my agenda is a questioning of the over-intellectualized bases of much that has been written and advocated. This is probably inevitable and not totally a misfortune in a new area of curriculum development. Inevitable because academics rather than teachers working at the chalk face tend to take the initiative in these matters; not a misfortune because sound academic foundations are crucial for any educational activity. However, we must be careful that courses are not inappropriately academic; not so much in the sense of being too difficult for any given class, for that can be easily monitored, but in the sense of undervaluing the practical character of the courses. A useful distinction has been made between 'teaching politics' and 'political education'. The latter term is taken to mean something like preparation for citizenship and should therefore incorporate economic and legal education on such topics as trade unions, taxation, house purchase, social security as well as strictly political matters. 'Rights, duties and how to use the system' would be another way of putting this. The question concerning syllabuses that then becomes appropriate is, 'What does the adolescent need to know and be able to do if he is to make effective use of the system as it exists?' Professor F. F. Ridley of the University of Liverpool, who has seen the disaffection of young people in a city of very high unemployment, has expressed himself very forcefully in these terms in other forums.

To query the validity of politics as a classroom subject at least for some pupils is to raise also the question of the desirability of focusing too myopically on the school as the sole, or even the main, institutional context for political education. Harold Entwistle helps us to consider this matter. One serious gap in the list of contributions to the present volume, as previously noted, is the rather amorphous though perhaps nevertheless vitally important area of youth clubs and educational provision while in employment. In Britain, for example, the government has recently provided substantial sums of money to encourage political education in youth clubs; while general studies programmes taken alongside craft training courses in Colleges of Further Education are a feature of day-release schemes. We need to know more about the effectiveness of such work and how widespread similar practices are.

Each country has its own characteristics in terms of traditions, political, economic and educational systems. In that sense, programmes of political education must be individually tailored to particular countries' needs. And yet the countries of the Altantic quarter of the globe have much in common. For example, students from numerous countries with whom I have spoken at the United World College of the Atlantic in south Wales, admittedly an intellectual élite, discuss political matters within a common framework of discourse. Those of us engaged in political education can possibly learn from each other rather more than we have been inclined to do in the past. As professionals we need to know with much more self-assurance what kinds of teaching or learning experiences are really effective. Let us be honest and admit that in solid, concrete terms, we know precious little. Through that all too frequent ingredient in the day-to-day classroom mixture, namely boredom, we may be having a seriously negative effect.

True, a start has been made with the launching of the *International Journal of Political Education* under the vigorous captaincy of Willem Langeveld. But more readers and contributors are needed if it is to perform this onerous task effectively. Even so, it is only a start. For truly effective cross-national exchange of experience, we need something like the following. Programmes of political education, devised for different age and ability ranges and different socio-economic backgrounds, should be carefully monitored and assessed for their immediate impact and long-term effectiveness. An international dossier of particularly successful schemes could then be compiled. They should, of course, not rely heavily on particularly skilful teachers or particularly lavish resources, since these are not universally available. Useful progress has been made in many countries; the momentum must be sustained.

Notes on Contributors

Harold Entwistle has worked as a teacher in primary and secondary schools and as a university lecturer in education. Since 1969 he has been Professor of Education at the George Williams Campus of Concordia University, Montreal. He is the author of *Child Centred Education* (1970), *Education, Work and Leisure* (1970), *Political Education in a Democracy* (1973), *Class, Culture and Education* (1978), and most recently *Antonio Gramsci: Conservative Schooling for Radical Politics* (1979).

Judith A. Gillespie is the Director of the Program in Educational Policy and Change in the Workshop in Political Theory and Policy Analysis at Indiana University, Bloomington. She has written several books and has conducted research and development projects in political education in the United States.

Derek Heater is Head of the Humanities Department at Brighton Polytechnic, UK. Formerly he was Chairman of the Politics Association and editor of the journal *Teaching Politics*. He is the author of *World Studies: Education for International Understanding in Britain*.

Willem Langeveld is Lecturer in Political Education at the University of Amsterdam. He is editor of the *International Journal of Political Education*.

Austin Mitchell is Labour MP for Grimsby. Previously he taught at universities in New Zealand and at Nuffield College, Oxford, and worked as a presenter in commercial television.

Fred M. Newmann is Professor of Curriculum and Instruction at the University of Wisconsin. He has worked on developing curricula for the analysis of public controversy and community-based citizen participation and has assisted in the design of an 'alternative' secondary school. Currently he is researching the conception and implementation of meaningful roles for citizens and the revitalization of community life.

Alex Porter is Lecturer in Political Education at the University of London Institute of Education. He is co-editor (with Professor Bernard Crick) of *Political Education and Political Literacy* (1978).

Dieter Schmidt-Sinns studied history, education, English language, and physical education at the Universities of Göttingen and Heidelberg. He has taught in grammar schools and now works at the Federal Centre for Political Education in Bonn.

Robert Stradling was Director of the Political Literacy in Further Education Programme and is now Co-director of the Curriculum Review Unit.

Judith Torney-Purta is Professor of Psychology at the University of Illinois at Chicago Circle. She has been active in the fields of political socialization research, global education and international human rights. She is co-author of *International Human Rights and International Education* and *Civic Education in Ten Countries: An Empirical Study*.

Mary Jane Turner is Staff Associate in the Social Science Education Consortium, Boulder, Colorado, and Co-director of the Basic Citizenship Competencies Project.

Robert Weissberg is Associate Professor of Political Science at the University of Illinois, Urbana. He has published books on political socialization, public opinion, political analysis, and American government.